Understanding Crime in
JAMAICA

Understanding Crime in
JAMAICA

New Challenges for Public Policy

Edited by

Anthony Harriott

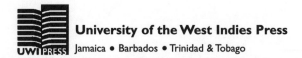
University of the West Indies Press
Jamaica • Barbados • Trinidad & Tobago

University of the West Indies Press
1A Aqueduct Flats   Mona
Kingston 7   Jamaica
www.uwipress.com

07 06 05 04 03   5 4 3 2 1

CATALOGUING IN PUBLICATION DATA

Understanding crime in Jamaica: new challenges for public
policy / edited by Anthony Harriott.
p. cm.
Includes bibliographical references.
ISBN: 976-640-144-6

1. Crime – Jamaica. 2. Crime prevention – Jamaica. 3. Crime
– Political aspects. 4. Crime – Economic aspects. 5. Women
– Crimes against – Jamaica. 6. Tourists – Crimes against –
Jamaica. I. Harriott, Anthony.

HV6868.5.U64 2003   364.97272

Cover design by Robert Harris.
Book design by Roy Barnhill.

Printed in Canada.

Contents

Acknowledgements

This book had its beginnings in a conference on crime and criminal justice in the Caribbean which was held on the Mona campus of the University of the West Indies in February 2001. A number of the articles in this volume were first presented as papers at the conference. I wish to thanks the authors for their patience and cooperation in the effort to shape them into a somewhat unified and coherent volume.

The effort would not have been possible without the generous support of the principal of the Mona campus, Professor Kenneth Hall; the dean of the Faculty of Social Sciences, Professor Barrington Chevannes; and the head of the Department of Government, Professor Stephen Vasciannie, all of whom facilitated my leave of absence from departmental duties to take up a Mona Research Fellowship which afforded me the time to complete the work on this volume (among other things).

Ms Shivaun Hearne and other members of the staff of the University of the West Indies Press put considerable effort into preparing the manuscript for publication. I wish to acknowledge our debt of gratitude to them.

Chapters 5 and 10 were published – in somewhat different forms – as articles in the *Caribbean Journal of Criminology and Social Psychology* and *Wadabaji*, respectively. I thank the editors of these journals for their kind permission to publish these chapters.

Editor's Overview

Despite the severity and seemingly intractable nature of the crime problem in Jamaica, the literature on this aspect of life has been fairly sparse. The decades of the 1980s and 1990s saw the publication of only two books on this problem (Ellis 1992; Headley 1994) and the publication of the proceedings of an important seminar (Phillips and Wedderburn 1987). Of course there were also a number of articles published in scholarly journals, but in sum, the quantity of the output and the range of issues dealt with were rather limited.

We may think of "Caribbean criminology" – a term that may be given many different meanings, but by which I simply mean the literature on crime in the Caribbean, not a special perspective on crime that is grounded in a peculiarly Caribbean way of perceiving and knowing – as developing in two phases.[1] I believe that a second phase is just now beginning to distinguish itself. With few exceptions, the work associated with the earlier phase of criminological research tended to be centrally concerned with theoretically informed speculation about the root causes of crime, but revealed very little empirical work (cf. Pryce 1976). This was perhaps consistent with the times – the close proximity to the colonial order and the need for public policy to take new directions in engineering a new social order that would correct the historical injustices. These value-related issues remain as central as ever and have always been a major issue in crime control and in public policy generally.

In the current period, however, there is the urgent need to undertake the empirical work required to advance our understanding of the crime phenomenon in the Caribbean and to allow for better informed, evidence-based judgements and policy, by more critically evaluating theory and existing crime control programmes. This developing second-generation literature is and ought to be more empirically grounded, more methodologically rigorous, closer to the crime phenomenon – that is, more engaging rather than relying solely on official crime statistics, and more varied in perspective, with researchers from different disciplinary backgrounds working separately and together, within and beyond the traditional disciplinary boundaries.

Much of this is evident in the chapters included in this volume. The volume makes a modest but important contribution to the literature by filling some of the gaps and by providing new perspectives on old themes. It makes new empirical contributions and advances in the methodological rigour with which the subject matter is treated. This latter point is not peculiar to this volume, but is a feature of the new wave of literature, a sample of which may be found in the volumes of the *Caribbean Journal of Criminology and Social Psychology* (see, for example, de Albuquerque and McElroy 1999; Frost and Bennett 1998; Deosaran and Chadee 1997). It also makes a useful contribution in terms of advancing the understanding of the role of politics in the development of the crime problem in Jamaica, makes some preliminary efforts to evaluate the impact of crime on economic and political development, and presents some policy insights and considerations.

Very few of the chapters in this volume attempt to explicitly and systematically elaborate policy. This book is, however, an attempt to contribute to the knowledge base that would allow for a better understanding of the Jamaican crime problem and, on that basis, to engage in more effective problem solving. Many academics, including most of the contributors to this volume, may be too distant from the day-to-day problems to actually develop practical problem-solving innovations and generate blueprints for action. But many still see their mission as helping to develop the knowledge base that would enable more effective engagement with acute social problems and, despite the difficulties, to even go beyond this to active involvement with change processes in government and in civil society, especially at the community level. That is the spirit of much of the Caribbean academic research on the crime problem, and it is the spirit of this book.

Within the covers of this volume, economists, political scientists and sociologists all make their contributions to the debates. This introduces differences in perspective even at the level of epistemology, with highly positivistic articles as well as some that are presented in a more subjectivist style. But the variety of these contributions will only serve to further enrich the literature and our understanding of criminogenic processes. The authors explore four major themes, as follows: the links between crime and politics, crime and poverty, the impact of crime on the developmental process, and the development of appropriate policy responses.

Crime and Politics

In Jamaica, as noted earlier, crime cannot be fully understood without reference to politics. A major contribution of this volume is in the systematic discussion of this theme – moving the discussion of the relationship between crime/violence and politics beyond the limited scope of political violence. Four of the ten chapters in this volume are concerned with this theme. Some of these chapters tend to give politics a central place in understanding ordinary criminality and social violence. Figueroa and Sives's chapter highlights the dangers of politics as crime and identifies the garrison infrastructure as an important aspect of this problem. The significance of the garrison lies not just in its role as a place where politics and crime intersect and which provides a protected site for criminal enterprise, but also in its being a mode of political administration that subverts democracy. The garrison is regarded as an ugly expression of our mainstream political methodologies and a symbol of the dangers to democracy that inhere in mainstream politics. Others have taken the diametrically opposed and more contentious view that the garrison constitutes a "counter system", or "counter hegemonic" influence (see Charles 2002). Political crimes and crime-politics relationships may be most sharply manifested in the garrisons, but are evident in political activities outside of them.

In their chapter Figueroa and Sives rightly treat electoral fraud as a special and dangerous type of crime. It is special in terms of its harmful consequences for society, which include direct contributions to the problem of violence. Electoral fraud may serve to precipitate violent clashes between the parties, as the victim of the fraud may respond violently. It also delegitimizes key political institutions, including the parties, and tarnishes the electoral system. But its significance extends beyond this. It represents a distinctive case of elite-mass criminality in that it brings together the powerful and the relatively powerless, people from different locations in the social hierarchy but with similar motivations, in organized criminality, openly and on a mass scale. This raises the issue of the political parties being criminal organizations. They are, of course, not criminal organizations in the same sense as organized crime networks, that is, their *raison d'être* is not criminal engagement. On the contrary, their primary objective is to form the government of the country, and both major political parties have a record of developmental achievements. Nevertheless, the resort to criminal means of gaining office, and the alliances with criminals that are used for this purpose, give criminal networks considerable leverage on the parties, and lead to the use of criminal means to systematically plunder the resources of the state once office is acquired. These activities of the political elite have profound implications for ordinary criminality, especially the normalization of crime which is reflected in the view that criminality has become conformist behaviour or, as cynically expressed in Creole, "all a wi a thief".

This large-scale (in some urban constituencies) institutionalized electoral fraud, other crimes associated with the routine working of the political system, and the embeddedness of ordinary criminality in a web of political relations at the level of urban communities, including broader attachments to the party system (and thus the importance of the political factor in the explanation of crime), present challenges for theorizing crime in the Jamaican context.

Prevalent criminality may be *dissolved* as a social problem by naming it as fundamentally a political problem requiring a political solution. Most readers, even those who are familiar with the Jamaican situation, would rightly bristle at this kind of reductionism. And I believe that this is largely avoided by the much more subtle treatment of the political variable by the chapters included in this volume. But it may be illuminating to press the line of investigation of the political to its fullest. In his contribution to this volume, Gray proffers the notion of the "predatory state", by which is meant a form of power that "weds structures of clientelism and democratic institutions to extra-legal processes associated with criminal and political underworlds". This predation, as Gray argues, undoubtedly provides justification for criminality, perhaps even as resistance to the predation and thus a type of political action approximating social banditry. One may make this argument without politically dissolving ordinary criminality and naming it as "resistance". As is the case with social banditry, in some instances there may indeed be no clear boundaries between ordinary criminality and sociopolitical action. For many citizens, party politics is an important avenue for opportunity. For some in the marginalized urban communities it is the only avenue, the only link to the mainstream of society. It is a source of both legitimate and illegitimate opportunities and a means of resistance and resource access. Given the existing political arrangements, people easily shift from being political outsiders to insiders and vice versa, and thus their responses to socioeconomic conditions may easily shift from political forms of resistance and mobilization, via electoral channels, to corrupt access to state resources, crime and more conventional responses. There are no sharp boundaries between the forms of response. There is a long tradition in the social sciences, especially in the work of Merton, that treats rebellion and crime as different responses to structural strain, that is, as stemming from similar roots (Merton [1938] 1996). Modernization theory could also be used to explain the politics-crime nexus as a vestige of backward patron-client relations, and the use of clientelism as a method of political mobilization (cf. Stone 1987). But some of the contributions in this volume seriously question this.

The seeds of the crime-politics phenomenon in Jamaica were planted and nurtured over decades of competitive party politics. In her chapter Sives tracks the long career of political violence in Jamaica and how it intensified after the achievement of self-government. Indeed, the problem pre-dates the period reviewed by Sives, with roots extending to the post-emancipation period, prior to the formation of the two mass parties of today (the Jamaica Labour Party [JLP] and the People's National Party [PNP]) and before universal adult suffrage (Wilmot 1982). The problem of political violence and violent crime has had a long gestation period. It is not simply a matter of particular individuals whose personalities may accentuate or embody the current conflicts, nor even only a matter of the patron-client relations that attend the distribution of the resources of the state. As Sives correctly notes, deeper problems of identity are at the root of the violence. These matters are further explored in the contribution by this writer, who extends the discussion to its expression as everyday social violence.

Much has been said about the crime-politics nexus in popular discourse, and some of this is shared by authors in this volume. But here this problem is not treated as an alternative discourse and is not intended to deflect the attention of the public or policy makers away from the *social roots* of crime. Rather, this discussion serves to highlight an important dimension of the problem: how the existing political relationships and methodologies of political mobilization operate as root causes of crime, not just as facilitators of crime. The challenge is, of course, to integrate these explanations into a more sophisticated system-atized theory. This discussion also forces a consideration of policy and the issue of fundamental change in political relations and social organization.

Crime and Poverty

Consideration of fundamental change presumes contemplation of the social roots of crime. The relationship between poverty and crime is an old theme, and perhaps the central issue in the discourse on crime in the Caribbean and particularly in Jamaica. The discussion of this relation-ship has taken many forms, but it has been the central discourse over the thirty years since the emergence of any systematic study of crime in the region. The discussion has involved explorations of the direct effects of immiseration (Ellis 1992), the effects of relative deprivation (Stone 1987), and of inequality (Headley 1994). There has been considerable concern with the complexity of experiences of poverty and how various mediating variables such as family type and educational achievement structure the effects on different types of crime. How poverty may influ-ence the social processes that lead to high rates of criminal offending is not exactly a settled issue.

This issue presents some political difficulty once a positive relation-ship between crime and poverty is asserted. The assertion of a positive relationship, it is feared, may cast doubt on the moral integrity of the poor or, worse, blame them as the subcultural carriers of criminogenic values and violence-engendering attributes such as toughness and aggressiveness.[2] In some societies the result of this is the stigmatization of the (urban) poor as criminal and dangerous, which sets them up for discrimination and repression. There is also quite a different, perhaps completely opposite, concern. It is that such an analysis implies a policy shift that would divert resources to the poor under the guise of fixing the crime problem. Of course, some quickly forget their objections to the assertion of a positive relationship between poverty and crime when this becomes a language that is appealing to external donor agencies and yields grants and loans. Clearly, the arguments should be evaluated without imputing moral judgement or implicit policy advocacy. In order to advance this discussion, careful argumentation and a fair degree of empirical rigour and innovation are required. Marlyn Jones enters this debate in a new way, via the thesis that the feminization of poverty may account for increased female offending. This contribution should stimulate further empirical work on the criminogenic effects of poverty and gendered poverty, as these are important developmental issues.

Crime and Its Impact on Economic Development

The problem of a relationship between crime and economic development is the source of great speculation based on common-sense notions. According to Francis et al. (2001), "The supply of offences is substantially an economic phenomenon." One cannot help noticing that the political scientists tend to make a similar claim for the centrality of the political variable. Indeed it could be argued that grasping the centrality of the political is essential to properly understanding crime in Jamaica. And, of course, criminology has long been regarded as the "sociological notion of crime". But these positions should not be dismissed as simply disciplinary biases or claims to turf. Although the study of crime and criminal justice processes is not seen as belonging in the domain of any particular discipline, and the contributions of the various disciplines within and beyond the social sciences are recognized and valued, within the Jamaican context the arguments should be evaluated on their own merit. Further work based on these claims may yet serve to better illuminate the peculiarities of the Jamaican crime problem. From the economic perspective, crime may be treated as the effect of opportunity costs (unemployment, education), economic growth and other such variables. But crime may also be treated as "cause" – for example, as a source of disinvestment in industry or capital flight (for fear of extortion rackets and other types of business victimization). These are not matters to be left to intuition and common sense (which may be very misleading). They are to be empirically investigated. The authors have advanced our knowledge of these relationships; they provide a stronger foundation on which to systematize explanation.

Some of the articles on this subject (crime and economic development) are quite understandably more concerned with informing policy than with building theory. The three chapters in this volume on the impact of crime on tourism, while raising theoretical considerations, seem to be primarily concerned with informing policy. McElroy is specifically concerned with the vexed issue of harassment, and locates the Jamaican problem within a global setting. The chapters by King and by Alleyne and Boxill are more narrowly concerned with the effects of crime. King examines the perceptions of travel safety that are held by travel agents and how these influence "tourist decision making". Alleyne and Boxill attempt to model the relationship between crime and the growth of tourism. They contest popular intuitive notions about this relationship and report that the effect of violent crime on tourist arrivals does not appear to be significant, and is neither immediate nor simple. This is a valuable contribution. However, the general effect of crime on *tourism* may be more long term, based on an established reputation as a violent place or the stigmatizing effect of high rates of violent crime. Acquiring the reputation of being a high-crime destination may also have a long-term effect on the type of tourists who visit. The upscale middle-aged person may stay away, while the younger person who may be enchanted with the image of reggae and rebellion may not be deterred. The high rate of violent crime in Jamaica may have served to alter our place in tourism markets. Further work is needed; this is a promising line of research which could enrich the debate on applicable theory in the region and which ought to inform further work on policy.

Insights into the negative impact of crime on tourism and on economic development more generally would provide a framework for policy responses that deeply shape the political development of the country. Political administrations may seek to protect economic development by repressing crime in ways that further retard the country's political development. These are dangers which may be avoided by prudent policy making.

Policy

In the final section there is some explicit discussion of policy. All of the chapters in the volume carry policy implications, but Robotham explicitly engages this issue. Policy development in the field of crime control is sadly lacking. There are a number of reasons for this but we may highlight three: (a) an overly simplistic popular view of the crime problem that decries professional research as a waste of money (and perhaps some of it is); (b) a lack of rigour in past work; (c) a weak state bureaucracy with

very limited capacity to develop policy work in this field. These problems have led to an emerging intellectual dependence on external assistance and consultancies. These consultants bring with them the
experience of their countries, and in some instances a wider experience,
but they have no knowledge of the local situation and no time to learn
about it. They may also bring considerable ideological luggage with
them, as expressed in fads associated with the rotation of political
administrations in their home countries which are not interrogated
from the viewpoint of the concrete realities of Jamaica (and other developing countries). For example, the ideological influence of New Public
Management is evident in the modernization programme of the Jamaica
Constabulary Force (see Harriott 2000). This is not to suggest that
aspects of this perspective may not be useful; the point is that the appli-
cations are not the outcome of critical interrogation of these ideas and
experiences based on sound knowledge of the local environment. In
some instances, Froudian plans are elaborated without an understanding of even the basic patterns of crime and the ground covered in the
published literature on the region, and in ignorance of the evaluations
of the very programmes which they recommend to the Jamaican government.[3] The outcome of much of this is that crime control policy has
largely been reduced to law enforcement. Again, the point is not to
underplay the importance of law enforcement. Rather, the issue is its
limitations and ineffectiveness (in its concrete Jamaican institutional
expression) as a stand-alone or even primary tool.

Robotham advances the discussion of appropriate policy and extends
the discussion in this volume by incorporating various factors in his
analysis of the crime problem and thus arguing against economic reductionism in any policy response, although he suggests that "the long term
sustainable solution to the crime problem is the recovery of the formal
economy". His analysis highlights the importance of a developmental
approach to (among other things) improving the education system,
resolving the difficulties associated with labour force reintegration, and
the need for effective enforcement – "a combination of socioeconomic,
political and law enforcement measures". It is educational attainment,
not simply school attendance, which facilitates access to the social
goods desired by those who aspire to upward mobility. Thus, the challenge is not just to provide access to education, but rather to quality

education. Similarly, with labour force integration, the quality of jobs matters. Labour force participation is important not just for economic reasons but for cultivating attachments to the society and its institutions, for fostering notions of respectability and thus self-imposed conventionality. For this reason, as well as the economic realities, the quality of the jobs matters. Still, it may be necessary to make the point that for a struggling developing country, in the short term, the problems of access and quality are unlikely to be solved as conjoined goods, that is, as open, mass access to quality education and quality jobs.

If in the short term not much can be done on these fundamentals (and this must be questioned as, for example, it seems possible to begin to correct some of the problems with the education system), there are other strategies which could yield some immediate results. As implied in chapter 5, sustained peace building offers considerable potential for reducing the homicide rate. Having the institutions of the state treat people with greater respect (a valuable intangible that costs nothing) would facilitate its role in controlling crime and preventing conflicts from becoming violent. Effective anticorruption measures would help to restore a measure of confidence in the institutions of the state. These measures cannot succeed if crime control is highly politicized and treated opportunistically. If politics and public policy have contributed directly and indirectly to the crime problem, it is politics that will have to rescue the society from violent crime. And with regard to policy, if nothing else, we hope that this volume will serve to highlight the need for an integrated, multifaceted approach to crime prevention and control, for a coordinated parallelism, not a pot-pourri of unconnected responses which are presented as a misconstrued "holism".

Notes

1. For a good discussion of this issue, see Birkbeck 1999.
2. See, for example, the work of Walter Miller (1958), which discusses this issue in the context of the United States.
3. James Froude was an Oxford don who spent a few weeks visiting a number of Caribbean territories and became an instant expert on the region. He wrote a book entitled *The English in the West Indies* (1888) which simply reflected the prejudices and arguments which he had arrived with and which he used as tools in support of colonialism. Naming this unthinking

and canned approach to the study of the region *Froudacity* was the work of John Thomas, who wrote a sharply critical reply to Froude, entitled *Froudacity: West Indian Fables Examined* (published in 1889). Recently my daughter invited one of her American friends from school to visit us in Kingston. He is eighteen years old, just out of high school and on his first visit outside of the United States. Twenty minutes after picking him up at the airport, he was confidently telling me how the problems of Jamaica should be fixed.

References

Birkbeck, C. 1999. "By Your Theories You Shall Be Known: Some Reflections on Caribbean Criminology". *Caribbean Journal of Criminology and Social Psychology* 4, nos. 1–2.

Charles, C. 2002. "The Zeeks Riot: Garrison as Counter-Hegemonic Space". Paper presented at Third Annual SALISES Conference, University of the West Indies, Mona, Jamaica, 4–6 April.

de Albuquerque, K., and J. McElroy. 1999. "A Longitudinal Study of Serious Crime in the Caribbean". *Caribbean Journal of Criminology and Social Psychology* 4, nos. 1–2.

Deosaran, R., and S. Chadee. 1997. "Juvenile Delinquency in Trinidad and Tobago: Challenges for Social Policy". *Caribbean Journal of Criminology and Social Psychology* 2, no. 2.

Ellis, H. 1992. *Identifying Crime Correlates in a Developing Society: A Study of Socio-economic and Socio-demographic Contributions to Crime in Jamaica, 1950–84*. New York: Peter Lang.

Francis, A., et al. 2001. "Crime in Jamaica: A Preliminary Analysis." Paper presented at the Second Caribbean Conference on Crime and Criminal Justice, University of the West Indies, Mona, Jamaica, 14–17 February.

Frost, B., and R. Bennett. 1998. "Unemployment and Crime: Implications for the Caribbean". *Caribbean Journal of Criminology and Social Psychology* 3, nos. 1–2.

Harriott, A. 2000. "Police Reform in the Caribbean". *Caribbean Dialogue* 6, nos. 1–2.

Headley, B. 1994. *The Jamaican Crime Scene: A Perspective*. Mandeville, Jamaica: Eureka Press.

Merton, R. (1938) 1996. "Social Structure and Anomie". In *Robert K. Merton on Social Structure and Social Science*, edited by P. Sztompka. Chicago: University of Chicago Press.

Miller, W. 1958. "Lower Class Cultures as a Generating Milieu of Gang Delinquency". *Journal of Social Issues* 14, no. 3.

Phillips, P., and J. Wedderburn, eds. 1987. *Crime and Violence: Causes and Solutions.* Kingston, Jamaica: Department of Government, University of the West Indies.

Pryce, K. 1976. "Towards a Caribbean Criminology". *Caribbean Issues* 11, no. 2.

Stone, C. 1987. "Crime and Violence: Socio-political Implications". In *Crime and Violence: Causes and Solutions,* edited by P. Phillips and J. Wedderburn. Kingston, Jamaica: Department of Government, University of the West Indies.

Wilmot, S. 1982. "Race, Election Violence and Constitutional Reform in Jamaica, 1830–1854". *Journal of Caribbean History* 17.

1

The Jamaican Crime Problem
New Developments and New Challenges for Public Policy

Anthony Harriott

At the time of writing the Jamaican people are celebrating their fortieth year of independence. The country is also approaching its sixtieth anniversary of internal self-government, which was achieved in 1944. Although it is still a young nation, the country has engaged in intensive debates about its development and has acquired considerable experience in nation building. Unlike the citizens of some developing countries which are ripped apart by ethnic polarization, failing national institutions and other politically debilitating problems, Jamaicans are well equipped to understand and effectively respond to the major developmental challenges confronting the country. Crime, especially violent crime, is one of these challenges. Although this problem presents new and difficult challenges to the country's development, it is not insuperable. In this first chapter, the aim is simply to present a brief overview of the Jamaican crime problem, to specify its main features and to highlight the challenges that it presents for policy makers.

Young ex-colonial nations are usually concerned with issues of identity, economic development, social transformation and institutional re-engineering. These issues are usually not resolved or solved by pursuing them sequentially, but rather by engaging them in intersecting and intertwining processes. Economic development and successful social transformation, for example, are hardly likely without the supporting institutional change. In the case of Jamaica, at the dawn of independence, economic development and social transformation were regarded as the central issues. This was clearly reflected in the frequent, approving reference to the view of Norman Manley that the mission of his generation was to end colonial rule and secure "political independence", and that the mission of the post-independence leadership was to "reconstruct the social and economic society and life of Jamaica" (Manley 1971, 380–81). As one of the leaders of the anticolonial movement, Norman Manley seems to have had a fairly profound grasp of the socioeconomic problems and political challenges facing Jamaica at independence. But with hindsight we may now suggest that even Norman Manley and Alexander Bustamante (a co-leader of the independence movement and the country's first prime minister) may have underestimated the scope of these challenges – the grave problems of social injustice that were inherited from colonialism, the intensity of the alienation from the institutions of state, and the need to reform and perhaps even reinvent some of these institutions and the system of governance. As in the first decade of independence, today the task of economic development is also emphasized (cf. Robotham 2002). All of these problems, however, cannot be reduced to economic solutions, although in some cases economic development may be a necessary condition for their solution. The failure to properly resolve these issues and to develop some consensus on them has contributed to the present problematic outcomes and social malaise.

The reality is that these problems, especially violent crime, are now more acute and complicated than ever and are impatient of properly planned, systematic and long-term treatment. Perhaps Jamaica must first truly become a nation before it is able to develop the unity of purpose and broad consensus that is necessary for sustained effective treatment of these problems. Nevertheless, it is evident that mal-administration and the ineffectiveness of some of the state institutions have contributed to the problems. Public policy always affects social outcomes, especially in developing societies where the economies are weak and the state plays a significant role in the allocation of social goods. For example, policies that result in greater socioeconomic inequality are likely to indirectly contribute to increased social violence. Public policy matters, and policy makers must therefore take responsibility for the outcomes. But misguided or even ineffective policies should not be equated with mal-administration, by which is meant official (not just political) malfeasance, and the corrupt manipulation of the authority and power associated with public and state administrative offices. Mal-administration has resulted in a discrediting of the elites, especially the political elite, as it is believed to be implicated in the corrupt accumulation of capital by selected members of in-groups and in facilitating the activities of networks that plunder the resources of the state via various forms of enterprise crimes – usually in construction.[1]

Mal-administration tends to reduce the effectiveness of the state. This ineffectiveness of the state institutions was perhaps most evident in two recent incidents in small-town Jamaica. The first incident occurred in the usually peaceful town of Spaulding in the parish of Manchester, where the rate of violent crime tends to be relatively low. There, in response to a series of incidents of violent crime, citizens mobilized themselves as vigilante groups and rioted and attacked a police station in an effort to "lynch" three men whom they erroneously thought were criminals and who had sought refuge in the police station.[2] More recently, in July 2002, there was a similar incident in Clarks Town, Trelawny (another parish with a relatively low rate of violent crime), where over three hundred residents attacked the local police station with the aim of punishing four alleged offenders who had been detained by the police for violently victimizing a prominent member of the community.[3] These are unusual events, but they nevertheless show the extent to which citizens seem to have lost their patience with the crime problem, and lost confidence in the ability of the police to protect them and in the capacity of the state to provide effective institutional responses to the problem.

By their actions, albeit at times of the dangerously lawless type, the people are demanding a change in the way that the criminal justice system operates. The ineffectiveness of the system and the prevalence of negative perceptions of it have meant that the structures and methods of operation of these institutions (not the *idea* of such institutions) have very few overt defenders.[4] Talk of change is quite acceptable; the extent and character of change is, however, a different matter. With a few notable exceptions, administrators in the criminal justice system seem to have adjusted (downwards) their expectations of the role of their institutions, and have become more concerned with *managing* the crime problem. To suggest that simply managing this and other social problems is not enough, and that instead serious efforts should be made to try to "solve" them, may appear as idealistic and wishful thinking, but this is the kind of "luxury" of intellectual engagement that the academy thankfully affords some of us. To think in these terms means keeping the fundamental challenges in view and, despite the difficulties of the moment, suggesting that new crime control and prevention strategies may be needed. Suggesting even that, in the light of our experience, perhaps the crime problem has not been properly characterized and should be renamed, and that the police force and criminal justice institutions should be reinvented, not just "modernized".

Jamaicans have become very anxious about violent crime (Harriott 1998), yet the society is in danger of becoming very tolerant of crime, especially if the victims are not readily identifiable. The society is slowly yielding to higher thresholds of tolerance of crime, even as the population becomes progressively more concerned with this problem. Durkheim accepted the notion of a normal-functional level of crime in society or, as he put it, crime may be regarded as "an integrative element in any healthy society" ([1895] 1982, 98). Jamaicans have been adjusting the threshold of normality in both the moral and statistical senses in which the term may be used – that is, shifting the definitional boundaries of what is socially regarded as crime, and also adjusting upward the crime rate or statistical norm at which public opinion asserts itself and some mobilization against criminality occurs. As a part of the process of adjustment to living with high levels of violent crime, urban Jamaica has been trying to seek a new accommodation to it.

This process of normalizing criminal behaviour includes attitudes to some categories of street crime but is most evident in the attitudes to white-collar, corporate and governmental crimes whereby these latter types of offence are largely treated as mismanagement and errors of judgement.[5] What, after, all could be more innocently normal than an error of judgement? The link between politics and crime, an issue explored in some of the chapters in this collection, has contributed handsomely to this process of normalization. Corrupt ways of accessing the resources of the state are often treated as the normal way of doing business with the government. Tolerance of crime in the society has in some cases led to outright support for criminal networks, if not for criminality, as is evident in the relatively new roles being accorded street criminals and organized crime. These roles include the provision of services such as policing the communities, punishing criminal offenders and providing protection services to commerce. Such relatively new roles are added to old roles such as that of the party mobilizer who disrupts the activities of the opposition and fraudulently delivers the votes on the day of the elections. Here again electoral crimes are, in some areas of the country, treated as normal political activity, the expected and, in some measure, the accepted way of conducting electoral campaigns.

The process of adjustment and accommodation to crime is radically reshaping urban life, reducing the effectiveness of the state institutions responsible for responding to crime and sapping the will of the population to resist. Indeed, elsewhere I have characterized the current situation in Jamaica as a crisis of public safety (Harriott 2001). This should not be confused with a crisis of national security. The state, the regime, is not seriously threatened politically by either external or internal forces – although the threats posed by drug trafficking should not be underestimated. It is, however, the citizens' security that is problematic, indeed manifestly problematic, as the incapacity of the state to protect its citizens from criminal violence becomes more evident.

Another way of stating the idea of a crisis of public safety is that Jamaica is at a crossroads or turning point. It is vital that the present moment or point in the process of coping with violence in the society be properly understood. If indeed Jamaica is at a crossroads with respect to its crime problem, then the public policy response may definitively shape the long-term outcomes. It could help to abort the socially destructive processes that are emerging, or serve to consolidate and culturally entrench them. Despite the existence of a crisis of public safety, a broader social crisis and a stagnant crisis-prone economy, the sudden collapse of Jamaican society into total disorder and near anarchy is unlikely. The country has a strong, competitive two-party system and, despite the high level of conflict and the low level of trust between groups and in our state institutions, there is always considerable capacity to manoeuvre and fairly good prospects for renewal from within the system. The attempts to accommodate crime and to placate and even incorporate some of the major crime networks (even into aspects of city governance) are not just expressions of the pathologies in the political system, but are also expressions of the capacity of political administrations to manoeuvre in crisis conditions.

A continuing accommodation to crime, however, and the emergence of new normative expectations and behaviour patterns will make it increasingly difficult to ensure the rule of law and may further undermine the legitimacy of the institutions of state which are compromised by these processes. If we are at a historic crossroads, obviously in another decade we will, with hindsight, be better able to judge. But how are we to know without the benefit of hindsight? Perhaps we may better illuminate this idea of a crossroads by examining similar moments and roads taken in the past.

One such crossroads in the recent past was in the period 1976–77. As noted elsewhere, during these years Jamaica departed from the traditional pattern of crime which was characterized by a high ratio of property to violent crime, to one where the incidence of violent crimes was greater than the incidence of property crimes. The trend lines for these two categories of crime actually crossed in 1977 and continued to take opposite trajectories, with the rate of property crimes declining and the rate of violent crimes increasing (Harriott 1996). This was clearly a period when the policy makers and the general public felt that Jamaica was in a new and difficult situation in relation to the problem of violent crime (which had been a major issue since the mid-1960s). The government responded to this danger by intensifying its "fight against crime", declaring a state of emergency and imposing the Suppression of Crimes Act, which considerably extended the powers of the police and diminished the rights of the citizenry and, in addition, made the military a regular day-to-day actor in policing. Consistent with the approach of the previous government led by Prime Minister Hugh Shearer in the mid- to late 1960s, in 1972 the prime minister, Mr Michael Manley, renewed the declaration of war against crime and violence in the Jamaican society and made a call for national discipline and an end to what he called "goonism".[6]

These policing measures, as is well known, did not alter the upward trajectory of the rate of violent crime. Considerable human rights abuses (and protests against them) were associated with the routine use of these tools, and yet despite the mobilizations against this, and the subsequent changes in the law, many of these practices have persisted. Nevertheless, it is difficult to see another administration being able to impose more draconian "war"-type measures unless some extraordinary events were to occur, thereby allowing public opinion to congeal around support for such measures. It would be very difficult to impose harsher disciplinary measures, to up the ante, without going beyond the existing regime constraints, that is, without seriously violating democratic norms. Some respite came in 1980 with the decline in political violence, as the programmes and ideologies of the two parties again tended to converge. This brief decline was followed by another steady increase in the rate of violent crimes, this time as primarily social, not political, violence.

Even though the responses to it have not changed much, Jamaica's crime problem today is radically different from in the mid-1970s, that is, at the time of the first turning point. The rate of violent crime is now much higher. The homicide rate has increased from 17.6 per 100,000 citizens in 1976, to 43 per 100,000 in 2001.[7] This is an extraordinarily high homicide rate when compared with most of the other countries of the region, and indeed the world (Harriott 2000). It is a statistical outlier. But the changes are not simply quantitative. Beyond the figures are the development of organized crime, transnational networks of organized crime that are based on drug trafficking and drug dealing in the main consumer markets of North America and Europe, the burgeoning of the extortion and protection rackets, frequent gang warfare in the cities and, importantly, the *new social power* and enhanced political influence of some of the major crime networks. The Zeeks riot was one of the clearest expressions of this power.

In September 1998 Donald Phipps, otherwise known as Zeeks, the leader of an area in downtown Kingston, was arrested by the police for allegedly "sentencing" and punishing someone for criminal violations committed in *his* area or, rather, the area in the city that falls under his protection. His arrest resulted in three days of rioting, demonstrations and armed clashes between the security forces on one hand, and gangsters and community gunmen on the other. The violence left some five persons dead, including a soldier; seven shot and injured, including four policemen; a number of torched police vehicles, including an armoured vehicle that the police were forced to abandon; and the eventual release on bail and subsequent acquittal of Mr Phipps.[8] Some time after the riot these forces participated in helping to crush opposition-inspired political protests against a new government tax on the price of gasoline, thereby improving their political stocks. The relationship between crime and community, and thus between community crime networks and the political parties, is being redefined on the basis of the emergent social power of the inner-city poor and those who claim to lead them. Disorder in the form of street vending, and even riots, may be more effectively controlled with the assistance of those networks that govern aspects of the lives of the urban poor and that determine which political parties should be allowed access to the communities of the urban poor and be awarded their votes *en bloc*. It is fairly evident that a new pattern of crime and its relationship to the party system and perhaps even new and quite dangerous methods of governance are merging.

There is nothing in the available historical record to suggest that the nature of the 1976–77 turning point was properly understood at the time. At best the period was seen as a historical juncture at which social and political violence intersected and new synergies between the two were developing. The danger was then largely presented as being primarily politically inspired violence.[9] Of course, the appropriate measures for dealing with political violence are quite different from the measures for social or ordinary criminal violence. Yet data available at the time would have clarified the emerging changes in the patterns of ordinary criminal offending and would have indicated that, while the problem may have been intensified by political competition and armed militancy, it could not be completely reduced to the political. The true significance of 1976–77 was that a fundamental shift in the structure of crime occurred at this point. In 1976–77 Jamaica radically departed from the traditional pattern of crime of preceding years, whereby the number of property crimes was always greater than the number of violent crimes. The difference between the two had been gradually narrowing since the waves of violent crime in the mid- to late 1960s, but in 1977 the lines crossed. This was the first crossroads of the post-independence period. Thereafter a rapid escalation in political and ordinary criminal violence occurred, with the homicide rate peaking at 41 per 100,000 in 1980.[10]

The new crossroads is thus more problematic – more difficult to solve (political violence may be *resolved*), and more difficult to discern without the benefit of hindsight.[11] This new crossroads is indicated by the following markers, which are not exhaustive:

- An extraordinarily high rate of homicides and social violence more generally.

- Emergence of a new dynamic to this violence which includes a shift from interpersonal to intergroup violence, thereby making the situation more volatile and given to sudden escalations.

- The normative structuring or disciplining of this violence, and thus the prospect of the institutionalization of violent self-help methods of dealing with social conflicts.

- Violence becoming a business, a field of entrepreneurial activity. Groups and individuals now sell their ability to employ violence as a service (this is what the protection racket is all about) or use it to extort money from legitimate business firms. Those who control groups of armed men may exploit this as an economic asset by dominating an area and forcing persons who operate businesses within their area to pay a "tax".

- The power of organized crime and armed groups, and their entrenchment in some of the urban communities and their role in controlling and punishing rule violations.

- Community self-regulation and non-cooperation with the crime control agencies of the state.

- Incapacity of the formal institutions to effectively cope with the crime problem and their continued weakening as they tend to abuse their powers, offer poor service and fall prey to corruption.

- Crime, especially organized crime, is no longer responsive simply to local opportunities and conditions. As players in a larger international drug market, Jamaican criminal networks also respond to developments and opportunities abroad which may serve to strengthen their capacity to survive and to nullify control initiatives in Jamaica (or any single country).

Some of these developments are more fully discussed in chapter 5. It seems, however, that violence in Jamaica is developing a dynamic that is relatively independent of its "root causes". Jamaica may be approaching the point where dealing with root causes may not have much of an impact – unless coupled with other measures, including more consistent and just law enforcement. For example, organized crime has now developed a parasitic relationship, and in some instances a symbiotic parasitism, with business. The growth of the economy, the creation of opportunities for the unemployed, may also lead to the creation of greater opportunities for organized crime. Economic growth by itself may thus result in a strengthening of organized crime – unless it is accompanied by measures designed to deal directly with this form of criminal enterprise. In developing an effective response to the crime problem, more complex combinations of measures and processes may be required.

In this context there are new challenges for understanding and theorizing the crime problem and developing appropriate policy responses to it. There is a great need for research, including action research based on active engagement with the problem. The popularly held view that enough is known about the crime problem, that all that is needed is for policy makers to muster the political will to deal with the problem, grossly oversimplifies the reality. This idea is perhaps based on the erroneous view that all that is needed are tough policing measures, or to throw money at the inner-city communities. It is not an idea that is to be found among researchers or professional practitioners in this field, and it would be considered very strange by researchers, not simply because there are no final answers to the issues already explored in the academic literature, but also because there is so much that is of policy relevance which is either not known or about which no systematic work has been done.

Any reading of the academic literature on crime in the Caribbean will reveal very modest knowledge claims, and even more modest claims to policy inventiveness and innovation. This is not to suggest that more should be known before any concerted action is taken to control the crime problem, but rather that there should be learning and acting, and learning to act more effectively. Much is yet to be done.

Notes

1. There is ample evidence of this in the annual reports of the contractor general and in the recent report by the Angus Commission.
2. See the *Daily Gleaner,* 20 April 2002.
3. See the *Daily Gleaner,* 29 July 2002.
4. See IDB 2000 for a report on the perceptions of their criminal justice systems that are held by Caribbean publics.
5. This type of normalizing process must, however, be distinguished from normalizing crime as crime.
6. See the *Daily Gleaner,* 3 July 1972, 1.
7. Computed from data on reported incidents of homicide provided by the Jamaica Constabulary Force, and population estimate taken from the Planning Institute of Jamaica.
8. For a description of these events see the *Daily Gleaner,* 24–27 September 1998; also Meeks 2000, 1–5.
9. See Charles 1977 for an activist's account of this period.
10. The peak in the homicide rate is associated with the intense political violence at the time. After 1980 the rate declined sharply, but, as noted earlier, in 1997 it peaked again, with this second peak in the rate deriving its impetus from ordinary criminal violence.
11. Of course, with the benefit of hindsight this problem, this notion of a turning point may prove to have been contrived by the imagination of the author.

References

Charles, P. 1977. *Detained: 283 Days in Jamaica's Detention Camp, Struggling for Freedom, Justice, and Human Rights!* Kingston, Jamaica: Kingston Publishers.

Durkheim, E. (1895) 1982. *Rules of Sociological Method.* New York: Free Press.

Harriott, A. 1996. "The Changing Social Organization of Crime and Criminals in Jamaica". *Caribbean Quarterly* 42, nos. 2–3.

———. 1998. "Fear of Crime in a Reputedly Violent Environment". Paper presented at the conference on Crime and Criminal Justice in the Caribbean, Bridgetown, Barbados, 14–16 October.

———. 2000. "Police Reform in the Caribbean". *Caribbean Dialogue* 6, nos. 1–2.

———. 2001. "The Crisis of Public Safety in Jamaica and the Prospects for Change". *Souls* 3, no. 4.

Inter-American Development Bank (IDB). 2000. "Challenges of Capacity Development: Towards Sustainable Reform of Caribbean Justice Sectors". Vol. 3. Unpublished report.

Manley, N.W. 1971. *Norman Washington Manley and the New Jamaica: Selected Speeches and Writings, 1938–1968,* edited and notes by R. Nettleford. Kingston, Jamaica: Longman Caribbean.

Meeks, B. 2000. *Narratives of Resistance: Jamaica, Trinidad, the Caribbean.* Kingston, Jamaica: University of the West Indies Press.

Robotham, D. 2002. "Analyzing the Jamaican Crisis". *Souls* 3, no. 4.

2

Badness-Honour

Obika Gray

Defiance among the urban poor is remarkable for its preoccupation with matters of identity, honour and respect. Indeed, the pre-eminence of cultural concerns in the politics of the alienated urban poor suggests that culture is the terrain on which key social struggles are fought in Jamaica. Hostile responses to cultural insubordination among the poor, antipathy for their inversion of traditional norms and calls for a return to traditional values highlight how controversial contested notions of "self-respect" have become. What follows is an extended discussion of a particular form of cultural insubordination – badness-honour – and an examination of its implications.

In describing Jamaican politics, previous studies have yoked the concept of democracy and the notion of political clientelism. The co-joining of these two terms produced important insights into Jamaican politics, and those discoveries are still being developed. However, because of dramatic changes in Jamaican politics since the mid-1970s and because power in postcolonial Jamaica has never been a simple matter of democracy and clientelism, reassessments are in order.

Indeed, these two concepts may have outlived their usefulness. State clientelism has collapsed, and the civic culture necessary for democratic rule has long been in tatters. Democratic institutions are moribund, and illegal and flagrantly corrupt practices have supplanted democratic procedures. In short, the term "democratic clientelism" seems wholly inadequate to describe politics since the mid-1970s, and certainly the term does not now describe Jamaican political realities.

An alternative proposition is to recognize the existence of an inventive form of power in Jamaica – one that weds structures of clientelism and democratic institutions to extra-legal processes associated with criminal and political underworlds. More than that, we need an alternative formulation capable of recognizing the identity of a power that abhors sharp political boundaries and is intolerant of the autonomy of popular oppositional cultures. In sum, it seems useful to rename a power that can employ criminal and democratic procedures, rule by means of absorption of clashing political values, co-join dissonant institutional structures, and even organize the cohabitation of democratically elected representatives and their co-governors from criminal and political underworlds.

Democratic societies have typically engaged in sharp boundary maintenance. They have done so to prohibit resort to informal, unconstitutional political structures, to bar the mixing of incompatible civic values, and to rule out the combination of legal and illegal processes as the routine, even characteristic, way of exercising democratic power.

Power in Jamaica has never maintained such strictures. On the contrary, political power has been defined by permeability between ostensibly incompatible structures, overlapping of dissonant norms, and cohabitation of democratic representatives and allies from criminal and political underworlds. In revisiting the identity of political power in Jamaica, it seems reasonable to recognize the dilation of this power across incompatible social spaces, to appreciate its predation on dissonant value systems, and to acknowledge its brazen co-joining of criminal practices and democratic procedures. More than that, because Jamaican state agents have always sought to make power ubiquitous, we need to recognize the parasitic nature of their power. Such a power has embraced democratically informed procedures and off-stage, extra-legal repertoires rooted in popular oppositional norms and criminal subcultures.

This sociopolitical parasitism is remarkable for its protean qualities. Unlike "traditional" forms of autocratic power which often attempt to establish a divide between a dissident popular culture and the culture of the ruling class, state parasitism in Jamaica is more inventive. It reproduces dominant power by appropriating oppositional elements within popular culture, blurring and even collapsing the boundaries between antagonistic cultural forms of the alienated poor and those of their nemesis in the class system. It's important to note, however, that sociopolitical parasitism in Jamaica is neither an aberration nor an index of the failure of political power. Instead, it is best viewed as a repertoire of power, simply a mechanism to manage social contradictions unleashed by unequal relations of power in a peripheral society. The overall result has been the fashioning of a brutal form of rule that combines the cultural intimacy of clientelism with a form of punitive violence against the uncooperative urban poor that can only be called exterminism.

Responses to Predatory Power

Forms of engagement by the mobilized poor reveal distinctive responses to this form of power and domination. Unlike disadvantaged groups in poor countries who remained quiescent, rose up in revolutionary violence or overthrew oppressive states by insurgent "people power", discontent among the militant urban poor in Jamaica disclosed none of these polarizing traits. Instead, popular response to harsh disadvantage has assumed a novel form. It expresses itself as an agonism that has more to do with unrequited affairs of honour than with establishing coalitions of the oppressed or seeking the overthrow and seizure of state power.

A remarkable feature of alienation in Jamaica's urban ghetto is the intensity of group mobilization and high levels of social consciousness on the one hand, and the throttled expression of group social power on the other. On the one side, lower-class social and political alienation produced high levels of political activism and compelling varieties of culturally informed engagements. On the other, lower-class social discontent triggered massive violence, unleashed disruptive social dynamics and fed clashing, destabilizing relations of power. Still, these mighty exertions seemed more attuned to securing lower-class social honour and escaping atomized personal and group power, than to toppling state actors or even embracing an alternative dissident elite.

Emotionally laden and deeply felt antisocial identities linked to racially charged concerns have informed lower-class activism in Jamaica. Across ghetto communities, heightened awareness of stigmas and cultural injuries has fed individual and group belligerence. While the urban poor could hardly ignore political matters, political considerations have not dimmed alertness to urgent group cultural needs. Indeed, in post-independence Jamaica group cultural claims seemed overwhelming in their influence. It is arguable that lower-class quests for wealth, power and cultural standing depended less on the official political liturgies of the day than on affirming the poor's own doctrinal commitment and belief in an inviolate black personhood. In the slums, a near-sacred defence of imperiled black humanity fed racially saturated claims to honour, power and economic need. Hence a dominant preoccupation in the ghetto was not the overthrow of the existing political order by means of a united and concerted opposition by all strata of the urban poor. Rather, self-ownership, social ambition and competitive individualism in the cause of personal and racial-group achievement became core values. Consequently, volitional rights and cultural respect for subordinated *black persons* became common sense in poor communities. These twin considerations, and an arch response to their violation, fed and maintained defiance of authority.

Variations notwithstanding, the multiple involvements of the alienated urban poor had one thing in common: anxieties of black personhood and acute sensitivity concerning reputation, social honour and respect. The urban poor made them priorities, and the social power of the group used these cultural claims to defend a variety of interests well beyond cultural matters. This preoccupation was so powerful that the mobilized poor seemed less concerned with unseating predatory power than with assuring that both state and society respected the volitional identity and the status claims of a racially proud but throttled population.

In reaching for this elusive goal, disadvantaged groups and over-loyal fanatics fought less for freedom of political opinion and unconstrained political choice for the partisan poor in the slums than for the indivisibility of cultural respect and lower-class volitional rights. In brief, regardless of their agendas, the socially mobilized, alienated urban poor were not so much champions of free political choice in the ghetto, as they were exponents of that durable and unyielding brand of cultural fundamentalism we call personal freedom.

Poor people's fundamentalism for themselves as honourable, inviolate persons of a particular ethnic group insisted, above all else, on volition, self-management and black dignity. This lower-class cultural essentialism made personal honour and racial-group respect the *sine qua non* of social existence, and insisted that both state and society defer to these core values. For the most alienated contingents, this fundamentalism of personal freedom and racial-group honour is best described by the concept of badness-honour.

A Theory of Badness-Honour

By the early 1970s the mobilized urban poor had established multiple claims to group power and had created manifold sources of identity. Outlawry-as-identity, particularly among the alienated young, had established its hegemony over all other identity claims, and its supremacy identified rebels in the slums as a volatile, non-compliant constituency that was ill-disposed to easy moral governance and cheap political blandishments. Despite its vogue in the slums, however, hardened defiance was typical of only the most alienated elements. It should be remembered that the rebelliousness that led to crime, banditry and general mayhem among the poor was the work of only a tiny minority. Not all slum-dwellers and residents of working-class districts were driven to outlawry. A majority of these residents still remained law abiding, even as more and more of the unemployed young in working-class communities were fast becoming morally uncaptured rebels.

Motivated variously by devout religious faith, commitment to civic morality and ambition for upward mobility, the lawful majority still adhered to racially inflected norms of excellence as the means to group uplift. As community exemplars whose inclinations ran neither to partisan violence nor to antisocial rebellion, this majority contingent offered to the restive young and other marginals a racially informed culture of uplift tied to traditional values.[1]

Yet, despite the fortitude of these role models, contrary trends weakened the force of their example. As the dynamic alliance between the parties and militant slum-dwellers unfolded, and as social inequalities widened during the early 1970s, the restraining influence of this majority group was steadily eclipsed. That authority was supplanted by the heightened moral sway of the lumpenproletariat. As this group became immersed in the cut and thrust of constituency-and-street-level politics, its desperate supplicancy and pioneering demand for racial justice imposed tremendous moral pressures on law-abiding groups and on the political parties.

Party leaders and activists responded positively to these demands. Indeed, as the parties sought to manipulate this supplicancy, the struggle for benefits encouraged further antisocial defiance among the rebellious poor. That defiance was represented by the popularity of what I shall call the norm of badness-honour. As I shall explain below, badness-honour is the oral-kinetic practice in Jamaica that enables claimants, usually from disadvantaged groups, to secure by means of intimidation a modicum of power and respect.

By 1971 badness-honour as a cultural practice had won moral dominance within the society of the Kingston poor. There a stylized outlawry ("badness" in Jamaican parlance) provoked fear in the larger society, but earned raves in the slums for challenging the norm of civility and for affirming a racially charged defiance as a new basis for social identity and respect (honour).[2] Defiance of conventional norms by juvenile gangs and political enforcers gave such rebels in the slums a martial, violence-ridden identity totally at odds with widely held norms of respectability and obedience to law. By the end of the 1960s acts of badness-honour and the sensibility that informed them were commonplace in Kingston's ghettos; by the early 1970s that outlaw sensibility had deepened its hold on both the society and the political culture of the parties.

Of course, outlawry and violence as signature features of politics in urban Kingston were neither new nor solely the acts of desperate supplicants. In the decades-long association between parties and urban masses, the moral concerns of the alienated poor had preoccupied the parties and dominated the calculations of their leaders and activists. Material want among the urban poor and their boisterous outlawry in the service of partisan politics and self-help had compelled the parties and their strategists to acknowledge this alienated constituency.

One effect of this association was that urban politicians and activists were compelled to exhibit their own forms of braggadocio, outlawry and aggression if they were to survive in Kingston with its violent political culture. There is little doubt, then, that mass pressure from below and the suzerainty of hardy politicians in Kingston had long made violent outlawry a feature of Jamaican politics that was not confined to the ranks of the militant poor. What was new in the early 1970s, however, was the increased authority that badness-honour assumed as a cultural force in political life. To the satisfaction of the lumpenproletariat and their allies in the parties, political contestation drew increasingly on the contentious symbolism, combative dramaturgy and pugnacious etiquette of urban street life and culture.

Displays of badness-honour had become *de rigueur* in urban politics and party culture. Political activists and leaders bid up their dramaturgic claims to respect in these years. The histrionics of partisan competition with its outlaw tinge confirmed, for friend and foe alike, that politics in urban Jamaica were increasingly being regulated by a stunning cultural imperative: the adoption on all side of martial identities. They became the carriers of new social claims and the basis for the allocation of status honour.

Politics and access to power on the hustings therefore paid increasing homage to an aggressive corporeal etiquette. An important claim to personal authority now relied on a capacity to deploy militant social identities that would cause others to take pause and possibly concede respect. The lumpenproletariat became outriders in proclaiming this new right to honour among the poor. State agents backed this normative turn in the slums and complemented this endorsement with their own forms of badness-honour. This legitimation of outlawry by state agents had two effects: it won the political support of violent suppliants, and it awed them with the political patrons' equally militant claims to respect.[3]

In the society of the mobilized poor, it therefore became customary to break laws and to flaunt social customs as ways of decrying racial and social injustice. Outlawry, social indiscipline and violation of norms of respectability were justified in the name of rolling back imbalances in social power and affirming the poor's right to racial honour. Badness-honour among the poor had therefore become a retort to unequal power, class discrimination and ethnic injustice in Jamaica.[4]

Rival politicians seeking office and trying to establish their credentials with the militant poor matched this outlawry in the slums. This showmanship by politicians helped win political office; it also worked to regulate the delicate relations of power between boisterous supplicants on the one hand and their party sponsors on the other. Supplicants' irrepressible aggression for benefits solicited politicians' histrionic counterstrikes against these feisty loyalists. Braggadocio, threats of violence and ritual aggressive displays by middle-class politicians set the oral-kinetic terms under which equally martial supplicants were compelled to grant due deference and social respect to political sponsors. Politicians' aggressive histrionics tempered violent histrionics from below while affirming the patrons' own right to deference. In this way displays of badness-honour among party notables and middle-class organizers gradually established, in the eyes of the poor, the terms of submission to power, the basis for the cultural authenticity of political patrons, and the legitimacy of their right to rule in the violent urban cauldron.

As we have seen, those relations were driven by mutual need: politicians needed votes and the muscle of their backers, while supplicants needed the benefits and the political protection of their sponsors. However, as these relations unfolded it became clear that it was the urban poor who were dictating the terms for evolving claims to cultural authenticity and personal respect. State agents adapted themselves to that lead while boldly harnessing the violent gamesmanship among the poor. Racial agonism in the slums and a violent street culture dictated the etiquette by which votes were sought, they defined how constituencies could be secured against challengers, and they set the terms for claiming a heroic individualism within and beyond partisan engagements. A durable, boisterous gamesmanship had therefore migrated from the streets of Kingston. It compelled the society to take contentious notice and it entered the political fray, where it was both welcomed and condemned. This agonism of the powerless therefore provoked controversy with its claims on both politics and society. Because of its centrality to Jamaica's sociopolitical life, the concept of badness-honour warrants further examination.

As indicated earlier, in Jamaica this coupling refers to a distinct dramaturgy in which claimants to respect and social honour employ intimidation and norm-disrupting histrionics – "badness" in popular

Jamaican parlance – to affirm their right to an honour contested or denied. Although currently high rates of homicide and lawlessness have encouraged pundits on the island to associate these developments with a peculiarly aggressive "Jamaicanness", acts of badness-honour are not uniquely Jamaican.[5] On the contrary, such practices should be seen as one of the mundane and ubiquitous "everyday" weapons of the weak. At this juncture, it may be useful to elaborate on the specificity of what I have been calling "badness-honour".

Acts of badness-honour occur among the poor across all societies. It is the assertive form that moral alienation takes in contexts of inequality and social domination. It is the social behaviour that can result from sharp deficits in power, group respect and material well-being. In postwar urban Jamaica aggressive public displays of personal violence and defensive postures to secure an imperiled self in the ghetto qualify as forms of badness-honour. Thus, the racial indignation of the Rastafarians and the nihilistic outlawry of the "rude boys" were quintessential expressions of badness-honour in the 1960s. Their dramaturgy, and that of allied groups, confirms badness-honour as a social norm and a publicly displayed repertoire employed by alienated but highly mobilized social forces who want to change their disadvantaged circumstances. Badness-honour is evident therefore in the public, kinetic expression and corporeal gestures employed by social agents in contexts of domination and social inequality. Badness-honour is a repertoire that employs language, facial gesture, bodily poses and an assertive mien to compel rivals or allies to grant power, concede respect, accord deference or satisfy material want.

Badness-honour is therefore a cultural style which may be used to intimidate others through menacing or histrionic gestures. It may also be employed to bargain and negotiate the terms by which power, social respect, deference or resources are granted or denied to claimants. Acts of badness-honour constitute a gestural-symbolic system and a carrier of moral communication. Through badness-honour, intersubjective understandings about the basis of identity and the terms of power are conveyed by intensive corporeal acts of speech and gesture. Such acts exercise moral compulsion on social subordinates, group allies and social superiors.

While the norm of badness-honour may employ violence, it does not rely solely on the use of violence to be effective. Ominous threat, rather than actual violence, is the stock-in-trade of those exhibiting badness-honour. Menaces and histrionics to overawe and compel are often enough to secure the claims of practitioners. Of course, when these compulsions are inadequate they are indeed buttressed by resort to violence. As a repertoire in the arsenal of disparate groups and social actors, violent forms of badness-honour may well be amplified where harsh social domination and sharp inequalities exist. Provoked by conflicts and social tensions in these societies, exponents of badness-honour may employ histrionic gestures to rally allies or to intimidate and overawe adversaries. These exponents, who can come from diverse social backgrounds, typically apply these compulsions not through the violent machinery of the state, but through the aggressive display of unpredictable and ominous *corporeal power.*

Gestures of badness-honour may form the basis for a heroic individualism in contexts of deprivation. And while badness-honour is a form of personal charisma, it is surely the dark side of that magnetism. Indeed, where an optimistic populist charisma had once been the primary stock-in-trade of politicians and notables in Jamaica, that heroism was rapidly eclipsed in the postwar period by a snarling, violence-provoking disposition among both urban politicians and their ghetto supplicants. The former used violence-ridden histrionics to overawe and compel respect from boisterous, reckless supplicants, and the latter embraced a similar aggression both as a mark of social distinction and as a leverage on discriminatory political processes.

Badness-honour is therefore a variable repertoire available to disparate groups engaged in struggles to satisfy material want and to protect or claim imperiled values such as status rights and personal and group respect. Badness-honour is a major weapon of the powerless, for whom corporeal aggression is a real form of social power. As commentators remind us, the powerless in contexts of domination may not tolerate abuses indefinitely. If degraded and abused they have often resorted to volcanic oral-kinetic expressions as compensatory forms of leverage over both status allies and power holders (see Scott 1990).

Yet, as indicated earlier in this discussion, badness-honour, for all its usefulness to the poor, is not a resource available only to the disadvantaged.

Indeed, power holders have also found this repertoire useful for their purposes. Slave masters, colonial authorities, rural patrons and party bosses in postcolonial societies have also employed it for their own designs. Hence, both rulers and ruled resort to badness-honour, and may do so in contexts where "traditional" values and the societies that uphold them are subject to challenge. These societies with massive and unyielding inequalities in power, honour and wealth are the ones most likely to provoke dramatic and hardcore expressions of badness-honour among both rulers and ruled.

Despite this association between badness-honour and traditional settings, badness-honour as a repertoire of *subaltern* power may also appear in modern and highly industrialized societies. As the activities of street gangs in Los Angeles and the violent lyrics of "gangster rap" in the United States make clear, affirmation of a violent, stylized outlawry *in the name of rescuing a racially impugned self* is not limited to small and economically underdeveloped countries. Moreover, as the American example also makes clear, acts of badness-honour appear in democratic as well as in authoritarian political systems. Badness-honour is therefore a distinct repertoire of power and a tool of politics available to disparate groups enmeshed in power relations in many kinds of societies.

Despite these generic qualities and the ubiquity that identifies badness-honour as a worldwide cultural phenomenon, mere domination and inequality need not lead to the adoption of this dissident norm by the poorer classes. Poverty and economic hardship are not sufficient conditions for the display of badness-honour. That may depend on other determinants. Depending on the history of the country in question, disadvantaged groups may respond to domination without resort to our description of badness-honour.

Popular responses to domination have included revolutionary activity, political self-organization or covert non-compliance. Poverty has also led to resignation, disengagement or even flight by the poor. Deprivation need not lead to rebellion, and it need not provoke the kind of outlawry discussed here. Badness-honour seems to be only one of many kinds of political option exercised by the disadvantaged as they respond to different kinds of social domination. Political indeterminacy, not political regularities, seems to shape the options that the poor employ. It may be only when a combination of factors exists in poor countries that norms of badness-honour are chosen over other political options.

It is arguable, for instance, that badness-honour in poor countries tends to occur in contexts where the exercise of power is harsh, pre-emptive and ubiquitous, yet not so totally monopolistic that popular defiance becomes impossible. Badness-honour may occur in contexts where certain cultural traditions are absent, while other relevant ones are decisively present. Thus, badness-honour that is reflected in wide-spread outlawry may be heightened in settings where a sustained martial and revolutionary tradition among the people is *lacking,* even as intense social and political mobilization of the poor is acutely present.

Similarly, badness-honour in the form that I have described may also unfold in peripheral societies where individualism and personal ambition for upward mobility are intensely shared and are among the premium values of that society. Badness-honour may be facilitated in contexts where the status-honour of the mobilized poor is actively impugned and degraded, and their material wants stubbornly denied. Indeed, acts of badness-honour may become the typical defiant response from below where state and non-state actors mobilize the poor for political agendas, even as these state actors simultaneously throttle – by violence and co-optation – the ambitions of the poor for democracy, cultural self-regard and material betterment.

Badness-honour as outlawry and challenge to traditional norms of civility may similarly thrive in contexts where cultural self-regard and social cooperation among the deprived population are contradictory and ambiguously felt in contexts of high competitive individualism. In such societies acts of badness-honour may take on idiosyncratic guises. In these contexts personalist defiance and group agonism may displace other options in the challenge to political power.

Indeed, highly personalized forms of badness-honour and group agonism may occur and assume particular force in contexts where face-to-face encounters, ethnicity and other "intimate" interpersonal relations are the dominant bases for social interaction, the distribution of power and the granting of social respect. In such contexts affective ties and deeply felt ethnic sentiments, rather than impersonal norms, usually govern the formation of identities and the access to power. In sum, badness-honour of the kind discussed here may thrive where significant social power and respect derive from networks of interpersonal ties and forms of "intimate" power relations, rather than from the play of distant, impersonal ties or bureaucratic-organizational routines.

As a consequence, norms of badness-honour leading to social outlawry may well be invigorated in those "traditional" societies where oral cultures remain strong, where patron-client relations persist, and where demands for personal loyalty and the securing and protection of reputations are intense, and are achieved through small social networks and face-to-face interactions. Such societies, with their struggles over wealth, personal power, and individual and group honour, can provoke intense and sustained displays of badness-honour among the poor as they seek to rectify social disadvantages and alter relations which injure their reputation and social standing and bar their access to power.

Where ethnic discrimination and resistance to it are decisively part of this contestation, such societies may not just provoke conflicts over wealth and political power, but also trigger acute disputes over personal reputation, public honour and social worth. Hence, where the urban poor are alienated and highly mobilized around issues of ethnic discrimination, they may turn to norms of badness-honour as means to redress grievances, particularly those pertaining to disparities in power and obstacles to individual or group achievement. In such circumstances the play of power may operate at such a level of intimacy in the lives of the downtrodden that a concerted and focused group opposition to systemic power is blocked. In these contexts the intimate play of power can elicit atomized, throttled responses that are informed either by blind anger towards patrons or by cunning efforts to align with or evade them in order to minimize hardships.

In Jamaica this throttling has produced a distinct oppositional form in the postcolonial period: episodic protest, desperate supplicancy, exaggerated loyalty to patrons, and deep personal enmity for party bosses and their supporters. The overall effect of this disposition is that instead of provoking concerted action from the united poor, this patronizing power elicits throttled and atomized responses from them, but also a modicum of compulsion and empowerment within a corrupted system, as the following examples show.

Badness-Honour and the Struggle for Benefits:
The Case of George "Feathermop" Spence

The activities of the late George "Feathermop" Spence of the People's National Party (PNP) provide an excellent example of what can happen when members of the urban poor belonging to the parties' political underground make a bid for social power and respect by using badness-honour to get their way. George Spence was a PNP political enforcer and a recipient of its patronage in the 1970s. As a PNP loyalist from the ghetto, Spence was awarded small government contracts. One contract he received involved repairing gullies in Kingston that were damaged and blocked by flood-waters.

Spence, it should be remembered, came from the ghetto and shared the urban poor's cultural inclinations and political sentiments, including holding Rastafarian sympathies. Even though Spence was undoubtedly a PNP loyalist and could wreak havoc on party enemies, the badness-honour he engaged in to satisfy his own appetite infused his client status with a disruptive disposition. In time party bosses would come to see it as a form of disloyalty and insubordination.

Spence, for example, earned a reputation for using threats to demand monies owed for contracts. PNP activists report that he stormed into municipal offices and demanded by ominous threat disbursement of government monies. In doing so Spence showed a readiness to challenge his own party's implicit rules for the distribution of benefits to loyalists like himself. After all, the custom of both parties explicitly and unmistakably emphasized deference and respect for the party leader and his authority. Party culture also required enforcers' acceptance of handouts, without a fuss, through established channels and procedures. Party political culture was therefore intolerant of behaviours that could be deemed a personal insult to the leader and his authority, or regarded as a gross violation of rules concerning the distribution of benefits.

To be sure, customary practice in the PNP did not entail constant humiliation and personal abuse of key loyalists like Spence. Camaraderie between party bosses and members of the ghetto political underground certainly existed, and disagreements could be aired. Consistent with this flexible relationship, PNP party enforcers had some autonomy, but not so much that they were allowed to impugn the leaders' authority or engage in unsanctioned activities that could bring public embarrassment to the party. In other words, the unequal relationship between PNP bosses and their enforcers, while allowing for some give and take, emphasized tight management of power by party bosses and affirmed the supplicant, subordinate status of their political enforcers.

This hierarchical relationship began breaking down inside the PNP as the level of state patronage to the rank and file increased and as popular pressures for support monies and benefits intensified. By the mid-1970s the distributionist policies of democratic socialism produced related but conflictual phenomena. On the one hand, the policy of handouts reinforced perceptions among the disadvantaged that the PNP was engaging in the traditional "share out" of benefits to its supporters, even though the party was describing these as socialist measures. The supplicant poor recognized the disposition of political spoils for the patronage it was, and they jostled to feed hungrily on the new largesse that had come their way. On the other hand, increased public dismay regarding waste and corruption in politics increased pressures on the parties, and especially the PNP, to rein it in.

Heedless of a growing public outcry on this score, and driven by desperate competition to get at benefits, PNP supplicants like Spence often overstepped boundaries, committed acts of indiscretion and exposed to public view the sharp intra-party factionalism that attended the political distribution of benefits. Hence, when it was publicly disclosed in 1975 that Spence had received nearly double the original amount of a contract to repair the Lilford gully in Kingston, the disclosure of the overpayment severely embarrassed the PNP. Indeed, public outcry and pressure from the political opposition forced party leader and prime minister Michael Manley to begin a police inquiry into the matter (*Daily Gleaner*, 4 July 1975, 1; and 6 July 1975, 1). That Spence engaged in theft and other severe violations of protocol while on an official visit with the party leader to Cuba shows how much of a loose cannon he had become. More importantly, Spence's behaviour indicated how much disdain he had for the party bosses' demand that underlings from the ghetto defer to middle-class party leaders' cultural and political sensibilities.[6] Spence paid the price for these cultural and political infractions as he became *persona non grata* in PNP circles, and few mourned his passing when an assassin cut him down late in 1975.

Sexual Extremism as a Form of Badness-Honour

For Jamaicans of all classes who embraced traditional values and orthodox norms of moral propriety, public and unabashed displays of sexuality – "slackness" – was cause for vigilance. For the guardians of moral
propriety and those who shared their perspective, slackness, especially
among the urban lower classes, was a transgression of Jamaica's traditional norm-identity. For dominant groups, Jamaicanness was premised
on traditions rooted in the island's protean cultural inheritances. In the
late twentieth century, these were a christianizing European colonialism, Afrocentric Ethiopianism and a secular North American materialism. The intersection of all three had produced a norm-identity of
Jamaicanness that privileged the dominance of white over black,
"haves" over "have-nots", and the scribal classes over the orally and
kinetically profuse masses. Status consciousness and celebration of the
Christian-modern, over fears of the profane and the savage-primordial,
completed these polarizing beliefs.

Although all Jamaicans breached these binary opposites and lived
their everyday lives according to a jamboree of values, antinomies
formed part of the normative chain-link fence that barred the black
urban poor from full moral membership in Jamaican society. For dominant groups, slackness was the distillate of all the cultural deficits preventing the black poor from being accepted fully into the Jamaican
community.

Slackness as moral indictment therefore regarded the "careless sexuality" of the black poor as a moral crime. Slackness meant indecency,
public sexual licence, moral degeneracy and erotic lawlessness among
the rebellious black poor. In the realm of popular culture, "dancehall
culture" with its sexually explicit lyrics, its revealing costumes worn by
women, and the frenzy of its music and erotic dancers, confirmed this
degradation arising from ghetto culture.[7] Consequently, slackness and
the moral weaknesses associated with it were not conditions that
afflicted the guardians of moral propriety. To the guardians of public
morality, slackness was confined to the erotic. It was not associated
with theft from the public purse. Nor was it related to rampant private
greed and the widening graft of merchants, entrepreneurs and state
bureaucrats. On the contrary, slackness was a debased moral condition
of sexual extremism from which the ghetto poor had to be rescued.

For the "uptown" and privileged classes, the slackness of the "downtown" lumpenproletariat was more than a menace; it was a civilization threat. For the uptown elite, the black rabble and "dutty criminals" from the slums, with whom the term "culture" could not be associated, were threatening to substitute their debased norms for the civil "values and attitudes" of their social betters. The values evident in popular music, ghetto lifestyles, dance forms and "roots plays" were regarded as a cultural blight, appealing only to the lowest common denominator and to the basest of instincts.

To the better-off classes, and to the moral purists among workers, peasants and the urban poor, slackness was to moral culture what street violence was to politics. In this view the violence of the black poor had invaded and corrupted national politics, causing the better-off classes to flee from it. Now, the critics argued, slackness endangered the national culture in the same manner. For the defenders of moral orthodoxy, slackness threatened to replace social etiquette, civility and moral propriety with debauchery.

The intensity of the outcry that greeted the turn to sexually explicit lyrics in reggae music and the denunciations of the morality of the related dancehall phenomenon highlighted, as perhaps no other issue, fundamental social divisions in Jamaican society. These polarizations threw into sharp relief conflicts between power holders and the black lumpenproletariat. Such contestations also provoked clashes between black lower-class champions of the new, radical otherness and their more "respectable" working-class and urban poor kin. This intra-class conflict even arrayed defenders of earlier, antisystemic cultural and political orthodoxies against exponents of the turn to sexual extremism.[8]

The intensity of these differences over slackness was so acute that it rent Jamaican society, tearing apart traditional alliances, exposing sharp class divisions and triggering moral panics. Most interesting of all, slackness unleashed an inchoate mix of discourses. On the one hand, proponents of respectability slid into a species of cultural exterminism directed at expunging black lower-class moral influence on the society. On the other, defenders of the poor saw in the debate a potential for democratization of the society, acceptance of cultural differences and even the recession of social oppression.

To discern why rival claims to sexual propriety in the form of out-rage against slackness should simultaneously have destructive and recu-perative potentials requires closer examination. My own view is that slackness among the poor is a form of sexual transgression, and as such was merely another repertoire employed by the black lumpenproletariat in its ongoing clash with dominant groups. Just as racial identity and class allegiance disrupted social relations in earlier periods, slackness as a form of badness-honour now provoked huge social divisions. Slack-ness had this effect in the 1980s because the social crisis had ignited a stubborn issue underlying historic conflicts among the Jamaican people-nation, namely the moral status of disadvantaged but combative blacks.

Dominant groups in the late twentieth century echoed the fears and concerns of powerful groups a century earlier. In the 1980s dominant groups affirmed the "savage" identity of rebelling blacks, and won-dered whether they could be rescued for civilization. What made slack-ness so incendiary in the 1980s was partly conflictual social relations that gave moral culture predominance as symbol and crystallization of the social crisis. Criminalization of the state, breakdown of law and order, and predation within and beyond the slums provoked debates over moral and political culture. That moral injunctions were being handed down by political and economic elites who were themselves weakened politically and compromised morally only worsened matters. Yet this double handicap did not deter powerful elites in their claim to moral superiority. Not surprisingly, political debility and perceptions of elite moral weakness led to clashes between these elites and an uncap-tured lumpenproletariat equally determined to assert its own moral claims. That many of these claims revolved around disputed sexual norms only sharpened the conflicts.

Racially embedded sexuality had in effect converged with disputes over unequal social relations. This wedding set off major social tremors. This was the case because many Jamaicans agreed that, together with crime, undisciplined black sexuality in the ghetto was the final rupture of the civilization-identity of the people-nation. Raw sexuality in the ghetto further strained ideas of a "common culture" invoked by some sections of the dominant classes to hail the ghetto poor in the postcolo-nial period. Contested notions of "race" in the 1960s and after had already undercut dominant notions of a common culture. Now a disputed black sexuality posed new challenges to dominant notions.

But while "race" remained a potent cultural marker and incendiary cultural force in Jamaica, sexuality and gender identities also generated conflict and change. Sexuality and gender, like race and class in this postcolonial society, were bases of social stratification and determinants of social inclusion and exclusion. Sexual identity and the uses of the erotic helped to determine cultural membership in Jamaica's postcolonial society. In this racially divided and class-stratified society, the more the black poor policed their sexuality and kept their erotic displays out of public view, the better were their chances of social approval and the more likely their inclusion in the community of the respectable people-nation.

At the same time, however, the dominant society's emphasis on disciplining a fugitive sexuality among the rebellious black poor made that membership increasingly tenuous. Errant sexuality in the ghetto in the late 1980s was as much a threat to stable cultural relations as riotous acts of defiance were to peaceful political relations. Full cultural membership for the black poor in Jamaica was therefore premised, in part, on acceptance of a dominant-class norm-identity that privileged black submissiveness and black docility. Uncritical deference to power, not the norm of moral infrangibility, became the measure of black lower-class civility and the criterion for moral inclusion. Sexual docility in the slums was therefore as important to dominant-class power as political submissiveness.

The black poor undoubtedly recognized these compulsions and challenged them. Ghetto youths' and popular performers' celebration of unrestrained sexuality in the 1980s seemed to announce to guardians of propriety the end of their moral sway over the black lower class. In the performing arts and in everyday street culture, orthodox sexual morality gave way to uninhibited celebration of all things libidinal. Sexual extremism for its own sake, and as a repertoire for challenging social conventions, now became the dominant form of expression within an otherwise variegated ghetto culture.

The erotics of power was therefore wrested from moral guardians in a manner not too dissimilar from the violence seized from the control of politicians. By their sexual extremism, the black lumpenproletariat appropriated, stylized and inverted a form of power that defined the boundaries between the morally legitimate and the morally depraved. Undisciplined black sexuality on public display was now used not merely for libidinal release, but also to intimidate and to threaten. Flaunting sexuality was now a means of social struggle and an expression of badness-honour. The racial, sexual and social-class tensions that were latent in the postcolonial period were now awakened by the slackness-civility conflict.

In Jamaica's tormented history as a former slave society and colonial territory, sex and power were inextricably linked, and both sex and power saturated race and class relations. Dominant classes which were white or "brown" feared black lower-class sexuality, deeming it a source of anarchy and an agent of cultural disruption. It is arguable that throughout Jamaica's modern history middle- and upper-class fear of "unbridled" lower-class sexuality was as intense as fear of unchecked lower-class political violence. Both imperiled the public weal, if not the identity of the people-nation. The policing of black lower-class sexuality was thus central to the management of social and political power, as much as the policing of black lower-class violence.

Sexual extremism in the ghetto was therefore not an accident. It was instead a conscious, wilful political choice in reaction to dominant-class power. Inversion of the dominant sexual norms in the 1980s was merely the latest tactic of a black lumpenproletariat engaged in a protracted class war. In the 1980s and after, this war was fought on the terrain of moral culture. The ideological lines were sharply drawn between the depraved and the civilized.

Unflattering as it might appear, sexual extremism in the slums did not occur because the ghetto poor did not know better. Even the most alienated of them knew right from wrong. Many gangsters deferred to Christian values, and a few even read their bibles. More than that, the rebelling poor strove constantly to juggle dominant norms of propriety with contingent resort to moral licence. But the eroticism of dancehall queens and the licence of gun-praising DJs were raw expressions of shared cultural practices in Jamaica.

This did not make extremist behaviours morally right. Black sexual extremism in the ghetto primarily offered the negative emancipation of instincts, and not solutions to the poor's most urgent needs. Moral depravity was as disabling for the ghetto poor as it was for better-off groups, even if the latter were spared withering public criticism for it. Contrary to the pronouncements of apologists for the self-satisfied "uptown" classes and defenders of the rebelling "downtown" poor, there were not two cultures on the island, one depraved and the other civilized. Rather there was only a single culture, in which excess and licence, and their condemnation, were widely shared.

Having said that, it is worth noting that black nationality and its nexus with class inequality had trumped sexuality as source of conflict and fulcrum of change in the early postcolonial period. Black nationalism and lower-class insurgencies based on it forged new identities and secured significant social change in the period 1962–72. By the late 1980s, however, sexuality and its nexus with race, class and power had redefined social conflicts, complementing the earlier incendiary markers.

In the 1980s expressions of black sexuality in the ghetto were akin to the celebration of black nationality in the 1960s. Exhibitionist erotic displays in the dancehall, and explicit sexual lyrics in song and in theatre, mocked the sexual etiquette of the middle and upper classes. "Dancehall culture", with its celebration of the erotic, the sexually vulgar and the gangster lifestyle, had therefore opened another front in the war on a tottering and defensive society. Sexual indiscipline by ghetto youth, by male and female dancehall DJs, and by middle-class defenders of the dancehall, was another and later means by which the black lumpenproletariat raised the ante in an ongoing social struggle. "Slackness" had become the terrain of conflict and a highly charged cultural force in the 1980s.

In this respect, the sexual extremism of slackness made it a potent "weapon of the weak". Much like "terrorism" in politics, the hurling of slackness into an inflamed society was a disruptive, even seditious, act. The inversion of the core value of civility endangered the whole society and imperiled its norms. Slackness compelled social actors to choose sides. And that often produced unorthodox alliances and contorted ideological positions.

In doing all this, slackness as the sexual extremism of the black poor called attention to historic grievances, highlighted the hypocrisy of dominant groups and rallied respectable defenders to its cause. By provoking acute social divisions over the uses of sexuality, the transgressive slackness of the lumpenproletariat raised anew old and delicate issues of civilization.

Badness-Honour, Morality and Crime: The Hunt for Wayne "Sandokhan" Smith

As the foregoing has shown, state predation fed on the society's racist contempt for the urban poor, using it to both mobilize and throttle ghetto supplicants. This experience spawned a peculiar agonism that combined badness-honour and martial identities with the disillusionment of the downtrodden who believed they were socially dead. While communal clashes provoked proud partisan identities, and although criminal gangs and political gunmen built solidarities based on derring-do and heroic outlawry, both groups did succumb to the dark side of identity formation in the ghetto, namely the impulse to self-immolation. Orgiastic political and criminal violence overwhelmingly consumed the poorer classes, not the well-heeled or complicit politicians. Yet this stark reality of life in the ghetto should be qualified. Cultural contempt, class marginality and ceaseless predation undoubtedly drove the poor to despair, rage and social cannibalism. These dispositions won favour with politicians, and badness-honour was harnessed by them and canalized by party competition.

At the same time, deprivation also fed a species of redemptive immolation. It was premised not so much on the quest for a transcendent collective ideal as on an atomized rejection of the psychic effect of political predation: the mobilized-but-throttled self. This was a condition in which social and political mobilization offered prospects of social freedom and personal autonomy, even as the quest for these was simultaneously denied rebellious blacks. For the militant poor social inequality, and the state predation that backed it up, merely confirmed perceptions of themselves as persons who were socially dead. Reggae music culture, popular culture and everyday talk in Kingston's congested ghettos constantly strummed this theme of social death, in which the enjoyment of moral frangibility in the national community was constantly denied.[9]

However, rather than lead only to despair, massive social and political mobilization in Jamaica also fed notions of compensatory honour. In the 1980s the "ready fi' dead" attitude among the lumpenproletariat clearly expressed this sensibility, in which hopelessness and hopeful honour were joined. In these terms the self-immolation of the mobilized poor carried both nihilism and redemptive impulse as cultural freight.

On the one hand, hopelessness and blocked aspirations produced "born fi' dead" and "done dead a'ready" attitudes among the enraged poor. On the other, the agonism of the poor betrayed not just nihilism, lack of hope or obsession with death; rather, ghetto contention also disclosed a determination that violent extremism and physical death were better, even redemptive options – preferable to the far worse fates of social death and crucifying violence that the society deemed as a normal, if unfortunate, part of life in Jamaica. By the late 1980s this was undeniably the common sense among the most alienated groups in Kingston's ghettos.

Gang leader Wayne "Sandokhan" Smith, holed up in the Waterhouse community in the West Central St Andrew constituency, typified this outlook among criminal gangsters beyond the confines of the West Kingston and South St Andrew constituencies. Smith's tortured career as a drug don and community patron offers another vantage point for examining the conjunction of state politics, social inequality, crime, the moral culture of badness-honour and notions of community in the ghetto.

Wayne Smith was born on 2 May 1962. By the time he was seventeen years old he had dropped out of school three years previously, and was facing imprisonment for larceny (*Daily Gleaner*, 10 September 1988, 29). After his release he returned to the Waterhouse–Olympic Gardens community, which had become a battle-scarred zone in the 1979–80 political upheavals.

Like other gang leaders across Kingston who saw an opportunity in the enervation of the state and the crippling of society, Smith rose to prominence as a don freed of constraining ties to political parties. In a lawless environment he and other gunmen laid down the law. For populations neglected by the state, he became the new patron. For women and others who feared rape and the terror of marauding criminals, he was both protector and avenging lawman.

The decay of civil society and the criminalization of the state were preconditions for Sandokhan's power. The debilities of state power in the 1980s permitted Sandokhan's ready access to guns and ties to the network of the international drug trade. By 1988 Sandokhan's links to the drug trade reached from Olympic Gardens to the far-flung environs of New York and Kansas City, where drug rings carrying his name had established operations. Sandokhan's power in the Waterhouse area was based, therefore, on the connections between drugs, money and guns in the international economy. Drug trafficking created the means to buy guns abroad, to recruit gang members at home and to distribute patronage to the poor. The guns, in turn, overawed opponents and protected the drug trade. All three factors fed Sandokhan's accumulation of social power in the poorer communities of West Central St Andrew. Between 1986 and the summer of 1988 the gunman's exploits confirmed this awesome power and highlighted the conjunction of power, crime, and alternative notions of law and community.

As the clash between the avenging gunman and the state unfolded, terror backed by law was matched by criminal terror in the West Central St Andrew communities. In the hunt for Sandokhan, lawmen persisted in reckless assaults on residents, arresting and beating citizens who had committed no crime. Grandmothers, children and women were hauled into the dragnet and threatened. Women and youths who refused to cooperate became, according to the *Sunday Gleaner,* "prime targets" of the police and were roughed up by lawmen (11 September 1988, 8A). The hunt for Sandokhan spared no one, as marauding soldiers and police squeezed the community to deliver the gunman. As one frightened woman confided to a reporter, "Dem say dem naah stop terrorize we unless we turn over Sandokhan" (*Jamaica Record,* 25 August 1988, 2).

For his part, Sandokhan was even more violent in dealing with perceived enemies. He not only targeted policemen for murder but was equally vicious with those in the community who threatened his enterprise. He summarily executed a likely witness to his deeds; he brutally murdered a youth he merely suspected of being an informer; he expelled rival gunmen by means of superior arms; and he and his small gang terrorized all who might have stood up to him. According to the police count Sandokhan, by the first week of August 1988, had killed nine persons (*Daily Gleaner,* 8 August 1988, 1).

This predation, together with state terror and Sandokhan's expulsion of other criminals, gave the gunman the community protection he needed. Indeed, residents expressed relief at the gunman's return after his latest prison break. According to one, "Since him come back me sleep wid me windows opened every night without fear because him always fight against the robberies and the rapes and me know say that the thief them nuh like that" (cited in *Jamaica Record,* 11 September 1988, 4A). Those who knew him best, his mother and his wife, spoke only of a gentle, kind and friendly person who bore no resemblance to the savage "Public Enemy No. 1" villain depicted in police notices and lurid newspaper accounts (*Sunday Gleaner,* 9 October 1988, 9A).[10] At the height of the punishing manhunt, even old women who crossed paths with Sandokhan thought him kind. One recommended the gunman to the neighborhood priest, who later recalled her telling him, "Father, help him, he is a good boy for when he is here the police and bad men can't trouble us" (cited in *Daily Gleaner,* 26 August 1988, 3).

Father Richard Albert, neighbourhood priest and American-born rector of St Patrick and St Jude's Roman Catholic churches, joined in the community's paeans to Sandokhan. In a speech to the Kiwanis Club Albert spoke as priest and sociologist to the elite gathering, observing that Sandokhan was akin to a Robin Hood who

> watched politicians use young boys for violent, political reasons and he knows the daily struggles of old people who look for food and shelter. I make no excuses for Sandokhan or for the crimes he might have committed: I in no way want to say to you that poverty gives any man the excuse to commit crimes . . . But, I do beg of you to try to understand that when the social conditions around you are so bad, when the health services do not come anywhere near fulfilling even the basis [*sic*] needs of the community, and unemployment, [and] political rivalries cause young men to search for other alternatives to support themselves, I want you to understand how a man like Sandokhan could emerge. (*Daily Gleaner,* 26 August 1988, 3)

This challenge to the society, and the priest's disclosure that he had met several times in public with the gunman to persuade him to surrender, produced a political firestorm. The security minister denounced the speech and expressed amazement "that a man in Father Albert's position could meet with and know of the whereabouts of Sandokhan and not pass on this information to the Police".[11]

The press, with rare exception, concurred in this opinion. One prominent columnist averred that the priest "ought to be given a taste of the lockup". Another opined that the clergyman's real crime was glorifying Sandokhan, and concluded that Father Albert was "too busy playing politics, advancing worldly causes and striking poses for the gallery to have retained a sense of moral direction" (Perkins 1988).

As the debate raged, Sandokhan penned a letter to the clergyman the day after his speech. In the two-page letter, written on the leaves of a schoolbook, the gangster acknowledged the priest's effort to arrange his surrender:

> The last time I speak with you it was great. Father you're influencing me to give in myself, but father you're a great friend of mine, and I've heard your speech on the radio yesterday and it was good. I know you don't want to see me die on the dungle, I know you care about me and my family.

The letter then turned to a complaint and issued a threat:

> Father, Tuesday the Police curfew water house and held my wife and that same Police D.C. Colt boxed up my wife and beat her up, and I want some action to take against the Policeman soon. If no action don't take against that policeman he's going to go on doing the same. And father I promise you I will never molest the Police, but if the Police continue doing things to my wife they will get me doing things to them. Father I want this cassette to play over the air. I know the police are not going to stop looking for me . . . action must be taken now on that policeman. If no action is taken against that Policeman, he's going to make things worse on other Policeman.[12]

The letter leaves no doubt about Sandokhan's hostility to the police. However, this missive to the clergyman is equally revealing of the gunman's other values and moral orientation. First, the outlaw revealed the importance of his family, and particularly of his wife, Jenice Smith, whom he had married in 1985 when she was fifteen years old (*Sunday Gleaner*, 11 September 1988, 2). He took the hardships she endured at the hands of policemen personally. However, the rough justice she received in detention backfired on the lawmen. As I show below, rather than cause his capitulation, the abuse intensified his contempt for the law.

Finally, though Sandokhan's case became a *cause célèbre* that riveted the nation and depicted a struggle between good and evil, the gunman's letter revealed a very different narrative. It expressed that distinct and recurrent feature of social conflict and power in Jamaica: its intimate and highly personalized character. Sandokhan, the letter shows, sought redress for his impugned honour. He wanted to settle scores with a particular policeman for showing disrespect to the gunman's family. In his fury at being disrespected, Sandokhan took note of the offending policeman by name and rank. It was not lawmen at this or that police station who angered him, but "D[etective] C[orporal] Colt" who earned his enmity. Because of this policeman's personal slight, Sandokhan sought to settle scores with him.

In the morality of the ghetto, hunting for a gunman and trying to kill him was one thing; those were the terms of the war in Kingston's badlands. But impugning Sandokhan's family honour was another. It had to be corrected by means of a personal vendetta against a single policeman and, by implication, the entire police force. For Sandokhan the Jamaican state was a distant entity; he knew it not as the "committee of the bourgeoisie", but only in the person of an arrogant lawman who had cut to the quick of Sandokhan's honour by slapping his wife. Fighting the state meant a vendetta against one policeman.

A reciprocal relationship of personal hostility held for the security forces. In this dramaturgy of mutual personal revenge, securing honour and reputation seemed more important than upholding the law. Policemen sought out Sandokhan, not merely as a lawbreaker, but as a rude, facetious "bwoy" who challenged their swaggering power. He had fired on them with impunity, killed three from their ranks, kept them at bay for months, and embarrassed them in the public eye. This was not only criminality, but also an offence that mocked their competence as armed men. Sandokhan had to be taught a lesson, not just to pay for his crime against society, but also to recover the integrity and manhood of other powerful men whom he had violated by his defiance and prolonged escape. The manhunt for Sandokhan therefore became highly "personal", as state agents in their role as dishonoured men sought their elusive quarry.

These cultural preoccupations informed the motivations of Jamaica's vigilante policemen and reduced gunfights to duels of offended honour between armed men. In these kinds of conflicts, it is arguable that law enforcement on the streets in urban Jamaica was less a matter of upholding public law than of defending the manhood of armed men whose integrity and respect had been "tested" and violated by armed and impudent criminals.

It is little wonder, then, that the policemen in West Central St Andrew dealt harshly with communities who threw up a wall of silence against them. In this battle for honour and struggle of personal wills, the Riverton City and Waterhouse communities stubbornly held out against the security forces. They did so not because they were irredeemably lawless, but because the state's power radiated to them in the form of known-by-name corrupted policemen who exacted punishments, as if settling personal scores with each victim. Indeed, one policeman alerted Sandokhan's wife to the personal vengeance he would take, when her twenty-two-month-old son became a man. She reported him as saying that "When the boy grow up, me goin' shoot him. Me goin' waste him and drop him off the causeway" (*Sunday Gleaner*, 11 September 1988, 2).

In this zone where crime, law and politics collided, traditional notions of community, justice and propriety collapsed. At the ground zero of mutual terror, ghetto moral culture and law enforcement culture became flexible and expedient, as both lawmen and rebels jettisoned proprieties. Lawmen killed with impunity, and victimized residents had no compunction in defiantly embracing the criminal who protected them from predators. Men like Sandokhan became one of "us", victimized residents, against "them", the predatory outsiders, represented by known-by-name policemen. Although vigilante gunmen seeking to lift the siege on their community eventually killed Sandokhan, the gunman's death could not quell the violence nor arrest the norm of badness-honour.

Cultural Contradictions of Power: Badness-Honour and Democracy

The foregoing discussion and case studies on forms of power in Jamaica leave no doubt about the vital impact of cultural obligations on national politics. Power relations showed a marked susceptibility to cultural inflection. Protagonists not only took cultural imperatives for granted in their encounters, they cherished and boldly affirmed them. Conflicts in which personal honour, reputation or group racial claims were repeatedly invoked exposed the cultural roots of power. Social rank and knowing one's place in a pecking order both smoothed and disrupted relations within and beyond the political arena. Aspirants to power within and beyond the ghetto increasingly made their authority claims on the basis of group competence and achieved status rights.

To be sure, protagonists in Jamaica undoubtedly fought huge battles in which unabashed, raw contests for advantage and booty were on display. However, encounters as various as the struggle over political turf, leaders' claims to class deference, and the war between the security forces and criminal gunmen were shot through with powerful cultural impulses. Matters of impugned manhood, anxieties concerning violation of class and ethnic identities, and agonism over transgression of rank in a social hierarchy aggravated encounters and raised the political stakes for all involved.

Not surprisingly, protagonists fought over competing claims to competence and respect. Fear of losing face, with its attendant humiliation, was a constant in these power struggles in which some form of black competence was at stake. Party bosses, top-ranking notables, criminal gangsters, performance artists, avenging lawmen and ordinary citizens all recognized and acted on these powerful cultural impulses. In these ways the culture of badness-honour became more than just a cohesive and disruptive force in Jamaican political life. It was also a normatively familiar lever of political and social power and a legitimate basis of authority claims. For both state and society, cultural inflection gave power its authority and transmitted deep personal meanings. Thus, cultural inflection defined the identity of power at all levels, and this inflection of power also became the source of this power's renewal. Indeed, decades-long habituation to the communication politics of badness-honour guaranteed this outcome. Based on this sketch of the power-culture nexus it is clear that the dilemma for Jamaica is the apparent and growing disjunction between this cultural expression of power – with its communication politics of "badness" and "slackness" – and the norms of democratic politics.

The contrast between democratic politics and the communication politics of predatory power and resistance to it could not be more extreme. Party activists, state elites, fanatical voters, criminal bandits, army and police forces, and ordinary citizens in Jamaica turned massively to violence and self-help indiscipline to affirm their claims. Aggression became a lever of power, a means of self-defence and a source of invigorated identity. In a society increasingly perceived to be gorgonian and socially cannibalistic, the struggle for self-protection displaced any interest in or support for the state's historic function as defender of the public interest and guarantor of public safety.

Provoked by both internal and external forces, the post-1972 crisis years in Jamaica therefore spawned a violent, disruptive political culture that became universal in scope and multi-class in character. Violence, incivility and indiscipline defined the emergent and broadly shared political culture. Needless to say, this uncivil political culture imperiled persons, and was profoundly threatening to democratic institutions and to citizens' respect for them.

Yet, as I have shown, this threat to personal safety and hostility to democratic values was no bar to the accumulation of social power across all sectors of society. Social disorganization produced disruptive but compelling forms of political and social power. Invasive state strategies, ubiquitous party politics, the penetration of a subversive global culture and the island's structural economic dependence shattered stable social relations, encouraged social oppression and provoked uncivil political responses. Yet these very destabilizing forces spawned awesome forms of power, shot through with deeply felt cultural motivations.

Weakened democratic institutions were no match for such disruptive forces. Raging violence coarsened social relations, and self-help indiscipline progressively displaced respect for law and public institutions. In this context, liberal-democratic ideals pertaining to the civic uses of power and the priority of the public interest collapsed. Factional political violence, the progressive "criminalization of the state", and the turn to a generalized outlawry at the level of both state and society drove such ideals and their defenders to the political margins. In sum, during the post-1972 crisis period, democratic forces and public institutions lost their vigour. Having been instruments of social oppression, public corruption and lawlessness for decades, democratic institutions lost legitimacy and public support.

A major contradiction thus lay at the heart of power and its exercise in Jamaica. The conditions for gaining political support, for securing an honourable identity and for maintaining power were all at odds with the conditions for creating a civil and democratic society. The one thrived on vicious factionalism and martial displays of honour, while the other required accommodation, trust in negotiation of difference and respect for law. Predation politics was manifestly inconsistent with democratic politics. This incompatibility weakened the appeal of democratic norms; it eroded respect for democratic institutions and trimmed public trust in their capacities.

It is clear, then, that the political culture which generated powerful personal meanings and buttressed state politics was not the political culture which invigorated democratic politics. Widely shared agonism and highly charged honorific impulses fed the contention and factionalism that gave vigour to proud martial identities. These vital identities were being formed, however, by resort to an aesthetics and a dramaturgy which were completely alien to democratic politics. Because predation politics summoned Jamaicans' status anxieties and fed their testy agonism, violent factionalism undercut democratic politics. Oddly enough, the very cultural impulses which undermined democratic norms were the same ones which gave power its authority and social groups their potent identities and measure of social honour.

Consequently, despite its dysfunctional effects, cultural summoning that invoked honour through combativity had great appeal for leaders and supplicants alike. State agents found in it a powerful repertoire of power, and the rebel culture of the urban poor used it to build an equally potent means of power and identity. Badness-honour in this context was the crystallization of a brand of cultural fundamentalism which was thoroughly opposed to civil politics. Badness-honour was more than merely disruptive; clearly, it was also socially productive. Badness-honour enhanced the authority of the politically powerful; it summoned ordinary citizens to its siren call; and it won massive allegiance from the criminal class and the mobilized poor.

Consequently, those seeking personal and social respect no longer looked to democratic institutions or civic norms to validate their identity claims. Rather, persons in search of social identity in a context of threat and uncertainty drew on a historic agonism and widely held authoritarian values and set them to new purposes. In the changed circumstances of the time, authoritarianism and agonism in the guise of badness-honour were transformed into decisive influences. As they became ubiquitous, a myriad of relations succumbed to their influence. In the twenty-year span between 1972 and 1992, the norm of badness-honour went from being a local tradition among alienated subcultures in the urban ghetto, and for a minority of politicians and party activists, to being a near-universal political culture which roiled the society.

In light of these cultural conditions of power and their close nexus with social identities, it should be evident that Jamaica's social crisis will not be susceptible to quick solutions. There will be no easy road to the reinvigoration of Jamaica's fractured democracy. Indeed, the restabilization of society and the cessation of social aggression and incivility are probably not amenable to orthodox, short-term forms of political management, easy cultural fixes or simple economic remedies.

This is so for several reasons. First, the tottering Westphalian inter-state system will make recovery difficult. This structure which has formed the political edifice of world society since 1648 is now breaking up. National states outside the industrialized democracies have either collapsed or are experiencing major crises. A notable feature of this unravelling is the onset of civil strife across the world, around issues ranging from nationalism and ethnicity to religious fundamentalism. Collapsed civic norms, the dispersal of violence to non-state actors, and the rise of criminal gangsters and mafiosi as major social and political actors all testify to the erosion of state authority in a weakened inter-state system. Jamaica's turmoil is partly due to its membership in the crisis-ridden inter-state system. Its convulsions are inexorably linked to the local, "Jamaican" forms of upheaval and conflict. Any effort at recovery will necessarily have to acknowledge the continuing impact of this destabilizing connection.

Second, efforts to invigorate democracy in Jamaica will come to naught where structures of democratic factionalism that feed predation politics and reproduce racist images of Afro-Jamaicans are left untouched. An unfortunate aspect of Jamaica's membership in the inter-state system has been its leaders' embrace of a culturally compromised nation-statehood. That is, local thralldom to Westphalian structures based on cultural "modernity" and "progress", and on their gendered and ethnicized hierarchies, abetted political strategies and social ontologies that fed both gender subordination and racial domination.

In truth, Jamaica's reproduction of liberalism's ideology of modernity and progress produced a savage and destructive effect on poor Afro-Jamaicans. Political reform will require an end to state and party politics that impose forms of domination insistent on limiting political choice in the slums and purging the majority population of Africanist forms of civilization-identity.

Finally, any political renewal must address the crisis of widening allegiance to honorific fundamentalism. This brand of cultural fundamentalism among poor Afro-Jamaicans is historical in character, though variant in its manifestations. In the postwar years, the lumpenproletariat and the urban unemployed poor have been honorific fundamentalism's outspoken champions and its irrepressible vanguard. Their insistent claim to moral infrangibility based on equivalent identity and volition, and their demand for a better life and an end to the racism embedded in Jamaica's factional democracy, identify them not as a rogue culture but as the compromised avatars of liberation in Jamaica.

Honorific fundamentalism is not a claim to an exclusionary racialism, nor is it a demand for racial supremacy. Least of all is it a threat to a freer, more humane and fully democratic Jamaica. At its best, honorific fundamentalism is a powerful expression of Afro-Jamaican civilization-identity under duress. Its claim to the moral infrangibility of Afro-Jamaicans represents a sweeping radical thrust for the full democratization of Jamaican society. Short-term reform measures now under review, or currently being implemented, can certainly make a difference in the lives of the poor, but they are not sufficient.

Such measures as dismantling garrison constituencies, ending the benefits politics associated with them, reforming the police force, and passing anticorruption laws are all to the good. However, while honorific fundamentalism is certainly about the desire for free expression of political choice and opinion, and although it has always insisted on "full employment" and an end to police brutality, its claims are more far-reaching, and hence more threatening. Honorific fundamentalism among poor Afro-Jamaicans is premised on a radical reordering of class and institutional relations. Its demands have always carried an explicit challenge to all the forms of social domination discussed here.

There can be little doubt that decades of dissent during the postwar years have drastically reordered Jamaica's domestic relations. The urban poor have undoubtedly become more socially empowered, even as the group remains politically throttled and culturally demeaned. The huge contradiction between forms of social empowerment for the poor on the one hand, and marked political throttling and cultural scorn for the group on the other, weakened democracy and spawned the phenomenon of "badness-honour". As Jamaica makes its inevitable transition out of predation politics and democratic factionalism in an era of globalization, badness-honour may well be eclipsed. Barring a major upheaval in the interim, however, it is probable that the transition could well usher in newer and possibly more subversive forms of the fundamentalism of black competence.

Notes

1. In several neighbourhoods and enclaves throughout western and central Kingston, law-abiding citizens of both working- and lower-middle-class origins held onto the old ways. This group represented the self-conscious, if numerically declining, custodians of the stock of cultural capital in these communities.
2. Nowhere was this cultural turn more evident than in popular music: scores of male reggae singers proclaimed the message and authority of antisocial behaviour in the slums. One typical response came from Bob Marley, whose popular song "I Shot the Sheriff" offered the proud refrain from the urban rebel culture: "I shot the sheriff, but I didn't shoot the deputy."
3. I am grateful to Anthony Bogues, Jamaican political scientist, for explaining to me the honorific and disciplinary uses of badness-honour by top party figures in Jamaica.
4. In the late 1960s Walter Rodney, Guyanese scholar and Black Power activist, gave a boost to this challenge to state power in Jamaica by identifying with the cause and moral culture of the urban poor. He was expelled for his activism in the slums and elsewhere. See Rodney 1969.
5. One need only consult the current editorial and "op-ed" pages of Jamaica's major newspaper, the *Daily Gleaner,* to read the typically mistaken view that social outlawry is a uniquely Jamaican phenomenon.
6. For a report on Spence's activities in Cuba, see David D'Costa's account in the *Sunday Gleaner,* 4 June 1978, 13.
7. For a book-length discussion of Jamaican dancehall culture, see Stolzoff 2000.

8. For the varying political positions on dancehall culture, see Stolzoff, chapter 8.
9. I am indebted to Orlando Patterson for his discussion of the principle of moral infrangibility. See Patterson 1997, 139–42.
10. In a retort aimed at the negative media coverage of the gunman, Sandokhan's mother-in-law offered this lament to reporters: "Sometimes what oonu write, is like oonu working for the police."
11. Statement issued to the press (*Jamaica Record,* 28 August 1988).
12. Wayne Smith's letter to Father Richard Albert, dated 26 August 1988.

References

Daily Gleaner and *Sunday Gleaner,* July 1975–October 1988.

Jamaica Record, August–September 1988.

Patterson, O. 1997. *The Ordeal of Integration: Progress and Resentment in America's "Racial" Crisis.* Washington, D.C.: Counterpoint.

Perkins, W. 1988. "A Kind of Corruption". *Money Index,* 6 September.

Rodney, W. 1969. *The Groundings with My Brothers.* London: Bogle L'Ouverture Publications.

Scott, J. 1990. *Domination and the Arts of Resistance.* New Haven, Conn.: Yale University Press.

Stolzoff, N.C. 2000. *Wake the Town and Tell the People: Dancehall Culture in Jamaica.* Durham: Duke University Press.

3

The Historical Roots of Violence in Jamaica
The Hearne Report 1949

Amanda Sives

Introduction

On 16 May 1949 Norman Washington Manley and Alexander Bustamante both signed the first of many peace pledges on behalf of their
respective political parties. In this, both leaders appealed to the Jamaican people, and particularly to their own supporters

> not to use force in political campaigning and to remember that, regardless
> of their political views, it is in the interest of everyone to comply with this
> appeal so as to secure the preservation of law and order, the right of free
> speech and the right of everyone to exercise his privileges as a voter.
> (*Daily Gleaner*, 18 May 1949)

This led to a front-page editorial in the *Gleaner*, somewhat optimisti-
cally claiming that "Jamaica can now move forward politically, socially
and spiritually without the spectre of brutality haunting its dreams and
making a nightmare of its hopes . . . And so goodbye to bricks and
sticks, goodbye to the hatred which was severing the people into two
hostile camps" (*Daily Gleaner*, 18 May 1949).

Two months later, on 6 July to be precise, Benjamin Taylor, aged 57, of Tamarind Tree, St Andrew, was stoned, beaten and eventually stabbed to death in his yard. The attack was a political one, and was the culmination of a series of clashes between supporters of the rival parties, which had been occurring at political meetings over the preceding few days. The context for the murder was a by-election for the Kingston and St Andrew Council seat of Eastern St Andrew No. 2 Division, located in the Gordon Town area. The main candidates were Leo McDonald for the Jamaica Labour Party (JLP) and Allan Isaacs for the People's National Party (PNP). McDonald got 2,176 votes and Isaacs 2,134 votes, so it was an extremely close election.

Governor John Huggins took swift action; on 8 July it was reported that he had appointed Sir Hector Hearne to undertake a one-person commission of inquiry with the remit to "nail responsibility to the mast of the party concerned" (*Daily Gleaner,* 8 July 1949). The inquiry began on 9 July and ended on 29 July. Blame for the incident was firmly apportioned. In his report Hearne wrote, "The organization and instigation of violence must be placed at the door of the PNP" (*Daily Gleaner,* 6 August 1949). Norman Manley, in response, argued that the report was "intemperate and unbalanced" (*Daily Gleaner,* 9 August 1949).

This chapter will concentrate on the evidence[1] that emerged during this inquiry, as it provides a wealth of detail about the relationship between political party supporters and the place of violence within the Jamaican political culture. The issues which arose during the course of the inquiry were much wider than the murder of one political supporter during a by-election campaign. Instead, questions such as the role of the colonial state in policing the violence, the role of candidates in developing the violence, the levels of organization within the political parties and the tactics developed to ensure that campaigning could take place were debated. The evidence highlights the existence of loyal supporters ready to engage in violence against their rivals during this early phase of party politics in Kingston. This does not mean, however, that political supporters were on a predetermined path of conflict during the 1940s which would automatically lead to the different forms, intensities and levels of violence which were to emerge in the later period. Still, there is a clear sense in which the violence of the late 1960s flourished so *rapidly* because there was a history of interparty violence. Indeed, political party narratives of violence, from within both the JLP and the PNP, make reference to the incidents of the 1940s in constructing their explanations for the development of political violence in Jamaica.

While the violence of the 1940s was not as dramatic in its forms or outcomes as that of the later period, partly because sticks and stones were used rather than semi-automatic weapons, a strong sense of party loyalty and affiliation was in evidence. This chapter argues that we need to explore the roots of this partisan-political violence – which evidence suggests goes back into the post-emancipation era (Wilmot 1977) – in order to understand the development of politics and violence during the latter half of the twentieth century.

The Hearne Commission

The terms of reference of the commission were threefold. First, all political incidents subsequent to 2 July and relevant to the by-election campaign were to be investigated. Second, the commission was to explore all the events and circumstances leading up to the violence, and third, the commission was to identify the persons or political bodies who were responsible (Hearne Commission 1949; *Daily Gleaner,* 6 August 1949). While there had been previous commissions of inquiry into incidents of political violence, they were not as substantial nor did they take as much detailed evidence.[2] There would appear to be little doubt that Governor Huggins appointed the commission of inquiry because both parties had reneged on the peace pledge they had signed. Whoever was proven responsible for the death of Benjamin Taylor, there was no gainsaying that both parties had been involved in violence. In establishing the inquiry as one which required responsibility to be laid at the feet of *one* of the parties, Huggins was therefore clearly intent on punishing the party that had failed to "control" and "direct" its supporters.

In essence, the commission focused on events which occurred on the three nights preceding polling day (3, 4 and 5 July) and on polling day itself, 6 July. On the three pre-election nights, political meetings of both parties had been disrupted. On 3 July, in Dallas, a JLP brigade and band[3] had marched through a PNP crowd of three hundred, who were about to start a meeting. Stones were thrown by supporters of both parties, and six people were injured. On 4 July a JLP meeting in Gordon Town was disrupted by PNP supporters. They had been trucked up from Kingston to heckle the meeting, which ended in stone throwing. On 5 July two meetings by the rival parties were held close to each other – one in Gordon Town and the other in Mission House. Violence was averted by a strong police presence.

Polling day was 6 July. From the evidence given, it is clear that there were a number of incidents, beginning early that morning with allegations of JLP supporters intimidating voters in Industrial Village, and continuing throughout the day with pitched battles between rival supporters occurring in at least four areas. The main areas which experienced trouble were Milling's Spring, Maryland, Penfield, Tamarind Tree and Gordon Town itself. The murder of Benjamin Taylor occurred at mid-afternoon, when two trucks of PNP supporters were travelling past Tamarind Tree on their way to Gordon Town. Incidents continued and were only brought to an end when tear gas was released on a large crowd outside Gordon Town Square, following an altercation between Bustamante, Manley and Wills O. Isaacs.

"Strong-Arm" Politics

One of the striking facts to emerge from the inquiry, particularly noticeable in the context of the peace pledges, was the key role of candidates as agents of conflict rather than peace. This finding is not surprising given the heightened focus on candidates' activity in the political process, but it does point to the undermining of the role and purpose of peace pledges signed by politicians, and it highlights the hypocrisy of political movements which, on the one hand, preach unity and, on the other, defame their opponents "on the hustings", thereby encouraging conflict between supporters. The arrival of candidates increased tensions at meetings, and it is clear that rival crowds harassed them.

On election day itself Hugh Shearer pulled a revolver on a crowd, as did Mrs Leon's husband Arthur.[4] Candidates had felt threatened by crowds of rival supporters many times prior to 1949, as amply illustrated by Norman Manley's recollections in 1942: "I have been abused. I have been kicked when it suited them to kick. I have been stoned on his [Bustamante's] orders at meetings. I have seen my own workers in the Party beaten at street corners" (*Daily Gleaner,* 19 February 1942).

By 1949, seven years after Manley made this statement, candidates were well prepared for violent conflict during election campaigns. "Strong-arm" politics had become a feature of the political contest, leading the *Gleaner* to lament, when referring to the 1949 general election campaign, "Men who should be considered to be of high dignity too often appear in the company of persons known to be of evil reputation. The election is being conducted in some quarters as if it cannot be won without the support of criminals" (*Daily Gleaner,* 11 November 1949). Evidence was provided to the commission of both parties' preparations.[5] Not only did Arthur Leon brandish a loaded weapon at the gathered assembly, but he and his wife were travelling with what might loosely be called a bodyguard. Known as "Gungoo", the man was described by Mrs Leon as a professional boxer. She said he was "an aide in case of tyre trouble and was a person who could watch the car when the other occupants were not in it" (*Daily Gleaner,* 28 July 1949). Gungoo was identified by the police as Eustace Cox; he had three convictions for grievous bodily harm, wounding and loitering. The PNP had brought along their own strong-arm man – Aston Nelson, also known as "Jarman" – who was usually at 69 Matthews Lane and had two convictions: one for larceny of a bicycle and another for rioting.

The Wider Context

However, the focus of the inquiry was on the role of the PNP defence force, "Group 69" or the "Fighting 69th", as some of the group were present during the by-election. They had been bussed up to Gordon Town in response to allegations that JLP supporters were intimidating voters. Based at 69 Matthews Lane, Group 69 was formed to stave off attacks from the JLP, who made it extremely difficult for the PNP to campaign on the streets of Kingston. As Vivian Lewis, Secretary of the Central St Andrew Constituency, stated in his evidence, "They earned the sobriquet [Fighting 69th] because of the resistance which a small number of them put up against some Bustamante thugs in the Corporation Strikes of 1947."[6] It is here that the wider context is extremely important to an understanding of the murder of Benjamin Taylor, particularly as the PNP were blamed for orchestrating violence during the by-election. As Norman Manley recalled in 1949, "I don't forget the boast that used to be made that below the Cross Roads line no PNP man dared hold any meeting."[7] The PNP had organized their supporters to resist the violent tactics of the JLP and, having developed a level of organization, were far more adept than the Labour Party during this period at protecting their supporters and reacting to any early signs of trouble.

The need to implement a strategy for defending PNP supporters arose from the repeated attacks suffered by the PNP during the post-1944 period. In fact, it is possible to trace it back to the period before the acrimonious split between Bustamante and Manley. As Richard Hart, an organizer for the PNP during this period, recalled,

> And he [Bustamante] often caused meetings that were held in the western end of the City to be broken up. I remember so well the technique that used to be used . . . [a] Bustamante union follower just gets up on the fence and conducts the audience in the singing of God Save the King . . . making the speaker quite inaudible and making it impossible to continue the meeting. (Hart 1996)

After the split between the two men in 1942 and the formation of rival political parties and trade unions, it became increasingly difficult for the PNP to hold any meetings on the streets of Kingston. Orville Brown goes as far as to state, "When the JLP *declared war* on the PNP in 1942, JLP ruffians began to attack PNP meetings."[8] Following the 1944 election, the PNP developed a strategy to resist the JLP thuggery. As Frank Gordon, a long-time political activist, recalled,

> People would attack you because you was PNP. You couldn't keep a meeting on the street . . . We had a Councillor, Wills O. Isaacs, who says we must "keep a meeting and get all the roughnecks to come out – have a meeting on the street . . . so you have to fight back." You had to build a counter-force. Group 69 was part of it, and others. (Gordon 1995)

The violence emanating from the JLP sought to hinder the development of the PNP and its trade union arm. Incidents of violence occurred, mainly on the streets of Kingston, between rival trade unions. Supporters of the PNP would be involved in Trades Union Congress (TUC) activity and JLP supporters would be active on behalf of the Bustamante Industrial Trade

Union (BITU). The violence was intense during incidents such as the asylum strike of 1946 (three people killed), the *Gleaner* strike of 1947 (two days of battles with the police) and the bus strike of 1948 (four bombs thrown at buses and gunfire reported). The battles in the union field were about recognition of the TUC; the violence was organized and effective in most cases. The language used by the PNP highlighted their determination to ensure that they could campaign and recruit members. As N.N. Nethersole stated in February 1946,

And we will resolutely oppose all and resist all demagogic thugs who attempt to reduce us into servility, and to suppress our rights to hold and express any individual opinions and to join and participate in the institutions and organisations that we support. We will defend those vital and fundamental rights to the death and we will defend our persons and property when they are attacked and threatened, and for those purposes we will fight our attackers in the streets, in the lanes, on the housetops, until we have driven them into the sea. (*Daily Gleaner*, 19 February 1946)

As well as the development of violence among rival trade union supporters, forcibly preventing some from gaining representational rights, partisan violence was also taking place between rival political supporters. A key victory for the PNP occurred during the 1947 parish council elections, at what became known as the "Battle of Rose Town". Ken Hill, a charismatic organizer for the PNP who had captured a great deal of support from the skilled workers, emerged triumphant from this battle, with the consequence that Bustamante vacated his West Kingston seat, moving to Clarendon for the 1949 election. The Battle of Rose Town demonstrated that the PNP had developed an ability to match the JLP on the streets of Kingston. The JLP were clearly uneasy about these developments, as debates in *Hansard* the following November highlight. The members discussed a ban on night marches, and Bustamante cited the Battle of Rose Town as one of the key examples of why the ban was necessary.[9] By 1949, then, the PNP could equally match JLP forces on the street. As a PNP witness who gave evidence to the Hearne Commission, Altamont Ried, stated: "My house had been attacked several times . . . The PNP were not attacking anybody but they would defend themselves *now that they were powerful and strong, they could match the Labourites*" (*Daily Gleaner*, 21 July 1949; my emphasis).

Levels of organization were highly developed in the PNP. This came out very clearly in the evidence given by Keith Gordon Martin, chairman of the Eastern St Andrew Division of the PNP. He related that upon hearing from a party worker that PNP voters were being intimidated, he had spoken with Vernon Arnett (PNP Secretary) and three trucks had been engaged in Kingston. They were instructed to collect PNP supporters from the Corporate Area, starting at Matthews Lane, and they "were to drive from polling station to polling station to see to it there was no violence or intimidation offered to workers or voters at the polling stations" (*Daily Gleaner,* 16 July 1949). No one was in charge of the truckload of supporters. Keith Martin, when asked that question, responded that he took it that there would be one to take the lead, that there were natural leaders among the people (*Daily Gleaner,* 16 July 1949). Supporters were effectively "policing" the polling stations, ensuring – as a partisan force with a history of antagonism – that polling could occur in a neutral manner. Norman Manley explained the premise behind this view: "Actually what happened was when you got your representatives at trouble spots, the trouble stopped. Of course, at times, things developed into a fight" (*Daily Gleaner,* 29 July 1949). A key question which Manley's testimony provokes is: Why did the party have to send its representatives to "trouble spots"?

The Colonial State and the Police

One of the key reasons for such PNP organization was the absence of adequate police protection – and the importance of a police presence was highlighted in the inquiry. On 5 July it was clear that the presence of police between two well-supported political meetings had averted clashes which, according to police evidence, both sides were well prepared for. In the absence of police deployment, what would normally begin as minor incidents of heckling could end as violent affairs where, in the past, people had been injured and often killed. If policing strategies had been properly implemented during that period, a PNP defensive force would not have been required.

Why was policing not more effective? One answer is the relatively small size of the police force, which numbered 1,448 in 1942 (Harriott 1994, 146). Allied with this was the large number of political meetings.[10]

According to the evidence, it is clear that the capacities of the police were overextended, as 63 meetings were held between 1 and 5 July, and on the night of 5 July there were fifteen meetings in the Corporate Area alone. A second reason was the unwillingness or inability of the colonial state to protect PNP supporters, primarily due to the antipathy of the colonial authorities towards the socialist policies of the party. By 1949, following a series of strikes and political battles, it was evident that the colonial state would have to step in to avert further bloodshed. As Richard Hart recalled, "When things could no longer be left to Bustamante to determine, the state began to intervene to preserve or restore order."[11] By that time, however, violence between rival supporters had almost become part of the political landscape.

Outcomes of the Hearne Commission

The concluding paragraph of the Hearne report was very clear: "I find that the incidents in Gordon Town were due to the mass importation of non-voting PNP supporters into the town for the purposes of forming a nucleus of aggression, and that they were actually provoked to violence by the sheer unprincipled conduct of Mr Wills Isaacs" (*Daily Gleaner,* 6 August 1949).

Little mention was made of the role of the JLP, except in referring to the incident in Dallas, about which Hearne remarked, "In my opinion the whole incident arose suddenly, spontaneously and was entirely local in character" (*Daily Gleaner,* 6 August 1949). What Hearne condemned was the *organization* of the violence, rather than its "spontaneous" appearance. This is an interesting distinction, and leads to the following questions: first, why was there spontaneous violence, and second, had this history of "spontaneity" originating from one political party not led the other to organize its supporters? Hearne fails to understand this broader context. In fact, in making his judgement he blatantly rejects the suggestion that he should have considered it. Manley wrote a critical response, in which he argued that the report was one-sided and failed to take account of the intimidation by JLP supporters. Indeed, there is little doubt that Hearne minimized the role of the JLP in harassing PNP supporters. The blame, as in many situations of conflict, cannot easily be apportioned on one side, and Hearne's failure to take account of the context undermined the usefulness of the commission in terms of moving the debate forward and seeking possible solutions.

An immediate outcome of the report was the resignation of Wills Isaacs as third vice-president of the PNP. His reasons rested "not so much in what I did as what I did not do and what I may have prevented" (*Daily Gleaner,* 10 August 1949). His infamous remark that a "broken skull or two was not much in the growth of a nation" (*Daily Gleaner,* 15 July 1949) was to haunt him for many years, and was certainly used to full effect by the JLP during the 1949 general election campaign.

Governor Huggins had also appointed a five-person commission to "examine existing legislation and to make recommendations for any amendments whereby the risk of an outbreak of violence, such as occurred in the recent by-election in Eastern St. Andrew, might be reduced as far as possible during any future elections" (*Daily Gleaner,* 29 August 1949). The Cundall Committee delayed responding until the Hearne Report had been completed. It recommended introducing stiffer penalties for election offences (including disenfranchising the voter for five years), putting the onus on the defendant to prove that sticks and stones are not dangerous weapons during an election period, empowering the police to search for concealed weapons, and allowing arrest without a warrant on grounds of reasonable suspicion (*Daily Gleaner,* 29 August 1949).

The key issue, in terms of outcomes, was whether the two commissions of inquiry (and the changes that were implemented as a result of them) had any impact on the levels of electoral violence. The evidence suggests that they did little to stem the development of violence. In a November 1949 editorial the *Gleaner* commented, "It is obvious that violence is being spawned in this political contest" (*Daily Gleaner,* 11 November 1949). Reports of clashes, riots, shootings and stonings were published over the course of the campaign, although election day itself remained peaceful. Changes to laws and more adequate policing were introduced too late. Experiences of party violence had already led to the formation of a hard core of political support in the Kingston area, and supporters were well armed and versed in strategies of attack and defence. Party supporters actually chose to live together, and refused to cohabit in certain sections with rival supporters during the late 1940s and early 1950s. As Richard Hart recalled,

> Then again, you would find that because of the hostility between the two groups, you would have a movement into a yard of people, who were of the particular party that dominated that yard, and a movement out of the yard, of those who were opposed. And so, you would have yards that became predominantly PNP or predominantly Labour. (Hart 1996)

Twenty years prior to the creation of the first "politically packed" housing scheme, there were elements of the population in Kingston who exhibited strong political identity without having received any political spoils. Loyalties to the political parties therefore need to be seen as a complex set of relationships, rather than one that has been founded simply on the division of political spoils.

Conclusions

By 1949 both political parties were engaged in violence to achieve political goals: the JLP to keep the PNP off the streets of Kingston, and the PNP to force their way back, to campaign for their party and their union movement.

It is important not to overestimate or underestimate the significance of violence in the 1940s. It was low key compared to the violence which was to follow. However, the key point is that organized violence and links with criminal elements were features of the political system during this period. In fact, the strong partisan loyalties that have assisted in perpetuating the political system were partially formed and entrenched through involvement in partisan violence. These experiences of political participation formed through violence on the streets, whether political-party or trade-union inspired, helped to define the way in which the relationships developed between individuals, their parties and their government on the streets of Kingston.

Most countries experience problems at the birth of their political systems, as new relationships are formed and consolidated. In this way, Jamaica is no different from many other states, particularly postcolonial ones. What is interesting is the extent to which this early history has become part of the party narratives. Senior JLP politicians will refer to the fact that the PNP was the first political party to organize for violence, and name Group 69 to support those allegations. The PNP, on the other hand, will refer to the fact that the JLP controlled the streets of Kingston, refusing them the right to campaign freely, forcing them to resort to the use of violence. The development of partisan political violence during the 1960s and 1970s led to these early forms of violence becoming important to the parties, allowing them to construct a party view which positioned them on the side of defending their supporters. These events became a crucial aspect of the parties' world views and therefore need to be taken seriously and investigated, even though the actual violence was of a lower intensity than that which followed.

The evidence from the Hearne inquiry allows us to make a brief foray into the party political perspectives that developed during this early period, and to uncover some of the conflicts and tensions evident between the two political parties. It also demonstrates clearly that the roots of political violence in the modern period pre-date independence.

Notes

1. The evidence presented to the Hearne Commission was covered extensively in the *Daily Gleaner*. I have taken the bulk of my evidence from this source. It is important to note two things. First, in 1947 the affiliated trade union of the PNP, the Trades Union Congress (TUC) had been involved in a protracted and bitter strike with the *Gleaner*. Whether this had any impact on the later coverage needs to be considered. Second, in line with this, both PNP and JLP witnesses wrote to the *Gleaner* complaining about the coverage their evidence had received. Cundall (the main interrogator) informed Judge Hearne that Wills Isaacs had written to him expressing grave concern about the fact that there were eight misreports of his evidence printed in the *Gleaner* (*Daily Gleaner*, 16 July 1949).
2. Another example is the Sandford Commission, July 1948.
3. Having bands at political meetings was actually illegal but, as Norman Manley stated in his evidence to the inquiry, "There seemed to be a tacit understanding that it would be ignored as both sides used bands throughout the election" (*Daily Gleaner*, 12 July 1949).
4. Arthur Leon was fined £5 for carrying an unlicensed firearm. Hugh Shearer was a JLP member of parliament at the time and later prime minister of Jamaica; Mrs Leon was a JLP member of parliament.

5. Bustamante had stones and two iron bars in the back seat of his car. In evidence, Mayor Newland (JLP) explained how the stones got in the back of Bustamante's car: "When Mr. Bustamante come there [BITU headquarters], I was relating to him what had happened at Gordon Town, and he noticed there were several persons piling up bricks in front of the union office and saying they wanted to go to Gordon Town. Mr. Bustamante instructed his chauffeur and some of his men to take the bricks away with them. He said that he would take the bricks to his home and leave them but he had forgotten and went to Gordon Town instead" (*Daily Gleaner,* 21 July 1949).

6. *Daily Gleaner* (19 July 1949). On the other hand, Shearer, a JLP candidate, described Group 69 as "a group of PNP adherents who had vowed to wreak vengeance and take life if necessary, and that they couldn't go to prison because they had Manley to defend them" (*Daily Gleaner,* 20 July 1949).

7. Address by Norman Manley to the PNP Conference on 21 August 1949, printed in *The Report,* no date.

8. Unpublished manuscript by Orville Brown, information officer for the JLP in 1995.

9. See *Hansard,* 17 November 1948, 517.

10. On the night of 5 July, for example, there were three officers and one hundred policemen covering the two political meetings (*Daily Gleaner,* 13 July 1949).

11. Correspondence with Richard Hart, April 1995.

References

Daily Gleaner, February 1942–November 1949.

Gordon, F. 1995. Interview by author. Kingston, Jamaica, July.

Harriott, A.D. 1994. "Class, Race and Political Attitudes of the Jamaican Security Forces". PhD diss., University of the West Indies.

Hart, R. 1996. Interview by author. London, April.

Hearne Commission Report. 1949. 4 August.

Wilmot, S. 1977. "Political Development in Jamaica in the Post-Emancipation Period, 1838–1854". DPhil thesis, University of Oxford.

4

Garrison Politics and Criminality in Jamaica
Does the 1997 Election Represent a Turning Point?

Mark Figueroa and Amanda Sives

Introduction

In coming to terms with Jamaica's high rates of violent crime, we need
to track the development of the garrison phenomenon. The growth of
the garrison communities has been one of the key factors in the development of crime and violence in Jamaica. These communities also represent an important set of sites where the political process has been
linked with criminality. Located in the heart of the urban areas, and created by the sharp political divisions of the 1960s and 1970s, the garrisons have fostered the escalation of political violence and nurtured the
growth of gun and drug crime. It is relatively easy to use available data
to establish a link between the garrison communities and the very high
rates of crime that occur in and around them. However, presenting a
full picture of the connections between the garrisons, crime and the
political process is a much more difficult task, and research in this field
could pose dangers for the researched and the researcher.

The relationships between politics, the garrison communities and
crime exist on a number of levels in Jamaica. Gun crime and violence
have received a great deal of attention in Jamaica, but it should be
noted that electoral fraud, intimidation and the related political violence

are criminal activities in and of themselves. On election day the garrisons are therefore major sites for crime, as the laws governing the conduct of elections are routinely disregarded in these areas; in the context of Jamaica, however, these crimes have rarely been prosecuted. The fact that politicians have failed to take action against the perpetrators of electoral abuse within their own constituencies and, in some cases, rely on such perpetrators means that they are compromised, even if they are not directly involved in criminal activity. This makes it extremely problematic for political representatives to disengage from elements in their constituencies who are involved in political manipulation and criminal activity. In addition, even where violent crime is not politically motivated it often takes on a political mantle because the actors are closely associated with a political party or with a garrison community that has been closely associated with a political party.

This chapter tackles the difficulty of undertaking detailed research in this area by concentrating on the electoral manifestations of the garrisons. The significance of this approach is that it seeks to make the most of publicly available data to gain an insight into processes that are fundamental to the generation of high violent-crime rates. Using a box-by-box approach, the returns for the 1997 general election are assessed to determine whether there has been a significant break in the trend (evident up to 1993) towards a strengthening of the garrison phenomenon. Homogeneous voting, recorded voter turnouts and reports of electoral malpractice are analysed in detail. While we argue that the analysis undertaken here does indicate a break in the trend, there were several factors that coalesced around the 1997 election which distinguished it from previous elections.

In the rest of the chapter we discuss the relationship between the garrisons and crime, identify how we make use of electoral data and then focus on the 1997 election results. Following this, we assess the factors that made the 1997 election qualitatively different from its predecessors and conclude on the future of the garrisons, elections and crime.

The Garrisons and Crime

At one level a garrison community can be described as one in which anyone who seeks to oppose, raise opposition to or organize against the dominant party would be in danger of suffering serious damage to their possessions or person, thus making continued residence in the area extremely difficult, if not impossible. A garrison, as the name suggests, is a political stronghold, a veritable fortress completely controlled by a party. Any significant social, political, economic or cultural development within the garrison can only take place with the tacit approval of the leadership (whether local or national) of the dominant party.[1] The development of the garrison phenomenon is usually traced to the establishment of large government housing schemes in the 1960s and 1970s, where the allocation of units was done on a partisan basis. At that time an effort was made to create politically homogeneous communities by ensuring that all new residents were supporters of the ruling party. Chevannes (1992) and Figueroa (1994) have demonstrated that there are a number of other ways in which garrison communities have developed, and the phenomenon has become somewhat more complex over the years.

Rooted in the political struggle for turf politics (Figueroa 1985), the garrisons were quickly associated with positional gun warfare and the illegal gun trade. More recently they have been seen as fundamental to the transformation of the structure of crime in Jamaica (Harriott 2000, ch 1, esp. 15 ff.). They are "whole urban communities living beyond the state and law". They are "safe havens, where externally directed criminality is accepted" in which the "tight integration between local party structures and criminal gang organizations [ensures] a fair measure of political protection from police action" (Harriott 2000, xxv, 16). At their inception the significance of the garrisons had more to do with the securing of a safe seat within the politically volatile inner-city constituencies; concern with crime and violence centred primarily on elections and political campaigning. More recently the garrisons have received greater attention, as they have become increasingly linked to organized crime and the international drug trade.

In addition, the garrisons also have a broader criminogenic significance. In this regard it is important to note again that the widespread electoral fraud, intimidation and violence associated with the garrisons constitute criminal offences. On election day the garrisons are therefore major sites of criminal activity. The fact that wanton lawlessness is integral to the process by which lawmakers are elected undermines the legitimacy of legal processes in Jamaica. This is exacerbated by the history of elections in Jamaica, where election crimes have not been treated as such and perpetrators have been essentially immune from prosecution. In addition, members of parliament have increasingly been seen to associate themselves publicly with reputed criminals, and have done nothing to convince the public that they are working to undermine illegal electoral practices.[2]

The garrison phenomenon manifests itself in different ways. It is not static in either space or time, but rather should be viewed as a dynamic process. In effect, there is a wide spectrum of communities which have become more or less garrisoned. At one end there are communities which live in the shadow of the garrisons; they are located on the border or just within the periphery of garrison influence. They experience the impact periodically, notably during hot electoral contests, when the garrisons extend their reach to the limit. At the other end are the tightly controlled core garrisons, with their increasingly well-known area "dons". It is the large-scale core garrisons which provide a nurturing context for organized crime. In addition, the presence of major core garrisons in adjoining constituencies, as well as the presence of minor garrisons within constituencies controlled by the opposing party, provides a foundation for continued intercommunity violence. The perpetrators of this violence, even when it is not of an openly political nature, are able to take advantage of the divided political loyalties of adjacent communities to provide themselves with a degree of localized legitimacy, political cover and protection from the security forces.

Monitoring the changing characteristics of the garrisons represents an important element in the analysis of criminogenic factors operating in Jamaica. Evidence that suggests a strengthening of garrison processes needs to be analysed to determine the extent to which this could lead to an increase in crime and violence. Similarly, evidence that suggests a weakening of garrison processes needs to be analysed. Crime, violence, intercommunity conflicts and the associated outward movements in population, abandonment of buildings and collapse of infrastructure are all aspects of the garrison phenomenon. However, alongside these factors, the garrison also exhibits a series of political manifestations. Homogeneous voting (which signals an underlying form of political control) is one of the most striking. Electoral data can be used to monitor the growth and development of garrison areas. In this sense "we might consider a garrison community one in which the dominant party can, under normal circumstances, control the voting process" (Figueroa 1994, 6). It is the integral link between the electoral process and the garrisons which allows us to gain important insights into their growth and development through the use of electoral statistics. With this in mind we seek to examine what insights are provided by the results of the 1997 election.

Using Electoral Data

The methodology applied here has been used previously to track the growth of the garrison phenomenon from 1962 to 1993 (Figueroa 1985, 1994; Figueroa and Sives 2002). In essence, we see homogeneous voting as a sign of political control in the garrisons. The existence of this garrison-type voting signals a deeper manifestation of the garrison phenomenon.[3] Ideally this analysis should be carried on at the level of the community, as garrisons are communities. We are unable to take such an approach here. The mere identification of the boundaries of all the relevant garrison communities would be a considerable undertaking. Matching them to electoral boundaries over time would be even more difficult, due to the regular changes that are made to the boundaries of individual polling districts. An alternative approach that focuses on entities with more stable boundaries has been used. The only political/administrative boundaries that have not changed since independence are parish (municipal) boundaries. Thus, although there are limitations to the use of such a large and non-homogeneous unit, it is the starting point for our analysis. This is supplemented by a discussion at the constituency level.

The study is restricted to one-half of the sixty Jamaican constituencies. These cover the four parishes with urban communities that have exhibited the garrison phenomenon. The parishes can be ordered from the mainly rural to totally urbanized as follows: Clarendon, St Catherine, St Andrew and Kingston. The capital city, Kingston, completely engulfs the parish of the same name and occupies much of St Andrew. It also forms a contiguous urban unit with a significant section of St Catherine. To make the analysis more precise, the twelve most garrisoned constituencies are singled out for special attention. The ratio of

Table 4.1   Percentage of Boxes where Losing Candidate(s) Got 0, or 10 or Fewer Votes in Eight Jamaican General Elections, 1962–1997: Selected Parishes

	1962		1967		1972		1976		1980		1989		1993		1997	
Parishes	0	≤10	0	≤10	0	≤10	0	≤10	0	≤10	0	≤10	0	≤10	0	≤10
Kingston	0	1	0	9	2	31	3	17	8	28	24	49	48	78	22	72
St Andrew	0	2	0	8	0	19	2	11	8	19	16	34	28	44	10	36
St Catherine	0	11	0	15	0	19	0	7	0	12	1	11	6	24	1	9
Clarendon	0	16	0	16	0	11	0	7	0	12	0	6	2	16	0	8
Four Parishes	0	7	0	11	0	19	1	10	4	17	10	24	19	38	7	27

Source: Calculated from reports of the director of elections/chief electoral officer, various years.

garrison-dominated constituencies to the total number of constituencies in each parish is as follows: Clarendon 1:6, St Catherine 2:9, St Andrew 6:12 and Kingston 3:3.

Two measures of homogeneous voting are used. The first, narrow measure counts those boxes where the losing candidate gets no votes. The second, broad measure counts boxes where the losing candidate gets ten votes or less. The narrow measure is almost always an indication that the box comes from a garrison community. The broad measure is quite crude, especially in the context where the number of electors on the list for each box varies widely. At the micro level it is not possible to conclude that a particular box which exhibited broad homogeneity represents a garrison box. Yet at the macro level there is no doubt that the broad measure also tracks the garrison phenomenon. Looking at table 4.1, we see that the trend in broad homogeneous voting follows closely the pattern of narrow homogeneous voting (at least after 1976).[4] The broad measure is a cruder index of the growth of the garrison phenomenon but it is useful, as the narrow measure clearly underestimates the strength of the garrisons and their impact on the Jamaican sociopolitical scene. One way of refining the usefulness of these measures is to combine them with an analysis of voter turnouts. Extremely high voter turnouts can be seen as an additional indicator of garrison-type voting, especially when homogeneous voting is present.

Data from the 1993 election were used to select the twelve most garrisoned constituencies, as this was the election in which garrison-type voting was most manifest. In all twelve of these constituencies broad homogeneous voting was present in more than 35 per cent of the boxes (average 71 per cent). The comparable figure for the thirty constituencies not considered in our study is 12 per cent. Within the twelve constituencies, there are five that stand out. In these five, narrow homogeneous voting occurred in 56 to 90 per cent of the boxes, compared to 0.5 per cent for the thirty constituencies not covered in this study. For these five constituencies broad homogeneous voting varied from 74 to 92 per cent of the boxes (see table 4.2).[5] The next six constituencies are somewhat less garrisoned, exhibiting narrow homogeneous voting from 15 to 38 per cent and broad homogeneous voting from 49 to 69 per cent in 1993. The last of the twelve is Clarendon Central, which is by far the least garrisoned. In 1993 homogeneous voting was 9 per cent and 38 per cent on the narrow and broad indicator respectively. To better understand the 1997 election, it is necessary to study a number of these constituencies.

The 1997 Election

Given the steady upward trend in homogeneous voting since independence, the results for the 1997 election represent a definite turnaround. In many cases the incidence of homogeneous voting returned to levels below those experienced in 1989. In some cases the level of homogeneous voting was actually closer to levels attained in 1980. This can be seen from the global figures presented in table 4.1. Of note is the steeper decline in narrow as against broad homogeneous voting. For the four parishes narrow homogeneous voting dropped from 19 to 7 per cent, a 63 per cent decline. The decline on the broad indicator is from 38 to 27 per cent, a 29 per cent reduction (see table 4.3). These global figures mask important differences between the garrison areas; we therefore need to examine particular constituencies in more detail.

As noted above, Clarendon Central is considerably less garrisoned than the other constituencies. In 1993 it exhibited broad homogeneous voting at a level just above one-half the average of the other constituencies. On the indicator of narrow homogeneous voting it was less than a

Table 4.2   Twelve "Most Garrisoned" Constituencies (1993): Recorded Voter Turnout and Percentage Boxes where Loser(s) got 0, or 10 or Fewer Votes, 1993 and 1997

		1993			1997		
Constituency		Recorded Voter Turnout (%)	% Boxes Losers Get 0 Votes	% Boxes Losers Get 0–10 Votes	Recorded Voter Turnout (%)	% Boxes Losers Get 0 Votes	% Boxes Losers Get 0–10 Votes
St Andrew	West Central	88	90	92	55	14	83
St Andrew	Southern	97	70	81	93	43	81
Kingston	Western	87	61	74	91	42	83
St Andrew	South Western	94	61	95	82	28	92
Kingston	Central	89	56	91	76	13	71
St Catherine	South Central	77	38	58	61	12	40
St Andrew	Western	70	32	63	63	11	47
St Andrew	East Central	78	21	56	55	2	32
St Catherine	Central	86	18	69	47	0	6
St Andrew	South Eastern	73	15	49	59	6	33
Kingston	Eastern	75	15	66	60	5	58
Clarendon	Central	78	9	38	67	0	13

Source: Calculated from reports of the director of elections, 1993, 1997.

quarter of the average of the others in 1993. In 1997 this latter indicator drops to zero. Clarendon Central was the marginal garrison constituency in 1993, and it essentially becomes "extra marginal" in 1997. It will therefore be excluded from much of the analysis that follows. In Central St Catherine broad homogeneous voting fell from 69 to 6 per cent, and narrow homogeneous voting fell from 18 per cent to zero. This strongly garrisoned constituency in 1993 was a special case in 1997: the sitting member of parliament was Bruce Golding, the former general secretary of the opposition Jamaica Labour Party (JLP). He had left the party and formed a new political party, the National Democratic

Table 4.3   Homogeneous Voting: 1997 and 1993, 12 "Most Garrisoned"
Constituencies (1993) Percentage Boxes where Loser(s) got 0,
or 10 or Fewer Votes

Constituencies	0 Votes			≤ 10 Votes		
	1993 (%)	1997 (%)	% Decline	1993 (%)	1997 (%)	% Decline
Top 5	66	32	52	86	84	2
Selected 10	47	20	58	73	65	11
Top 12	43	17	60	71	56	22
All 30	19	7	63	38	27	29

Source: Calculated from reports of the director of elections, 1993, 1997.

Movement (NDM). This produced an entirely new political situation in
the constituency which requires us to exclude it from much of the following analysis.[6]

The remaining ten constituencies are referred to as the "selected 10"
in table 4.3. When we look at the decline in homogeneous voting for
these ten constituencies we see that it was not as steep as the overall
decline for the four parishes. The narrow indicator fell from 47 to 20
per cent and the broad indicator from 73 to 65 per cent, representing
declines of 58 per cent and 11 per cent, respectively. For the five most
garrisoned constituencies the declines were even smaller: from 66 to 32
per cent and from 86 to 84 per cent, representing declines of 52 per cent
and 2 per cent, respectively. These figures underline the fact that not all
garrison communities are the same and their preponderance within specific constituencies varies widely.

In the 1993 election the garrison communities extended their influence
beyond their immediate borders and impacted on the voting patterns
across a very wide area in the heavily influenced garrisoned constituencies.
In 1997 this influence was not as widely felt. While the peripheral electoral
influence of the core garrisons appears to have diminished in 1997, there
is no evidence to suggest that within the core there was any significant
decline. The marginal 2 per cent decline for broad homogeneous voting
within the five most garrisoned constituencies demonstrates that the core
is intact. An examination of the recorded voter turnouts and margins of
victory helps to bolster this conclusion.

At first sight it appears that the voter turnout for the 1997 election was lower than that of the 1993 election. Votes recorded, as a percentage of the voters' list, amounted to 65 per cent in 1997 as against 68 per cent in 1993. Yet it would be quite wrong to see this as a decline in actual voter participation. For the majority of the constituencies there was in fact an increase in recorded voter turnout. The decline was most evident in a number of the garrison-dominated constituencies. This reflected a decline in electoral manipulation in the communities *outside* of the hardcore garrisons. By disaggregating the voter turnout into two groups we see a very different picture. For the twelve most garrisoned constituencies the votes recorded as a percentage of the voters' list declined significantly, from 91 per cent in 1993 to 78 per cent in 1997. For the other forty-eight constituencies there was actually an increase in votes recorded, from 63 per cent in 1993 to 65 per cent in 1997. Given Jamaica's history of electoral manipulation, especially within the garrison communities, we are inclined to take the latter figures as a truer reflection of the trend in voter turnout. The decline in recorded turnout in the most garrison-dominated constituencies is unlikely to reflect any significant decline in persons actually going to the poll. Rather, it most likely reflects a decline in what Winston Witter (1992) politely referred to as "bulk proxy voting". Indeed, anecdotal evidence from Citizens' Action for Free and Fair Elections (CAFFE) volunteers in some of these constituencies suggests that there may have been an increase in the number of persons who actually came out to vote.[7]

The recorded turnout was lower in only fourteen of the forty-eight non-garrison constituencies. Yet, in eleven of the twelve most garrisoned constituencies the recorded turnout declined. Kingston Western was the only garrison-dominated constituency where the turnout was marginally higher. This reflects in part the core garrison status of much of Kingston Western. It is also possible to explain this anomaly by factoring into the discussion the number of boxes where no votes were recorded in the 1993 elections.[8] The 1993 election produced far more boxes where no voting took place than was the case in 1997. If we exclude the voters' lists for the fourteen boxes where no votes were recorded, the turnout for 1997 would have been lower for Kingston Western than it was in 1993. Correcting for this factor would make the decline in voting in the garrison areas easier to see. Thus, a careful analysis would suggest that it is very unlikely that there was a decline in the number of persons who actually turned out to vote and actually cast a ballot. The most plausible explanation for the differences in the turn-outs recorded in the two elections was a decline in ballot stuffing and other forms of electoral manipulation in some of the garrison-dominated constituencies and the peripheral areas of others.

A more detailed analysis of the recorded voter turnouts provides an indication of the differentiation that took place between the constituen-cies. The most significant decline was in Central St Catherine, reflecting the completely new situation in that constituency in 1997. The decline in voter turnout in this one constituency was equivalent to more than half of the decline in recorded turnout for the whole country between 1993 and 1997. In 1993 the recorded voter turnout was 86 per cent. In 1997 this fell to 47 per cent, a decline of 45 per cent. For Central Clarendon the recorded voter turnout moved from 78 to 67 per cent, a decline of 15 per cent. The five least garrisoned of the selected ten con-stituencies slipped from 75 to 60 per cent, a decline of 20 per cent. Among these constituencies the decline ranged from a high of 30 per cent in East Central St Andrew to a low of 11 per cent in Western St Andrew, with the other three constituencies being very close to the average. Among the five most garrisoned constituencies there was a much greater variation with respect to the decline in registered voter turnout.

Two constituencies need to be singled out in terms of the pervasive-ness of the garrison phenomenon. These are Kingston Western and St Andrew South, the only two constituencies in which narrow homoge-neous voting was higher in 1997 than it was in 1989. These are also the only two constituencies where broad homogeneous voting was at the same level or higher in 1997 than it was in 1993. Recorded voter turnout actually rises in Kingston Western from 87 to 91 per cent (or falls from 93 to 91 per cent if you accept the correction discussed above). In St Andrew South there is a decline from 97 to 93 per cent (a comparable adjustment is not called for as there were no boxes in which voting did not take place in 1993). This marginal shift in voter turnout occurs nowhere else.

These constituencies remain almost completely garrisoned. The methodology we use to measure homogeneous voting tends to underes-timate the extent of the garrisons in these constituencies for two rea-sons. First, we tend to undercount the number of homogeneous boxes because we exclude all boxes where twenty or fewer votes were recorded (so as to avoid including boxes where genuinely homogeneous voting occurs). Second, for ease of data analysis we include those boxes where there are no electors when we are counting the total number of boxes. Due to urbanization and out migration, these two inner-city constituencies have a significant number of boxes that either have no electors or where the total number of votes recorded was less than or equal to twenty. For Western Kingston such boxes accounted for 21 out of a total of 162, while the comparable numbers were 31 out of 170 boxes for St Andrew South. If these boxes were excluded there would be a concomitant increase in the indicators of garrison-type voting.

In both cases the dominant party in the constituency controlled almost the entire constituency. This was reflected in the high margins of victory. The winner received 84 per cent of the votes cast in Western Kingston; in St Andrew South the winner received 91 per cent. The presence of smaller garrison communities controlled by the losing party is evidenced by the fact that in Kingston Western the losing party got 75 per cent of its votes from 15.4 per cent of the boxes. In St Andrew South the losing party got 75 per cent of its votes from 3.5 per cent of the boxes. Here we see some differentiation in the nature of these two constituencies. In St Andrew South there is a more complete bipolar homogenization. Communities in this constituency are sharply defined by political allegiance, and political control is paramount. The minority party has only a small foothold but it is concentrated in a tight garrison area. In Kingston Western there are more contested communities. These are areas where neither the JLP nor the People's National Party (PNP) completely dominates, hence the voting in these areas is less controlled. The presence of more contested areas often impacts on the level of crime. Where communities are less garrisoned there is an inbuilt competition for criminal spoils, which can develop into gang warfare. In addition, contested communities provide a basis for struggles between political rivals, which foster intercommunity violence. For both constituencies the only evidence of a decline in the garrison phenomenon is the fall in narrow homogeneous voting between 1993 and 1997. We do not attach great significance to this decline, for reasons discussed in detail below. Indeed, the conclusion to be drawn from an analysis of these two constituencies is that the core garrisons, far from being dismantled, may well have shown an element of consolidation.

Space does not permit a complete analysis of the profiles of all the garrison-dominated constituencies. This would no doubt reveal a range of additional details, in particular, the extent to which the garrison phenomenon is pervasive within the constituency, the degree to which one party dominates the constituency, and the extent to which the other party has a tightly controlled garrison within the constituency. The pervasiveness of the garrisons can be discerned from the percentage of homogeneous boxes. The degree of control can be measured by the percentage of the vote for the winning party. The extent to which the losing party controls garrison areas within the constituency can be seen from the homogeneous boxes it controls and the concentration of its votes within a small number of boxes. Analysing the most garrisoned constituencies could also be useful in providing some insight into future flashpoints for violence and continued havens for criminal activity. There is a limit to the detail that can be covered here, but it is important to make some brief comments on a number of other constituencies.

After Kingston Western and St Andrew South, St Andrew South Western shows the least change between 1993 and 1997. The decline in broad homogeneous voting from 1993 to 1997 was marginal (from 95 to 92 per cent), although the decline in narrow homogeneous voting was significant (from 61 to 28 per cent). Similarly, recorded voter turnout showed a decline from 94 to 82 per cent. This constituency is entirely dominated by one party, which gained 98 per cent of votes recorded. There are no garrison communities controlled by the minority party, which required 58 per cent of the boxes to get 75 per cent of its votes. This constituency comes a close third to the two most garrisoned constituencies discussed above. Yet it has a different history, not being as closely associated with government housing schemes as the other two. It remains firmly garrisoned but there is less of a tendency towards violence within its borders, as the minority party has no garrison presence. It provides further evidence that the core garrisons remain essentially intact. However, it also highlights that the relationship between violent crime and the garrison-dominated constituencies is complex. A key determinant of the level of violence is the presence of competing tendencies within the constituency vying for political (or criminal) control and turf.[9]

The other two constituencies in the top five most garrisoned, St Andrew West Central and Kingston Central, both showed similar declines in broad homogeneous voting (92 to 83 per cent and 91 to 71 per cent, respectively). The decline in narrow homogeneous voting (90 to 14 per cent and 56 to 13 per cent) and recorded voter turnout (88 to 55 per cent and 89 to 76 per cent) was more marked in St Andrew West Central. These two are the most contested of the top five garrisoned constituencies. In 1993 the minority party recorded 34 and 41 per cent, respectively, of the votes cast for these two constituencies, and St Andrew West Central actually changed hands in 1997.

There is a clear differentiation between these two contested constituencies and the top three discussed above. What they demonstrated in 1993 is the degree to which the garrison areas of a constituency, when fully unleashed, can influence the outcome of an election. This was particularly true for West Central St Andrew in 1993, where the party that lost (in the box) got no votes in all except two of the eighty boxes in which votes were registered. The total number of votes won by the losing party in these two boxes was three. When the outreach of the garrison communities is curtailed and the ballot stuffing limited, as was the case in 1997, we see a very different picture. Despite the problems faced in this constituency in 1997, which caused the competent authority to annul the election, it was a vastly improved situation to that which occurred in 1993.[10]

Our general conclusion is that garrison-type voting declined in the 1997 election to a significant degree. This was manifest in a universal fall in narrow homogeneous voting, a decline in broad homogeneous voting in all but two constituencies, and an overall decline in recorded voter turnout. The decline in Central St Catherine was dramatic, but this has to be seen as a special case. Despite these global trends it appears that the core garrisons remain firmly intact. We would suggest that the much sharper decline in narrow homogeneous voting should not be given too much significance. Garrison voting has increasingly become a target of those who are critical of the Jamaican political system. Just as overvoting was curbed in the 1980s (although it still occurs), it is possible that those who exercise control over the registration of votes within the garrisons now consider narrow homogeneous voting an untidy affair. In the better-organized areas instructions may well have been issued to restrict ballot stuffing to more modest levels and to allow a small number of votes to be registered for the minority party, given the level of scrutiny present for the 1997 elections.

Indeed, the pattern of voting suggests a possible consolidation within the garrison inner core, whereas the impact on the peripheral and border areas has been more restricted. The all-out effort to control the registration of votes that was evident in the 1993 election was not as widespread in the 1997 election – most notably in the constituencies where both parties have garrisons of comparable sizes. The garrisons are alive and well; however, while they continue to flourish, we need to recognize the differences between them. Each garrison community has a particular history of its own which manifests itself in the garrison's particular electoral profile as well as in its criminogenic tendencies. We have presented the available evidence with respect to the decline in garrison-type voting in 1997. The key question to which we now turn is, was this a mere decline in the electoral manifestation or is there a more significant underlying shift?

The Decline of Garrison-Type Voting in 1997

The factors accounting for the decline in garrison-type voting were triggered in the aftermath of the 1993 election. The levels of fraud and intimidation that occurred not only led to a demand for electoral reform but also signalled a growing cynicism with the political process. This wider social context created the conditions within which a specific political framework could be developed. Legislative changes were introduced, domestic and international observers were invited into the polling stations, and the police force developed a more professional approach on election day. This section of the chapter examines these changes and their impact on the general election of 1997.

The Impact of the 1993 Election

High levels of blatant electoral fraud marred the 1993 election, leading the Electoral Advisory Committee to consider "whether in a number of constituencies one can really say an Election has taken place or can take place because of the stealing of a high percentage of boxes and ballots" (*Daily Gleaner,* 31 March 1993). The report from the ombudsman for political matters, Justice Kerr, highlighted (not surprisingly) that the urban areas experienced the highest number of problems: "It is in these parishes that intimidation, stealing of ballot boxes and interference with the electoral process reached unprecedented extent and brazenry that caused these elections to be labelled the worst since adult sufferage [*sic*] came to the country in 1944" (Kerr 1993, 2). Election-related violence was also a problem and, while it was not on the same scale as during the 1980 election, it highlighted the fact that violence was still a feature of Jamaican politics. Between nomination day (12 March) and four April there were fifteen murders, fifteen shootings, three stabbings and three assaults (*Daily Gleaner,* 4 April 1993). However, it was the blatant fraud, rather than the violence, that captured the public imagination and led to the outpourings of condemnation in the newspapers following the election. There was considerable reflection and much public debate as to what could be done to avoid violence and remove electoral manipulation from the political system. This mood was reflected in statements from the government and political leaders, state sector officials, the business community, the press and various representatives of civil society (see, for example, PSOJ 1997).

While it was evident that the political parties and their supporters were involved in perpetrating electoral abuse, of even greater concern was the clear evidence of direct police interference in the electoral process. A number of statements were collected "that contain[ed] serious allegations of policemen involving themselves or turning a blind eye to blatant interference with the electoral proceedings" (Kerr 1993, 4). Condemnation also came from the churches, which had volunteers observing the process in the polling stations on election day. Reported incidents included open voting, marked ballots being brought to the polling station, poll books being confiscated, ballot boxes being brought into the station by unknown persons and so on (*Daily Gleaner,* 3 April 1993). The opposition released their own report on election malpractice (JLP 1993) and called for a commission of inquiry into the running of the elections. They also boycotted parliament from April to July, and called for the dismissal of the director of elections and the commissioner of police. Against this background the newly elected prime minister, P.J. Patterson, publicly committed his government to political and electoral reform.

Legislative Changes

On the recommendation of the Electoral Advisory Committee, changes in electoral law were introduced prior to the 1997 election. These amendments introduced much stiffer penalties, of up to five years' imprisonment, for individuals who were caught attempting to defraud the electoral system. More important than this, legislation was introduced which meant an election result in a specific constituency or polling station could be declared null and void and held again. This was a huge advance on the method of petitioning the court, which had proved to be an extremely costly and time-consuming process.[11] The introduction of this amendment ensured that bogus elections could be invalidated and held again within a matter of weeks or months following the general election. This, more than other legal amendments, placed a heavy penalty and responsibility on those candidates who presided over, or encouraged, illegal practices.[12] Attempts were also made to introduce safeguards against fraud, such as photographs in the polling station "black books" and identification cards. While there were a number of problems in the application of these safeguards on election day, such measures did show that the Electoral Office was introducing systems that could help to prevent abuse.

Scrutiny of the Electoral Process

There were some partisan divisions concerning the issue of election observers, but by September 1997 a domestic group, CAFFE, had been set up and the Atlanta-based Carter Centre had received a formal invitation.[13] This was the first time in Jamaican history that formal groups had observed the electoral process. International and domestic observer groups operate, and have an impact, on different levels and perform different functions. At the local level, the mere involvement of citizens in an electoral process, beyond their role as voters, is an important one. This is particularly the case in a country which has had a history of violent elections, highlighting, as it did, that people were not willing to stand aside powerless as others manipulated the electoral system. As one local observer stated, "I have always been complaining and I felt this was an avenue I could use to probably do something about it" (interview, CAFFE observer, July 1999). Their involvement sent an important message to those who had encouraged and perpetrated electoral fraud, with minimal repercussions for decades, that it would no longer be tolerated. The presence of CAFFE not only ensured that procedures were being observed; in some cases, volunteers became involved in the process as polling staff when officials failed to turn up for duty. They had an important impact on one of the problems that has plagued the Jamaican electoral process, namely the role of partisan polling officials.

International observers brought a different dimension to the process. The presence of such high-profile international figures such as President Jimmy Carter, Colin Powell and Evander Holyfield led to increased media scrutiny (nationally and internationally) of the election processes. The repercussions of electoral irregularities and violence were also magnified, as the process had become a matter of international attention and concern. Negative publicity would not only damage Jamaica's reputation, but would also impact on its credit status with international lending agencies and other governments. International observers, therefore, may well have acted as a brake on those politicians more inclined to encourage and condone illegal practices.[14]

Policing

The government's decision, following the 1993 election, to appoint a new police commissioner from outside the force had a very positive effect on the public's image of the police. Colonel Trevor MacMillan commanded respect as the result of a distinguished career in the Jamaica Defence Force and as head of the Revenue Protection Division (Harriott 2000, 127). MacMillan made it one of his key tasks to root out corrupt and partisan policemen. His time as commissioner was not without controversy, but there is no doubt that the reputation of the force was enhanced as a result of his tenure in office. His successor Francis Forbes took office in October 1996 and, while not creating as many waves, has certainly sought to associate himself with whatever positive legacy MacMillan left for him.

In 1997, for the first time, a comprehensive plan was developed to police the election. A management team which consisted of senior officials of all the major divisions was established specifically to plan for the election, and liaised on all election matters: monitoring actions of police personnel, overseeing and approving training, ensuring strategic issues were covered, assessing requests for resources, and liaising with the Jamaica Defence Force. In addition to adequate preparation and planning for election day, staff were also trained in the rules and regulations laid down under the laws governing elections. This contrasted with previous elections, when training had been on an *ad hoc* basis. Temporary special constables were recruited to ensure adequate coverage, and our informant from the police force stressed that part of the training involved the censure of partisan behaviour and an outline of the relevant sanctions. In previous elections the attitude on all of these issues had been more reactive than proactive (personal interview, superintendent of police, 5 August 1999).

Funding from the director of elections paid for special bibs for each police officer. These bore individual identification numbers in large type, making it much easier for members of the public to identify errant police. Citizens were urged in public broadcasts to phone a special hotline on election day if they witnessed police behaving in an unprofessional manner. The commissioner of police took the time to openly speak out against partisan behaviour by members of the force. As he stated after the election, "On election day more eyes were on them [his officers]. They were forewarned that their conduct would come under the microscope, not just to Jamaicans, but also to international visitors." This was a clear allusion to the positive impact that observers (a number of whom were stationed in the Joint Police Command Centre) might have had on restraining unprofessional behaviour. Allegations of misconduct were minimal, and there is little doubt that the conduct of the police in 1997 had a far more positive impact on the electoral process than in earlier elections.

Wider Considerations

The combination of all these positive elements impacted significantly, we would argue, on the general levels of fraud and violence. However, it is also important to recognize the political and social context within which these positive elements were introduced into the system. There was weariness in society regarding the continued abuse of the electoral system; this had been made clear in a number of ways since the 1993 election. In September 1996 the prime minister had appointed the National Committee on Political Tribalism in response to a debate about the continued existence of garrison communities. There was a public airing of the problems that beset these communities and the political relationships which lay at the heart of them. There had also been ongoing discussions about constitutional reform and, while they had stalled, they indicated a recognition that the system was not working. The creation of the National Democratic Movement (NDM, launched in October 1995) following the very public split between Edward Seaga and his heir apparent, Bruce Golding, was another important factor. Although the NDM never became a serious threat to the major political parties, it added a certain tone to the contest with its criticisms of the worst aspects of the political system, coming as they did from a party led by the member of parliament for a garrison constituency.

The split in the JLP came after a series of high-profile incidents of dissent in the ranks of the party. This led not only to the existence of a third party on the political scene but also to a weakening of the JLP position. It undermined the ability of the JLP to convince the electorate that they were a credible alternative to the ruling party. Following from this, it became clear from opinion polls and the prevailing public mood that the JLP would not win the election. Polls undertaken at the end of November and the beginning of December put the JLP almost ten clear points behind the PNP.[15] In the context of sure defeat, and with the eyes of the world watching, Seaga had nothing to gain by pulling out all the stops, and to do so could have resulted in irreparable damage to his reputation, which was already under serious pressure. It would have made sense for the leadership of the JLP to ensure that its supporters minimized electoral abuse.

Equally, it would have made little sense for the PNP to unleash massive electoral manipulation. P.J. Patterson had committed himself to cleaning up the electoral system to the point that, if it had not significantly improved, his own reputation would have been undermined. This was reinforced by the likelihood of his victory, and the consequent need to have international support following his electoral triumph. The PNP had little to gain from abusing its position of strength.

Allied with these developments in the wider civil society and at the level of the political elite, there have been changes manifesting themselves at the level of the garrison communities. It is evident, first of all, that the nature of the relationships between the politicians and the political/community leaders has become more fluid. Levels of dependence are not as strong as they once were. This ultimately means that there are fewer activists ready, willing and able to carry out the violence and fraud associated with electoral manipulation. Symptomatic of the changing environment was the conflict between Rema, Denham Town and Tivoli Gardens (all JLP garrisons) in February and March 1995. This conflict received unprecedented publicity via the Breakfast Club radio show (upper-middle-class audience), highlighting the complexity of the political relationships pertaining to the downtown area. During this conflict and the consequent media exposure, the overlaps between politics, crime, turf, drugs and community were exposed in many of their nuances. What became clear from discussions held on the programme was that the years of political warfare and the unending horrors of crime and violence had led to a certain partisan exhaustion. In addition, there were two other factors which further undermined the tendency towards partisan excesses.

The first had to do with the growth in the relative independence of the garrison "dons", gained through success in the international drug trade. In as far as the "dons" were less dependent on the state for patronage, and hence less dependent on politics, they were less inclined to engage in partisan activities. In as far as members of the community could depend on the drug "dons" for support as an alternative to political patronage, they were less inclined to participate in partisan activities. Added to this, it must be noted that organized crime had provided a number of opportunities for cooperation between the "dons" across party lines, especially in the drug trade and the protection racket. With less hostility between the leadership of the garrison communities, less need to win political favours and less dependence on politics and the state, the stage was set for a more quiet election.

This was made even more likely by the unprecedented national spirit that emerged in the "Road to France" campaign of the national football team, "the Reggae Boyz". Not since 1962, when Jamaica gained independence, had there been such a display of national unity. It was just one month before the election that Jamaica had held Mexico to a one-one draw at the National Stadium, to become the first English-speaking Caribbean country to qualify for a World Cup. The prime minister immediately declared a national holiday. The effect this had on the country's mood was dramatic, if short lived. For example, it was reported that on nomination day rival party supporters were hugging each other and dancing in the streets (*Daily Gleaner,* 4 December 1997). This is in sharp contrast to the usual situation, in which seasoned returning officers ensure that the party candidates arrive to be nominated a few hours apart so as to avoid tense stand-offs that sometimes develop into violence. One *Gleaner* columnist remarked on this transformation: "I am firmly convinced that this was no orchestration by political leaders, but a fall-out of the spontaneous unity celebrations of the Reggae Boyz football victory" (*Daily Gleaner,* 5 December 1997).

Conclusion

The 1997 election represented a significant shift in garrison-type voting but the garrisons remained a site for extensive electoral crime. In addition the shift that took place must be seen as primarily an electoral phenomenon, and not a foundation for a concomitant decline in violent crime and intercommunity conflicts. Garrison voting showed only a marginal decline within the core garrisons; indeed, there may have been some signs of consolidation. While there was a definite decline in the reach of the garrisons in terms of their impact on communities that are peripheral to their control, it is also possible that those who control garrison voting showed greater sophistication and sought to present a better image. However, it is also clear that there were significant developments of an institutional nature in a favourable sociopolitical context, that would have made it more difficult to spread the garrison-type voting beyond the core. Above we have made reference to the Electoral Office, the political ombudsman, the security forces and the judicial system, along with the parallel developments in civil society.

As important as these developments were, we cannot avoid concluding that they were mainly operating within the electoral sphere and therefore had very limited impact on the fundamentals of the garrison phenomenon. In addition, the election took place within a context that would have discouraged the active pursuit of garrison-type voting. The 1997 election does not signal the decline of the garrisons, but it does demonstrate that reform is possible. Improvements in the administration of the elections, legislative reform (including the creation of a competent authority with the power to void elections), transformation of the way in which the security forces deal with elections and other reforms indicate that it is possible to tackle a difficult problem and achieve improvements. It is important to continue to take steps to deal with electoral crimes, but it is equally important to deal with the underlying conditions that foster electoral and other crimes. What is necessary now is the identification of a combination of measures that can move beyond electoral reform to attack and undermine the fundamentals of the garrison phenomenon. If this is not done as a parallel process with electoral reform it is unlikely that the latter will succeed. Of equal concern is that the danger of a new upward spiral in electoral, inter-community and criminal violence will always be present, so long as the garrisons are not tackled in a far-reaching way.

Acknowledgements

This chapter was completed with the research and/or editorial assistance of Atania Davis, Shauna Douglas, Sherine Grant, Rachel Haye and Shellian Whyte, and is based on research funded in part by the Ford Foundation and the Dean's Office, Faculty of Social Sciences, University of the West Indies, Mona, Jamaica.

Notes

1. This widely accepted definition was first put forward by Figueroa (1994, 5). It was used by the National Committee on Political Tribalism (1997, 9), CAFFE (1998, 16) and Munroe (1999, 23).
2. For a more detailed discussion of how the garrisons undermine the rule of law, see Figueroa 1994; Figueroa and Sives 2002.

3. We use the term garrison-type voting to encompass all those elements of electoral manipulation – including fraud, intimidation and violence – that have come to be associated with the garrisons. There is no easy way to comprehensively record such occurrences. Homogeneous voting is therefore used as a proxy.

4. Prior to 1976 there was a non-garrison phenomenon operating that explains the presence of broad homogeneous voting, especially in the rural parishes. This trend is not relevant to our discussion here. Other, smaller breaks in the trend can be explained in terms of very wide swings that took place in a number of elections – notably in 1976, 1980 and 1989. For an analysis of this and other aspects of homogeneous voting in Jamaica, see Figueroa 1994; Figueroa and Sives 2002.

5. This approach actually understated the dominance of homogeneous voting. When we discount the boxes in which no votes were recorded, the number goes from 57 to 98 per cent for the narrow and 86 to 100 per cent for the broad homogeneous voting. See Figueroa and Sives 2002.

6. Note that although the NDM did contest the 1997 election in most of the constituencies they made a poor showing generally, and the party was not a significant player in the garrison phenomenon. As such, the analysis generally speaks only of two dominant parties, the JLP and the PNP.

7. This was reflected in the large number of mature adults who did not know the voting procedure and who were apparently voting in person for the first time. It was evident that someone else had voted for them in previous elections (informal interviews with CAFFE observers).

8. In very keenly contested (garrison-style) elections it is not uncommon to find a number of boxes where no votes are recorded. This is usually caused by the intimidation of prospective voters or other forms of electoral manipulation associated with the behaviour of partisan electoral officers.

9. The outbreak of violence in the Mountain View area in 2001 presents a contrasting case, where contestation has lead to open outbreaks of violence.

10. The seat of West Central St Andrew changed hands three times. The JLP won the seat in the general election. In March 1998 an election was held again in the constituency because the constituted authority declared the result null and void; the PNP candidate won the seat. In June 1998 a third election was conducted in four polling divisions, due to the second election being declared null and void. In this final election the JLP candidate regained the seat.

11. After the 1993 election twenty-two election petitions had been submitted, none of which had been heard by 1997.

12. While the amendment did not stop illegal activity, the authorities' willingness to apply sanctions was demonstrated when they declared an election null and void, in one area, on more than one occasion.

13. See Sives 1999 for more details about the creation of the election observer group and its impact.
14. Advertisements by both the PNP and the JLP immediately prior to election day called on supporters to exercise restraint. Leader of the Opposition Edward Seaga's message stated, "We can actually begin the healing process by proving to one and all that we can think and act as one people, even in stressful times" (*Daily Gleaner,* 15 December 1997). The importance of preserving reputation should not be underestimated.
15. A Stone poll published in the *Observer* (7 December 1997) showed that 23 per cent of those sampled said they would vote for the JLP, compared to 32 per cent for the PNP. The PNP had been consistently ahead from March 1996 (*Daily Observer,* 23 September 1997). This was true on practically every indicator. By 17 December 1997 polls were published for the "weather vane" communities that showed the PNP with 40 per cent and the JLP with 27 per cent (*Daily Observer,* 17 December 1997). The NDM consistently showed 7 per cent or less, and the rest were *don't know, not voting* and *won't say.*

References

Chevannes, B. 1992. "The Formation of Garrison Communities". Paper presented at symposium in honour of Carl Stone, Faculty of Social Sciences, University of the West Indies, Kingston, Jamaica, 16–17 November.

Citizens' Action for Free and Fair Elections (CAFFE). 1998. "The 1997 General Elections in Jamaica". Kingston, Jamaica: CAFFE.

Daily Gleaner, March 1993–December 1997.

Daily Observer, September–December 1997.

Figueroa, M. 1985. "An Assessment of Over-Voting in Jamaica". *Social and Economic Studies* 34, no. 3 (September).

———. 1994. "Garrison Communities in Jamaica, 1962–1993: Their Growth and Impact on Political Culture". Paper presented at symposium, "Democracy and Democratization in Jamaica: Fifty Years of Adult Suffrage", Faculty of Social Sciences, University of the West Indies, Kingston, Jamaica, 6–7 December.

———, and A. Sives. 2002. "Homogeneous Voting, Electoral Manipulation and the Garrison Process in Post-Independence Jamaica". *Commonwealth and Comparative Politics* 40, no. 1 (March).

Harriott, A. 2000. *Police and Crime in Jamaica.* Kingston, Jamaica: University of the West Indies Press.

Jamaica Labour Party (JLP). 1993. *Report on Election Malpractices: General Elections, March 30, 1993.* Kingston, Jamaica: JLP.

Kerr, J. 1993. "General Elections 1993: Report of the Ombudsman for Political Matters". Kingston, Jamaica.

Munroe, T. 1999. *Renewing Democracy into the Millennium: The Jamaican Experience in Perspective*. Kingston, Jamaica: The Press, University of the West Indies.

National Committee on Political Tribalism. 1997. *Report of the National Committee on Political Tribalism*. Kingston, Jamaica: National Committee on Political Tribalism.

Private Sector Organization of Jamaica (PSOJ). 1997. *Good Governance and Electoral Reform: The Case of Jamaica*. Kingston, Jamaica: PSOJ.

Sives, A. 1999. "Free and Fair? Monitoring Elections in Jamaica". *Journal of Representations* 36, no. 4.

Witter, W. 1992. "Patron Clientelism: Implications for Garrison Constituencies". Paper presented at symposium in honour of Carl Stone, Faculty of Social Sciences, University of the West Indies, Kingston, Jamaica, 16–17 November.

5

Social Identities and the Escalation of Homicidal Violence in Jamaica

Anthony Harriott

Studies of aggression and violence in Caribbean societies have been few and largely limited to exploring domestic (Gopaul and Cain 1996; Parsad 1988; Haniff 1995) and political violence (Sives 1998; Eyre 1984; Lacey 1977), or have been general discussions of violent crimes (Levy 1996; Moser and Holland 1995; de Albuquerque 1984) or even more general essays on crime that include a discussion of violent crimes (Headley 1994; Stone 1987). Specific studies of homicidal violence in Jamaica have thus far been limited to efforts by Wilbanks (1978) and more recently by this researcher (Harriott 2000b). In this chapter an attempt is made to further narrow and hopefully deepen the discussion of homicidal violence by examining the dynamics of its rapid escalation in Jamaica since the mid-1970s. More specifically, this chapter seeks to explore the role of given social identities in this process of escalation.

Studies of the escalation dynamics of homicidal conflicts may lend different meanings to the idea of escalation or simply focus on different aspects of it. The psychological approach tends to view escalation in terms of the stages of the homicidal act and attempts to map and explain the progressive severity of the violent act. Thus, one may explore an escalation from verbal aggression to physical violence, from dominance displays to death threats and, associated with this, the study of triggers and the pressures on inhibitors, the process of de-individuation and so forth (see Hall 1996). On the other hand, the more sociological approaches tend to focus on the structures and volatile, culture-bound relationships that tend to generate homicidal violence with some regularity.

Here it is argued that the extraordinarily high murder rate in Jamaica, and particularly in its capital city of Kingston, may be accounted for by an escalation dynamic associated with the formation of conflict-engendering social identities. Social identity refers to the groups or categories to which members of the society are socially recognized as belonging. Of course, any attempt to explain the murder rate should not be reduced to this. Elsewhere I discuss the socioeconomic realities of blocked legitimate opportunities and social exclusion, and the responses to this which include the construction of an alternate, illegitimate opportunity structure that engenders aggressive behaviour and violence, which are at the objective foundations of this problem. A high proportion of the initial conflicts that lead to homicides are linked to problems associated with transactions in this informal and underground economy (see Harriott 2000b).

These objective criminogenic conditions and relationships do not, however, sufficiently explain the subsequent mushrooming of some of these conflicts and the involvement and victimization of parties who have no apparent connection to the initial events. Social structure and social process explanations should not be seen as being mutually exclusive; a comprehensive explanation of violent criminality in the region requires a synthesis of both. The following discussion of the conflict dynamics associated with social identities may be seen as one layer of explanation that is important to understanding why Jamaica's homicide rate is so extraordinarily high, and why homicidal violence takes on some of the qualities that it exhibits. In other words, interests and identity are conceptually distinct but related aspects of the explanation. In this chapter we simply focus on the latter (which allows a closer view and better understanding of the violent *events*).

This chapter is part of a more general study of homicides in Jamaica that is being conducted by this researcher. It is based on a data set of all cases (N = 2,474) of homicide that were reported to or detected by the police during the years 1983, 1988, 1993 and 1997. In addition, a small purposeful sample of key informants (N = 5) in two communities that are research sites for the larger project was used to record case histories of incidents involving the intergroup escalation of homicidal violence which they had witnessed as members of these communities. At the level of the cases, a maximum variation sample would have been more appropriate, and, indeed, this is the approach being taken in the larger study, but this chapter is based on six cases of which two are reported in full. The conclusions in this chapter are therefore somewhat tentative.

The Problem of Homicidal Violence

In 1999 Jamaica's murder rate stood at 33 incidents per 100,000 citizens.[1] This represents the highest rate in the Commonwealth Caribbean, ranking Jamaica approximately fifth in the hemisphere and tenth in the world (Harriott 2000b, 8). Compared with the other 114 countries that submitted reports to Interpol in 1998 on reported crimes, Jamaica may be described as an extraordinary case.[2] At its highest point in 1997, the murder rate for Jamaica was 41 per 100,000. This figure was approximately twice the mean for Latin America, which as a region has consistently recorded the highest level of social violence in the world.

Since independence in 1962 the rate of increase has accelerated in a geometric-like progression from 3.8 per 100,000 to 41 per 100,000 in 1997.[3] This represents an elevenfold increase in the rate of criminal homicides. Two distinct waves of homicidal escalation may be discerned. The first began in the mid-1960s and was driven by the political struggle for party dominance in western Kingston. This area of the city, where many of the new "screwdriver industries" were housed, was at the time a receiving area for destitute, job-seeking, rural to urban migrants, and had a large concentration of unemployed and underemployed persons who suffered from poor housing, irregular water supply and a lack of all the basic social amenities. The concentration of a mass of socially excluded poor in this section of the city was not new, but in this period following independence the size of this population and the responses to this social exclusion had become more problematic. But even more problematic were the efforts at their political inclusion. Unlike the employed labour force, which was pulled into the political parties as part of the anticolonial and labour struggles of the earlier period (after 1938), the integration of these non-unionized, non-working poor into the political system was accomplished in a manner that served to consolidate the political methodology of patron-clientelism and the development of garrison communities as a way of ensuring one-party electoral dominance in these communities of the urban poor. Political identity was established on the territorial principle, by the manipulation of the carrot of public housing and the stick of violence to ensure party-homogeneous communities. Both Figueroa (1994) and Chevannes (1992) have ably described this multifaceted process, involving what have come to be called garrison communities. In this area of the capital city, community identity therefore tended to overlap with and was largely shaped by party identity. As noted elsewhere (Harriott 2000a), in these somewhat conflict-ridden and socially isolated garrison communities, community life tends to take on a near-communal character, with party affiliation rather than kinship bonds (although these may be extensive, given the relative isolation of these communities) serving as the primary organizing principle of internal social life and determinant of their relationships with outside others. This process was consolidated in the 1970s in the period of ideological polarization and the demonization of party opponents, and in the intense political violence of 1980 (Eyre 1984). These identities are reinforced by episodic political conflict (since the mid-1960s).

The second wave began in the mid-1980s and continued until the mid-1990s. Unlike the first wave, which was to a large measure driven by competitive electoral politics, this latter wave was associated with a more developed informal sector, including the drug trade and the emergence of transnational organized crime and the activities of youth or conflict gangs. Gang identity was overlaid on party and community identity. The territorial principle therefore continued to define these conflicts. This was the period of the most rapid escalation in social violence since independence. For this period (1983–97) the incidence of murder increased by some two-and-one-half times (245 per cent), while rape increased by 33 per cent, shooting increased by 29 per cent and robbery decreased by 13 per cent.[4]

An analysis of the data on all cases of murder for the years 1983, 1988, 1993 and 1997 clearly indicates a significant shift from interpersonal to

Table 5.1 Trend in Murder Rates by Category of Murder (per 100,000)

	1997	1993	1988	1983
Domestic	1.24 (31)	1.17 (29)	1.27 (30)	1.20 (27)[a]
Other Inter-Personal	0.95 (24)	4.49 (111)	3.22 (76)	4.30 (96)
Total individualized conflict	2.19	5.66	4.49	5.50
Political	0.20 (4)	0.57 (14)	0.51 (12)	1.42 (32)
Gang rivalry\control	14.10 (340)	7.04 (174)	3.61 (85)	3.12 (70)
'Undetermined'[b]	10.90 (273)	6.35 (157)	3.43 (81)	3.75 (84)
Total Inter-Group conflict	25.2	14.00	6.55	8 .29
Pursuant of other crimes	5.10 (129)	4.00 (99)	2.90 (69)	3.40 (78)
Other	8.61	2.64	3.66	1.51
Total Population	41.1	26.3	17.6	18.7

Source: Harriott 2000b.

[a] The first figure is rate, that is, number of incidents per 100,000 citizens. The second figure, in parentheses, represents the number of incidents.

[b] These are mainly victims of organized crime–type assassinations, community border control, and internal garrison control and community justice.

intergroup conflicts as the main category of conflict driving the murder rate.[5] The trend line for the former is fairly flat (declining towards the end of the period under review), while the gradient of the trend line for group conflict is fairly steep. There was little variation in the rates for domestic murders, as the rates for 1983, 1988, 1993 and 1997 were 1.20, 1.27, 1.17 and 1.24, respectively, per 100,000.[6] The pattern for all murders rooted in interpersonal conflicts and which remained individualized was quite similar but with a significant decline in 1997. On the other hand, there was a steady increase in the rate of murder related to intergroup conflicts, some of which have their origin in interpersonal conflicts. This declined somewhat between 1983 and 1988, but thereafter increased from 6.55 per 100,000 in 1988 to 25.2 per 100,000 in 1997 (see table 5.1). The reason that homicides which were the outcomes of intergroup conflicts were higher in 1983 than in 1988 may be explained in terms of the proximity to 1980, when there was an extraordinarily high level of political violence. After 1980 the prevalence and intensity of overt political conflicts progressively declined, but a significant number of intergroup and intercommunity conflicts, which were not attributed directly to politics by the police but which represented (in new ways) continuity with the earlier political battles, have persisted. Although less overt, politics has remained very much a part of gang and community identity and is often an unnamed undercurrent in many of these conflicts.

This growth in intergroup conflicts helps to explain the dramatic increase in the homicide rate. Intergroup conflicts tend to drive the murder rate more rapidly than individual conflicts, as:

- The scale of the conflict is multiplied as larger numbers of persons are usually involved in intergroup conflicts and more resources are easily mobilized for these conflicts, including guns.
- All members of the groups in conflict suffer liability for the actions of each of their members (this will be explained later). All group members are therefore treated as potential targets in the conflict, thereby considerably widening the pool of targets. Thus, many soft targets become readily available if the individual offender who precipitated the conflict cannot be found.
- The moral dynamics of intergroup conflicts are somewhat different from those of interpersonal conflicts. Moral neutralization is better facilitated when one kills or murders in the name of a group, as "soldiers" for the cause of the group, than when one kills for self-interest. To kill for the group is always regarded as morally superior to killing for self-interest.
- There are fewer social constraints on intergroup killing, as one's social ties are not threatened by the act of killing the "other"/enemy. Indeed, through such conflicts the social ties and communal bonds may be strengthened, identity affirmed and the main combatants treated as heroic figures. Their status and prestige as members of the group may be enhanced as "protectors" of the group.

Ideally, groups may be identified by the following characteristics: (1) they consist of two or more persons who have one or more characteristics in common; (2) they perceive themselves as forming a distinguishable entity; (3) they are aware of the positive interdependence of their goals or interests; (4) they interact with one another; and (5) they pursue their interdependent goals together. Groups which endure over a long period of time tend to develop (6) a set of norms that regulate and guide their interaction; and (7) a set of roles, each of which has specific activities, obligations and rights associated with it (Deutsch 1973, 48–49). Most groups share only the first three characteristics listed above. Deutsch therefore suggests that groups may be classified according to their degree of "groupness", that is, as "quasi groups" if they have only the first three characteristics, "functioning groups" if the first five, and "organized groups" if all seven characteristics.

This description of group thus implies a psychological bond, not just similar objective interests. The psychological bond provides great cohesiveness. Members tend to be easily influenced by one another, especially where there is intense interaction and communication in a context of an externally hostile environment, as is often the case in times of "war" or public condemnation (of mass killings or attacks on the security forces). These conditions typify the garrison communities of Kingston, and the inner core of criminal networks within these communities in many instances share all seven characteristics of organized groups that are listed above.

Group cohesiveness is further accentuated by the conditions of insecurity and uncertainty among the communities of the marginalized poor in the cities, where "survival" is the central issue for many. In these conditions group membership is vital to survival. Thus, as Jamaica becomes more modern and more individualistic, for the urban marginalized poor the group seems to become more important to their lives.

Where it is vital to preserve a high degree of in-group cohesiveness, as in the case of the garrison communities of Kingston (if they are to serve as safe havens for criminals and safe seats for politicians), a pattern of displacing internal conflict onto other groups may develop. A recent episode of intercommunity violence in western Kingston (April to September 2001), that was precipitated by the murder of an alleged drug don, is an example of this.[7] In this case emerging conflicts within a highly cohesive group were projected onto an old political enemy, leading to a number of killings and "war" between communities along the lines of the party-political divide. In the process, a four-year peace that had seen a dramatic reduction in the homicide rate in west Kingston was scuttled. Similarly, antipathy to out-groups may be used to discredit internal opposition, by naming such internal opposition as the agents of the external opposition. The intra-community "war" of 2001 between two gangs in the western Kingston area of Rema was resolved in a similar manner. Some of the persons who were at the centre of the dispute were successfully labelled as quislings of the traditional external enemy and were either killed or expelled, and the community reunited in violent opposition to the neighbouring pro–Jamaica Labour Party (JLP) communities. Regardless of the validity of these theses, it remains clear that countries with a high proportion of homicides being attributable to intergroup conflicts with these kinds of social dynamics are likely to have great difficulty managing this violence and the anxiety associated with the periodic moments of rapid escalation.

The process of escalation may be restricted to within-group mobilizations or may also involve the mobilization of allied groups from other communities who may share the most salient identity elements associated with the particular conflict. On either level these conflicts tend to be fairly protracted, as there are few available arbitrators (mainly the church) who are able to intervene effectively.

One consequence of the increased intergroup violence is the increased frequency of incidents of multiple and mass murder. And associated with this is the seemingly more indiscriminate group targeting of victims, the increased rate of killing of parties who may not be directly involved as combatants. Multiple killings as a proportion of *all* murders increased from 7.4 per cent in 1983 to 8.6 per cent in 1997, and in absolute terms from 31 fatalities to some 89 fatalities and a total 143 persons either killed or injured in the 37 incidents of multiple killings that occurred in that year (see table 5.2.). The incidents of mass murder, although few, became a recurring feature after 1988 and increased to four incidents in 1997 (table 5.2). By mass murder is meant the killing of at least four victims in a single incident.

The phenomenon of multiple murder (as a single event, not serially) is largely based on notions of collective responsibility and punishment for displays of solidarity (with offenders or initiators of conflict) that is linked to the salience or primacy of group identity in the conflict. In

Table 5.2   Incidents of Multiple Murders, 1980–1997

Year	Double	Triple	Mass	Total Victims of MM[b] as % of All	Total # Victims[a]
1997	28 (56)	5 (15)	4 (18[c])	8.6 (89)	143
1993	13 (26)	4 (12)	1 (5)	6.6 (43)	64
1988	14 (28)	0 (0)	1 (4)	7.7 (32)	53
1983	—	—	—	7.4	31
1980	24 (48)	7 (21)	2 (13)	9.2 (82)	...

Source: Harriott 2000b.

[a] With the exception of 1980, these data include all non-fatal victims from the incidents of multiple murder.

[b] MM is multiple murder. In this column the total number of victims of multiple murder is presented as a percentage of all murder victims.

[c] Unlike all the other data presented in this table, the number of victims of mass murder, not the number of incidents, is an estimate. As mass murder is defined as an incident in which at least four persons are murdered, the minimum number of murder victims would be sixteen, and there were no incidents in which more than six persons were killed, thus eighteen seems a reasonable estimate.

conflicts that are defined in intergroup terms, the entire sets of warring collectives are taken to suffer liability for the actions of individual members of the group. For example, an acid-throwing incident between two females from two communities with a history of conflicts between them could easily lead to community membership being treated as the most salient social identity element in the conflict, thereby leading to a rapid mushrooming of the conflict into a "war". In such a case the dyadic (seemingly interpersonal) conflicts are treated as more complicated intergroup representations. On the other hand, if their gender was seen as the primary social identity element and the conflict regarded as a typical conflict between females, the potential for escalation would be somewhat reduced (there would be no difference in the most salient social identity element of the participants in the conflict, thereby defining it in strict interpersonal terms). In the worst cases, that is, where there is great mutual demonization of the warring parties as groups, this idea of collective responsibility tends to lead to violations of common notions of innocence (killing of children, old people, women).[8] This partly explains the fairly high proportion (in 1997, 10.5 per cent of all murder victims) of women who are killed each year.[9] In some instances (where there is "war"), members of the opposing group may be treated as legitimate targets depending on their relational proximity (kin relations, crew members, paramours, participants in the community defence system as soldiers or suppliers of a supporting service) to the target and participation in the initiating trouble, particularly if the direct protagonists are unavailable and have made themselves too hard a target.

Interestingly, these practices seem to contrast with some of the developed cultures of violence where more sophisticated rules govern the process of retaliation. Such rules serve to better regulate the use of social violence and to avoid the killing of innocent persons and the kind of rapid escalation that tends to occur in Jamaica's inner-city communities. For example, in Albania, cited by Wolfgang and Ferracuti in their seminal work *The Subculture of Violence* (1967) as a paradigm case of a subculture of violence, there is the tradition of the *besa*. This tradition specifies what kinds of behaviour warrant punishment by death, who are permitted to pursue a vendetta, how the target(s) for retaliation may be selected and so forth. For example, in avenging a murder it is regarded as most honourable to kill the killer. However, one may kill a male relative or a specified number of relatives of the killer, depending on the egregiousness of the crime, *but one is not permitted to treat the friends of the killer as substitutable targets.* Homes may not be invaded to carry out a vendetta (Anderson 1999, 33).

These rules serve to avoid indiscriminate violence and, as in the case of the ban on home invasions, help to avoid putting socially disapproved targets such as females at risk. Importantly, there is a rule for ending the cycle of retaliation: If the target of the retaliation openly kills the person or persons pursuing the vendetta at a moment when they are actively hunting him, then he is free from further retaliatory action. The vendetta is at an end; his enemies are not permitted to "come for him" a second time (Anderson 1999, 33). These rules are part of a code of honour. One is as dishonoured for not avenging the death of a relative as one would be for breaking the rules associated with seeking vengeance. In these mature cultures of violence, although conflicts are settled outside of the framework of the criminal justice system, because self-help is so rule-bound, interpersonal conflicts do not disrupt the daily lives of whole communities nor threaten a generalized disorder. Indeed, some of these countries may exhibit lower homicide rates than others which have not been classified as cultures of violence.

In the Jamaican context, related to this notion of group liability for the actions of individual members is the idea of "being at war". In this condition all members of the group (usually the community) are encouraged to take precautionary measures to protect themselves from retaliatory attacks. The entire community has to be protected and the "dons" and leading combatants take charge of community life, usually enjoying an elevated status during this period of "war". Young males are able to assert themselves, display their courage and commitment, and move up in the "ranking" or status hierarchy of the group. One outcome of this process is that this kind of war leadership further entrenches itself in community life, which in turn serves to harden the perception of outsiders who associate the identity and reputation of the community with conflict – thereby increasing the potential for future "wars".

The Escalation Dynamic

As noted earlier, social identity is taken to mean how a group is perceived by others. There are cultural attributes and roles associated with these identity elements to which new members are socialized. As humans we are born as members of groups – as male, female, black, white, and in the case of some parts of Jamaica, as will be argued, as members of the People's National Party (PNP) and the Jamaica Labour Party (JLP), "Jungleists" and "Tivolites" (that is, in the case of the latter categories, with a designated near-communal identity).[10] Identity is usually taken to mean a stable sameness. Many inner-city communities exhibit a stable sameness in their political affiliation, in some instances regularly returning more than 80 per cent of their recorded votes for the same political party for a period of more than thirty years. For example, in the case of Tivoli Gardens in western Kingston, since 1969 this community has consistently returned more than 81 per cent of the legally valid ballots for the JLP, with the proportion for the dominant party progressively increasing. The 81 per cent was recorded in 1969 and represents the smallest proportion of the vote recorded for the dominant party in local elections during the period 1969 to 1998. Since 1981 typically more than 90 per cent of votes are cast for the monopoly party.[11]

"Labouriteness" or a pro-JLP affiliation is thus regarded as the most salient social identity element of the members of this community. This process has been replicated in a number of other urban communities, many of which are pro-PNP. But, as noted earlier, political affiliation may in some instances develop into a kind of communal identity. Where this occurs the members of these communities are derisively labelled political "tribalists". This problem is most acutely expressed in the phenomenon of the garrison community. As noted earlier, these communities are characterized by political and social homogeneity. Many of the benefits enjoyed by the members of these communities are derived *as group members,* not as individuals (Figueroa 1994, 14–15). This is perhaps the most important characteristic that marks these groups as being near "tribal" or gives them an approximate communal identity. These benefits may include preferential access to jobs, free government housing, free access to utilities and even cable television. Service providers are prevented from withdrawing these services by a combination of political leverage and the threat of group-organized violence.

These garrison communities tend to acquire conflict identities. Historically they have provided the shock troops for the parties during election campaigns – often engaging in forced mobilizations of the people living within the garrisons and their satellite communities, the intimidation of the opposition and illegal voting. These are all conflict-generating activities associated with electoral politics.

Electoral contests are seasonal, but the conflicts generated by the garrison are, as a rule, perennial. Two additional characteristics account for this. Perhaps the garrison's most conflict-generating characteristic is that it is fundamentally expansionist and galactic. It seeks to directly expand itself territorially as well as to create and control a number of satellite communities that are similarly organized as garrisons. It is also very protective of its members, including those who turn to ordinary criminality. This protectiveness has evolved as an aspect of the political methodology of patron-clientelism, which has deep roots in the nature of social relationships in the wider society. The essence of the patron-client relationship, as it is expressed in the political process, is the exchange of material aid and protection for votes. But where this exchange and the type of social relationships associated with it has become a method of administering the daily life and various activities of these communities, as has become the case with the garrisons, in the interregnum between elections it is an exchange of these goods for intangibles, especially loyalty and respect, that obtains.

This type of relationship and exchange may develop especially where the don (who is usually involved in organized crime) has become the patron of the community and its intermediary link to the political parties and state institutions. Such dons are obliged to protect their clients, and their reputations rest on how effectively they are able to do this. Collectively organized and supported retaliation is therefore very likely in cases involving conflicts between client-members of such communities and others that are organized on a similar patron-client principle. In some instances the protective relationship between the don and individual members of the community may have a material foundation. For example, criminals who operate individually may seek the protection of a don and may cement this relationship by paying regular tribute to the don – usually in the form of a percentage of the take from robberies or whatever the pursuit is. When the activities of such persons generate trouble, as may occur when they kill another protected or respected and valued person in a robbery, this may at times lead to very serious and protracted intergroup conflicts. These are the primary sources of the external conflicts that garrisons and garrison-like communities tend to generate.

Community identity and the intensity of the internal social bonds are shaped by relations of hostility with other communities. For example, to be a "Jungleist" or a "Garden man" is to have a conflict identity, as these communities are seen (for the reasons outlined above) as being in constant conflict with, or at least antagonistic to, other neighbouring communities. And as these communities and groups within them tend to be very protective of their members, conflicts involving individuals are likely to quickly involve the group.

Garrison communities are not typical. They are somewhat extreme cases in their mode of social organization and political administration. But many non-garrison, inner-city communities are similarly treated as homogeneous groups standing in opposition to other communities.

Some therefore suffer problems somewhat similar to the garrisons, with in-groups such as crews and conflict gangs engaging groupings from other communities. Despite their unrepresentativeness, the discussion of the problem of violence has centred on the social dynamics of these communities, as more than 60 per cent of all homicides occur in the inner-city areas which account for a minuscule proportion (less than 6 per cent) of the surface area of Jamaica. For example, in 1997, 73 per cent of all murders and 77 per cent of all shootings occurred in the Kingston Metropolitan Area.[12]

This reality of a proliferation of conflict groups in the inner-city communities pulls on the wider tradition of sharp political divisions and social segmentation that tends to lead to particularly hostile cross-group attributions, such as those associated with the class proxies of "uptown" and "downtown", "bigman" and "small man/person". Jamaica is highly segmented socially and has historically been ordered on the principle of sharp social hierarchies. Following this, social identity is similarly constructed on the principle of hierarchy, including, in this case, moral hierarchy. The following example should illustrate this point. In the wake of minor tensions between members of two neighbouring urban communities (which occurred during the fieldwork for this chapter), the members of one community derogatorily depicted the other as:

- Uninterested in education and legitimate opportunities to improve their life chances, that is, *by nature* averse to some of the more important norms of the society. For many Jamaicans the extent of one's commitment to education (and particularly the education of children) may be taken as a measure of one's commitment to conventional ways of making a living. The undervaluing of education is thus taken as a mark of moral degeneracy.
- Being envious of the achievement of others even though they did not make use of similar opportunities that may have been open to them, and even though they reject the kind of collective action and community self-help that is considered necessary to improve the quality of life in their community.

- Attaching less importance to cleanliness at both the public-community and private-personal levels. They are regarded as less concerned with the dirty state of their streets and other public places, and their homes are considered unkempt.
- Being irrationally violent and given to criminality.

These attributions are fallaciously seen as internal to the make-up of members of this community. This purported essence, as a cultural trait, is used to mark the differences between the two groups, and in times of conflict this essence is accentuated. The perceived differences are exaggerated so that the other becomes, in this case, deviant and essentially morally degenerate. Social psychologists refer to this as category accentuation (see Brewer and Miller 1996, 6–7).

Of course these attributes were seen to contrast sharply with the self-image of those who presented this image of another community with which they were in conflict. This is particularly interesting as, in this case, the communities were not divided by political affiliation. This idea of moral difference, of moral hierarchies (and even cultural hierarchies) in which the opposing group always falls lower in the ranking, provides ready justification for subjecting them to violent attacks as a group. This problem is further compounded in situations where the social and political distance between such groups is great but the physical distance between them is small, as is the case in Kingston.

As with communal violence, the escalation dynamic in these inner-city communities may be described in terms of the dual processes of focalization and transvaluation (Tambiah 1990). Focalization involves ripping incidents out of their contexts and aggregating them. New conflicts are always interpreted as incidents in a long and prior history of intergroup conflicts. By this process, new incidents tend to generate greater emotional intensity than would have been the case were they treated on their own merit and properly contextualized. For example, in times of peace between some of these communities, romantic relations may develop between members of formerly warring communities; if conditions change and tensions develop, a case of domestic violence between two such persons could be ripped out of context and interpreted as an expression of old intergroup hostilities.

Transvaluation involves assimilating events to a larger collective cause or interest. Thus, where personal pride and face may be perceived to be at stake, this may be redefined in terms of the face of the community or larger moral issues, perhaps related to party political conflicts. Individual interests are masked and the conflicts similarly redefined in terms of the more general interests of the community or party. Both processes (that is, focalization and transvaluation) serve to polarize the groups in conflict, intensify the emotive content of the reactions to conflict, and pull increasing numbers of persons and resources into these battles. They serve to extend the degree of social and moral support for "war" and to mobilize war resources – including guns – thereby multiplying the destructive power of the parties and increasing the accessibility of these weapons to persons who may later use them for ordinary criminal activity. This kind of interpretation of conflicts and mobilization also serves to entrench existing power relations (patron-clientelism) and increases the leveraging power of the dons.

Two Cases

The following two cases serve to illustrate the kind of escalation dynamic discussed above. They are taken from different periods. The first occurred between 1976 and 1980, when the processes associated with the escalation dynamic as described above were most pronounced, and the second case is current. Both are taken from the experiences of two inner-city communities in the capital city of Kingston and are based on their memories and perspectives.

Case 1

The first incident that triggered the pattern of events which constitute this case took place in 1976. This was a period characterized by increasingly sharp and intense political conflict between the two major political parties (the PNP and the JLP) and developing ideological and political polarization among the population – especially in the inner-city communities of Kingston.

The precipitating incident began with an attack on "Madge", who was intimately involved with a man whom we shall call "Reds" who had fathered her child. Madge lived in "Seaside", a solidly pro-JLP community, and Reds in "Beirut", a solidly pro-PNP community with similar politically homogenizing and controlling tendencies. Although at the time there had been fairly extensive and intensive social linkages between members of the two communities, including familial ties, and the physical distance between the communities is very small as they are separated by a narrow street, there was nevertheless a considerable and rapidly developing political distance between them.

Madge was stoned and as a result sustained some injuries to her body. The motivation for this attack was simply that she had maintained an intimate relationship with a member of the Beirut community; she was "sleeping with the enemy". Retaliation was swift and lethal. The following night Reds simply returned to Seaside and shot Madge's attacker and one of his friends who happened to have been in his company at the time. The main target of the attack survived, but the secondary target was mortally wounded.

Following this incident the entire Seaside community was mobilized and the conflict was now clearly defined in political terms as a "war" between Seaside and Beirut, PNP and JLP. Reds had interpreted the initial attack as being politically motivated, as an attack on his otherness and therefore unsuitability for Madge. Similarly, his retaliatory action, perhaps because of its excessiveness, was interpreted as a political attack on the Seaside community. The past conflicts and existing social identities of the parties to the conflict were factored into the interpretations and actions of both sides.

The night after the retaliatory shooting by Reds, a group from Seaside (no longer individual attackers) invaded a home in Beirut (a vulnerable place close to the border) and killed a young man. On the next day, shortly before noon, large groups from both communities massed on opposite sides of the street that formed the socially recognized border between the two communities. At some point in the verbal exchanges between the members of the two groups, one person came forward and, after making himself visible to all, openly identified himself as the killer of the previous night. Immediately thereafter he was said to have declared to the residents of Beirut, "A me kill ['John Brown'] last night. A same way mi a go kill the whole a onnu."[13] The following night this person, as was his regular practice, visited a nearby cinema. He was shot and killed while waiting in line at the box office. Someone from Beirut approached him from an unexpected direction and shot him to death in front of scores of witnesses.

After this incident an open "war" developed between the communities, with frequent attacks and counter-attacks being staged by both sides. These included two daylight killings. The fear of having to face a police investigation and possible punishment by the state had completely vanished, as both communities closed ranks behind their fighters and established considerable distance from the originating interpersonal conflict which set in train the subsequent events that escalated into the state of "war".

In this state of "war", few if any rules were operative. While the armed combatants and young males were the main targets of the attacks, they were not exclusively targeted. Women were not spared if they happened to be in the place where the attack occurred. Each side became more demonized in the eyes of the other; both celebrated the progressively less discriminating and more cruel acts of their fighters.

This process continued for the next four years and culminated in a widely reported "massacre" that became a major national political issue. In 1980, approximately four years after the initial event that precipitated the "war", a group of men from Beirut invaded Seaside and attacked a dance attended by hundreds of people, shooting and killing four persons. The idea behind this attack was to deliver a strategic blow to Seaside by attacking its nerve centre. The particular location was chosen because it was regarded as the hub of all the armed activity being conducted by Seaside. Reds allegedly provided the leadership of the attacking group, and most of the men who followed him (most of whom are now dead) were survivors of earlier retaliatory attacks during the vendetta and/or had been involved in it from the earliest incidents.

In total, it is estimated that over the four-year period some fourteen persons were killed in incidents directly related to the vendetta. This "war" between the two communities was eventually viewed as part of a larger national political conflict and was settled as such. Following the defeat of the PNP government, many of the leading figures in the vendetta – those from the Beirut side who had become involved in other violent and predatory criminal activities – were either killed, sent to prison or forced to flee the country.

Case 2

This case aroused interest and curiosity following the killing of two young men, whom we shall call Kemar Richards and Shamar Brown. They both lived and were killed in the Kingston community of Michael Town. Both killings occurred in rapid succession (in the year 2000) and both were carried out by members of the state security forces. At first appearance they seemed to have been cases of excessive violence by the security forces, while in the pursuit of their normal activities. The reality was, however, much more complicated. Investigations by members of the community led to the following beliefs and construction of the events (regardless of the accuracy of their account, this became a part of the reality of the conflict, as people acted on these beliefs):

Two years earlier, a gentleman who had been a "dads" or beneficent patron (not a don) of the people in his neighbourhood in Michael Town was robbed and killed. He was a small business man who was very generous with his money, and who could be relied on to help the poorer members of the community with school fees for their children and similar matters. Just before his death he had relocated his business and home to another area. This is significant, because his killer may have been mistaken about his community affiliation and would not have expected retaliation for his death based on his presumed community ties. Investigations by the residents of Michael Town led them to the conclusion that the killer was from the community of Haven Town, which borders on Michael Town. On realizing the real place of origin of his victim, the killer took evasive action and for two years successfully eluded any effort at retaliation against him. He was eventually killed, allegedly by one of the sons of the gentleman whom he had killed. However, in the process, another party who was not involved in the original incident but who happened to be in the company of the robber-killer when the retaliatory killing occurred was also killed. Two lives, including that of someone who was not involved in the original killing, were thus taken in response to the initial killing.

The relatives of the innocent victim of the retaliatory action were incensed by his death; it was seen as unwarranted and excessive. His mother is believed to have stated that she wanted the lives of six members of the Michael Town community as payment for the blood debt.[14] As the killings removed the only male from the family of the victimized, it was left to the females to organize the reprisals. The mother who had set the terms of the vendetta assumed the role of its organizer.

The first effort at a reprisal was attempted by a group of young men from Haven Town. Their plan involved a surprise attack on Michael Town via one of its neighbouring communities. They therefore attempted to seek the approval of this community for the avenging party to have safe passage *en route* to the invasion of Michael Town. The negotiations were not successful, as the group from Haven Town was not able to convince the other community that such a reprisal was just. It was noted that after the first killing as a result of the robbery, they (Haven Town) had refused to surrender the killer to Michael Town or to kill him themselves – an act that would have averted the killing of any innocent persons and the subsequent vendetta and intercommunity "war". Moreover, there would have been negative consequences for the neighbouring community, as granting any such permit to use their community as a staging area for an attack would have been treated as an act of "war" and a statement of alliance with Haven Town. It would have dramatically escalated the conflict.

This attempt having failed, the organizer of the vendetta then turned to an intriguing solution. She enlisted the help of a police officer – who is believed to be her lover – *as a party to the vendetta*. It is believed that he organized the party of police officers who then turned up in Michael Town, ostensibly on police duties, but with the clear design to opportunistically kill any young male in the area, as part of the vendetta. This proved to be not too difficult an assignment, as in anticipation of an attack by Haven Town the young men of Michael Town had organized their defences – as had been done so many times in the past during times of "war". Some of the young men of the community were armed and on guard in anticipation of an attack, and therefore exposed to countermeasures or routine patrols by the police. At the time of his death Kemar Richards had an illegal firearm in his possession, and this is usually taken (by some police officers) as sufficient justification for putting someone to death. However, there were no such confounding issues in the shooting of Shamar Brown. Moreover, even after this incident, citizens in the area claim that they have been told by this police officer that under the terms of the vendetta, they are also targeted for death.

By claiming such a large blood debt, the mother of victim number three (the innocent victim of the first reprisal) surely opened herself to retaliation from any threatened member of Michael Town. But Michael Town was thrown into confusion by the threat of further retribution, as the female organizer of the vendetta in Haven Town was believed to have powers of *obya* and the capability to kill her enemies via the use of her presumed supernatural powers.[15] It was believed that as a protective measure and an indisputable display of her powers, she had organized the death by *obya* of a witness to the execution of Shamar Brown. At the time of writing the belief that there was supernatural intervention in the vendetta had paralysed Michael Town and dissipated their forces, many of whom had lost any further interest in the fight.

Many aspects of this case are interesting, such as the long memories and lasting desire for revenge that is not simply tied to male notions of honour. But most interesting is the innovative solution to the absence of an avenging male. As this case suggests, even members of both arms of the security forces (the army and police) are from time to time drawn into these conflicts, ostensibly as members of the security forces, but in reality as players drawn in on the terms of the parties to the conflicts – as extensions of one or the other party. To the extent that this kind of conduct is seen as prevalent and unlikely to attract any negative sanctions from the leadership of the force, its implications for the legitimacy of the police force are most profound.[16]

This case remains open, and will become etched in the collective memories of both communities. Despite the belief that there was supernatural intervention in the vendetta, self-preservation may lead to new counter-reprisals, both against the members of the security forces who are seen as simply pursuing a personal vendetta and against the instructing agent in Haven Town. The potential for further escalation to a "war" between the two communities and for episodic shooting incidents between fearful members of the Michael Town community on one hand and the police on the other is considerable.

Conclusion

In the Jamaican inner-city context, self-help as a retaliatory response to conflicts generally leads to a sharp upward spiral of retaliations that in some cases may continue for many years. The salience of group identities and the history of intergroup conflicts in the inner-city communities tend to generate a self-perpetuating logic whereby intergroup conflicts lead to the need for group protection, thus spawning a proliferation of conflict groups and their increased involvement in interpersonal conflicts. These practices are already entrenched in the inner city, and there is the real danger of a spread of these practices beyond the Kingston/ St Catherine conurban area.

Self-help tends to develop and is sustained as a response to the ineffectiveness and unavailability of law enforcement and where there is considerable popular antagonism to it. This is clearly the case in urban Jamaica – and this should not be surprising given the historic relationship between the people and the state, the use of law enforcement in repressive and abusive ways, and the failure of successive postcolonial administrations to restructure these power relationships.

Notes

1. Computed from data provided by the statistics unit of the Jamaica Constabulary Force.
2. International crime statistics: Interpol.
3. Data provided by the statistics unit of the Jamaica Constabulary Force.
4. Computed from data provided by the statistics unit of the Jamaica Constabulary Force.
5. The period 1983 to the present was chosen because 1983 approximates the return to "normal" levels of social violence (that is, rates more consistent with the trend line) after the extraordinary years of 1980–81, which were characterized by high levels of political violence.
6. By a domestic murder is meant the killing of a member of the basic family or household unit. All the members need not reside in the same house, but are related by blood and did comprise a household either at some time in the past or at the time of the killing.
7. See the *Daily Gleaner,* 19 April 2001, for a news account of the events.
8. Impressionistic evidence suggests that women are also more involved in gangs and various forms of group-organized illegal activity.
9. Computed from data provided by the statistics unit of the Jamaica Constabulary Force.
10. These refer to activist citizens who reside in Tivoli Gardens and Arnett Gardens, otherwise known as "Concrete Jungle". These two communities are regarded as the most notorious galactic garrisons in Kingston.
11. These estimates are based on data provided by the reports of the Director of Elections – *KSAC and Parish Councils' General Election* – for the respective years.
12. This is based on data provided by the statistics unit of the Jamaica Constabulary Force. These data (for 1997) were then mapped using geocidal techniques. The estimate of the size of Kingston inner-city communities is an approximation based on maps drawn by the Survey Department of the Government of Jamaica.
13. This is Jamaican Creole; the translation is roughly as follows: "It was I who killed 'John Brown'. I intend to kill all of you in a similar manner."
14. I take this as a statement of her view of the relative moral worth of the citizens of Michael Town.
15. *Obya* is a form of magical belief and practice which has its roots in aspects of the African cultural traditions that were transported to Jamaica. For an interesting discussion of this, see Alleyne 1988.
16. For a discussion of this problem, see Harriott 2000c.

References

Alleyne, M. 1988. *Africa: Roots of Jamaican Culture*. Chicago: Research Associates School Times Publications.

Anderson, S. 1999. "The Curse of Blood and Vengeance". *New York Times Magazine,* 26 December.

Brewer, M., and N. Miller. 1996. *Intergroup Relations*. Albany: Brooks/Cole Publishing Co.

Chevannes, B. 1992. "The Formation of Garrison Communities". Paper presented at symposium in honour of Carl Stone, University of the West Indies, Kingston, Jamaica, 16–17 November.

de Albuquerque, K. 1984. "A Comparative Analysis of Violent Crime in the Caribbean". *Social and Economic Studies* 33, no. 3.

Deutsch, M. 1973. *The Resolution of Conflict: Constructive and Destructive Processes*. New Haven, Conn.: Yale University Press.

Eyre, A. 1984. "The Effect of Political Violence on the Population and Urban Environment of Kingston, Jamaica". *Geographical Review* 74, no. 1.

Figueroa, M. 1994. "Garrison Communities in Jamaica, 1962–1993: Their Growth and Impact on Political Culture". Paper presented at symposium, "Democracy and Democratization in Jamaica: Fifty Years of Adult Suffrage", Faculty of Social Sciences, University of the West Indies, Kingston, Jamaica, 6–7 December.

Gopaul, R., and M. Cain. 1996. "Violence between Spouses in Trinidad and Tobago: A Research Note". *Caribbean Quarterly* 42, nos. 2–3.

Hall, H. 1996. "Overview of Lethal Violence". In *Lethal Violence 2000: A Sourcebook on Fatal Domestic, Acquaintance and Stranger Aggression,* edited by H. Hall. Kamuela, Hawaii: Pacific Institute for the Study of Conflict and Aggression.

Haniff, N. 1995. "Violence against Women in the Caribbean: The Case of Jamaica". *Daily Gleaner,* 29 October.

Harriott, A. 2000a. "Controlling the Jamaican Crime Problem: Peace Building and Community Action". Paper prepared for the Caribbean Group of Cooperation in Economic Development, Washington, D.C., 12–15 June.

———. 2000b. "Making Dopies: A Study of Criminal Homicides in Jamaica". Paper presented at the Annual Meeting of the Academy of Criminal Justice Sciences, New Orleans, 21–26 March.

———. 2000c. *Policing and Crime Control in Jamaica: Problems of Reforming Ex-Colonial Constabularies*. Kingston, Jamaica: University of the West Indies Press.

Headley, B. 1994. *The Jamaican Crime Scene: A Perspective.* Mandeville, Jamaica: Eureka Press.

Lacey, T. 1977. *Violence and Politics in Jamaica, 1960–70.* Manchester: Manchester University Press.

Levy, H. 1996. *They Cry "Respect": Urban Violence and Poverty in Jamaica.* Kingston, Jamaica: Centre for Population, Community and Social Change, University of the West Indies.

Moser, C., and J. Holland. 1995. "Urban Poverty and Violence in Jamaica". Paper presented at World Bank–sponsored community stakeholders meeting, Kingston, Jamaica, 21 November.

Parsad, B. 1988. "Domestic Violence: A Study of Wife-Abuse among East Indians of Guyana". Paper presented at Caribbean Studies Association Conference, Guadeloupe, 25–27 May.

Sives, A. 1998. "Violence and Politics in Jamaica: An Analysis of Urban Violence in Kingston, 1944–1996". PhD diss., University of Bradford.

Stone, C. 1987. "Crime and Violence: Socio-political Implications". In *Crime and Violence: Causes and Solutions,* edited by P. Phillips and J. Wedderburn. Kingston, Jamaica: Department of Government, University of the West Indies.

Tambiah, S. 1990. "Presidential Address: Reflections on Communal Violence in South Asia". *Journal of Asian Studies* 49, no. 4.

Wilbanks, W. 1978. "Homicide in Jamaica". Paper presented at the Annual Meeting of the American Society of Criminology.

Wolfgang, M., and F. Ferracuti. 1967. *The Subculture of Violence: Towards an Integrated Theory in Criminology.* London: Tavistock Publications.

6

From the Footnotes and into the Text
Victimization of Jamaican Women

Marlyn J. Jones

Feminist criminologists bemoan the invisibility of girls and women in criminological literature. They critique *malestream* criminology, noting that it is produced by men, on men and for men, thereby ignoring women. In addition they argue that not only is the emphasis male, but because criminological theories are concerned with the etiology of crime and factors relating to offending, the focus is primarily male juvenile offending. They note, therefore, that "research of victimization rates and fear of crime often fails to account for the ways that victimization and fear of victimization differ between the sexes" (Belknap 2000, 7). Paradoxically, contemporary feminist criminological analyses have succumbed to their critique. Like their male counterparts who have ignored gender, Western feminists have ignored women in regions other than North America and Europe.

The politicization and subsequent criminalization of violence in previously endorsed relationships, such as the family, have generated a plethora of literature and legislation. Consequently, since the 1980s much has been written on topics such as violence against women, children and the elderly. However, despite a plethora of recent feminist criminological literature, a perusal reveals that the focus is disproportionately on Britain and North America. The result is that present criminological literature contains very little information on women's experiences in regions such as the Caribbean. The primary sources of information within the region are the United Nations, the World Health Organization and non-governmental organizations. Consequently, geography and ethnocentrism conflate to marginalize and double-ghettoize women of colour in developing regions of the world. bell hooks (1981), discussing the invisibility of women of colour in Western feminist analyses, notes that references to women generally mean white women and references to black people generally mean black men.

By failing to research the particularities of women in terms of factors such as geographical differences, feminist literature becomes prone to essentialism. While acknowledging that there are similarities in women's life conditions, this paper highlights the need to speak to women in diverse settings in order that the *particularities* of their life conditions are revealed. By so doing it addresses, in part, a gap in the literature. To examine a specific geographical context, this paper, using official statistics from the Jamaica Constabulary Force, discusses personal victimization of Jamaican women. It should be noted, however, that the statistics were collected for a doctoral dissertation in criminology; the dissertation explored the consequences of US drug policy on Caribbean drug transit countries rather than violence against women. Therefore, the paper is intended as a starting point to highlight the importance of undertaking criminological examination of women's experiences in different social and geographical spaces.

There are several reasons for choosing Jamaica. Most important, however, Morrow (1992) suggests that for English-speaking Afro-Caribbean groups the level of violence against women is lower than that typically found in other regions with similar economic characteristics. However, concerns have been raised about the vulnerability of women in Jamaica. Haniff (1998), using 1994 statistical data on assault on women in Jamaica, concluded that for women the forces that combine to keep them victimized are very powerful. She notes that female victims of domestic violence do not have the sympathy of the police, the community, or even their relatives. Instead, there is a high level of second victimization and victim blaming. Consequently, in Jamaica, for a female victim of violence from a male partner, her voice is silenced by the community and the legal system (Haniff 1998). Jamaica's criminal justice statistics indicate an increase in the victimization of women and children, with high rates of personal victimization reflected in official reports of murder, rape and carnal abuse. This paper is, therefore, a cursory look at this phenomenon.

Violence against Women and Children

Within the last two decades there has been an increase in the representation of women as victims, offenders and employees in the criminal justice system. For example, within the United States the rate of increase in women's offending exceeds that of males, with drug, property and violent crimes representing the bulk of offences for which women have been incarcerated (Greenfeld and Snell 1999). Similarly, the number of females employed at all levels of the criminal justice system has increased. Nonetheless, the rate of female victimization can be considered epidemic. The World Health Organization reports that in every country where reliable, large-scale studies have been conducted, results indicate that between 16 and 52 per cent of women have been assaulted by an intimate partner (WHO 2002). The US National Violence against Women Survey (Tjaden and Thoennes 1998) found that one in five American women has, at some point, been the victim of rape or attempted rape. The Federal Bureau of Investigation (FBI) crime clock for 1998 also indicates that within the United States one violent crime is committed every twenty-one seconds, with one forcible rape every six minutes.

The United Nations Population Fund (2000) reports that "around the world, at least one in every three women has been beaten, coerced into sex, or abused in some other way – most often by someone she knows, including by her husband or another male family member; one woman in four has been abused during pregnancy".[1]

Victimization, as defined in the *Little Oxford Dictionary*, means to "single out (a person) for punishment or unfair treatment". Within contemporary society, women are systemically, personally and institutionally victimized; thus, victimization as used herein refers to both formal and substantive inequalities within society to which women have been subjected, and the consequences flowing therefrom. According to the *Dictionary of Modern Thought*, systemic victimization may be understood to flow, wittingly or unwittingly, from "physical and social systems that enable complex and dynamic situations to be understood in broad outline". Within this context, then, women are systemically victimized through the institutional framework, or what Dorothy Smith (1987, 1990) calls "relations of rulings". Said victimization includes governmental policies and practices that disproportionately affect women as recipients and employees. Examples include structural adjustment programmes that reduce social service provisions, governmental inability or refusal to provide infrastructure and services, or their choice of which services to provide (Danner 2000).

Women are also more likely to be employed in sectors where wages are low and benefits non-existent. One consequence of systemic victimization is that, worldwide, women still earn less than their male counterparts. Recent reports based on US census data (2003) indicate that women's earnings, especially for women with degrees, are at record highs. Yet the wage gap remains, with women earning 76 cents for every dollar a man earns, an increase of 2 cents over the 74 cents earned in 1996.

Within many other countries, as with the United States, governmental resources are disproportionately allocated to law enforcement. This practice, known as the expansion of the prison industrial complex, results in the retrenchment of social services. Increased law enforcement activities exacerbate correctional overcrowding, and in turn strain institutional programmes and resources (Danner 2000; Pitch 1985). Paradoxically, the expansion of law enforcement increases the need for correctional facilities, leading Danner (2000) to note that incarceration of parents, both males and females, also leaves children behind whose economic care becomes the responsibility of other women. A Human Rights Watch report (2002) indicates that unsupervised children are at risk of becoming delinquent, thus creating a cyclical relationship. Nonetheless, retrenchment of social services has its greatest impact on women, who find themselves susceptible to physical and social harm simply because of their subordinate economic position.

Since women are the primary users and employees of social services, they are disproportionately affected by retrenchment of social programmes arising from reallocation of scarce resources. Commenting on the reallocation of resources into areas such as law enforcement and corrections, Danner (2000) asserts that "three strikes and it's women who are out". Thus, institutional and systemic victimizations include practices that systematically exclude or curtail women's full participation in the public sphere. Personal victimization, however, incorporates women's vulnerability and susceptibility to physical and social harm based on gender. Collectively, these forms of victimization can be understood as "relations of rulings" (Smith 1987).

The most dominant forms of personal victimization suffered by girls and women are (1) abuse within marriage and other intimate relationships and (2) coerced sex of adults, adolescents and children (United Nations Development Fund *c.*2000). Women are more likely to be victimized by a family member, whereas men are more often victimized by strangers or casual acquaintances. Thus, the nature and pattern of violence against women are qualitatively different from violence against men, with the major difference being that women are often financially and emotionally dependent upon their abuser. Some of the factors that perpetuate and sustain male dominance and abuse and increase women's risk of victimization in familial and other societal settings include low levels of female resources, social isolation, and patriarchal and violence-accepting cultural practices. In 1993 the United Nations adopted the Declaration on the Elimination of Violence against Women, resolution 48/102 (444). By so doing, the United Nations offered an official definition of "violence against women", which is defined in article 1 of the declaration as "any act of gender-based violence that results in, or is likely to result in, physical, sexual or psychological harm or suffering to women, including threats of such acts, coercion or arbitrary deprivations of liberty, whether occurring in public or private life".

As noted in article 2 of the Declaration, besides physical, psychological and sexual violence in family and community, other activities include spousal battering, sexual abuse of female children, dowry-related violence, rape (including marital rape), and other traditional practices, such as female genital mutilation, that are harmful to women. Non-spousal violence such as stalking, sexual harassment at work, trafficking in women and children, forced prostitution, and state-sanctioned or -perpetrated violence such as "rape casualties of war" also accounts for much of women's victimization.

It is now estimated that one in three women are beaten, coerced into sex or otherwise abused in their lifetime (Population Information Program 2003). Noting that violence against women is a major form of human rights violation that often continues to be perpetuated and sustained within many social and cultural contexts, many world organizations have started to speak out. Other notable organizations/events include the 1994 International Conference on Population and Development, the 1995 Fourth World Conference on Women in Beijing, China, and the Organization of American States Inter-American Convention to Punish, Prevent and Eradicate Violence against Women (1994). The World Health Organization resolution (WHA49.25) has also declared violence a public health problem. Many organizations now echo the UN slogan from the 1990s: "Women's rights are human rights" (Population Information Program 1999). So while it is important to eliminate personal victimization of women and girl children, it is equally important that systemic and institutional forms of victimization are also addressed. Simple ways of making inroads include governments becoming signatories to international declarations, resolutions and treaties that aim to ameliorate women's subordinate position within social, familial and cultural settings.

Country reports were produced on violence against women as part of the campaign to commemorate the fiftieth anniversary of the Universal Declaration of Human Rights. Intergovernmental organizations launched campaigns in every country in Latin America and the Caribbean to demand an end to violence against women and children. Integral to these initiatives was the acknowledgement that violence against women and girls is the most prevalent and universal violation of human rights. Based on information obtained from the Jamaica Constabulary Force, the emergency unit of the Kingston Public Hospital and non-governmental organizations, Jamaica's country report concluded that domestic violence is on the increase.

Within the Caribbean violence against women has started to garner much attention. De Albuquerque and McElroy (1999) examined violent and property crime trends for nine Caribbean countries, comparing 1969–73 murder, robbery and rape data with 1989–93 data. They reported that rape rates show significant increases, reflecting a uniform rise in violence against women.

Josephs, Weston-Henriques and Ekeh (1998), evaluating domestic violence legislation in English-speaking Caribbean nations, concluded that the existing legislation is inadequate. Specifically, definitions of domestic violence are too narrow, and punitive measures are insufficient to deter domestic violence. Similarly Bissessear (2000), evaluating the implementation of domestic violence legislation in Trinidad, makes two poignant observations. Her analysis suggests that the Trinidadian domestic violence policy was adopted nearly wholesale from the developed countries. Because it was not well thought out as far as the implementation of the policy was concerned, the Trinidadian legislation did not take sufficient account of the domestic situation. Bissessear suggests that the legislation did not adequately address factors that gave rise to crimes of violence, the need to provide economic security for the victims, or the need for the state to provide shelters for the victims. Consequently, the state was ill-prepared to provide the necessary services outlined in the act.

Feminist writers such as Brownmiller (1976) and Smart (1989) note a link between systematic violence against women and women's inequality. Explications of women's rationalizations for remaining in abusive relationships also highlight differences, such as women's economic position, that often contribute to women remaining in these situations (Belknap 2000, 288–89). Women's position of poverty makes them vulnerable to institutional, systemic and personal victimization. However, Grana (2002, 136), citing Shefield (1987), notes that while there is an extensive list of behaviours on the continuum of violence against women, the ultimate expression of women's victimization is femicide. The article now discusses victimization of Jamaican women, as reflected in the official statistics for murder and rape.

Murder

The Jamaican statistics only recently commenced making distinctions among murder victims by gender. However, as summarized in table 6.1, murder, attempted rape, rape and carnal abuse of females have increased during the last decade. Jamaica's violent crimes peaked in 1980, followed a downward trend during the 1980s, and again resurged in the 1990s. The 1990s crime rate peaked in 1997 with 1,038 homicides, a rate of 41 per 100,000 population. This inched upwards in 2001, with over 1,138 homicides. Harriott (1996) notes that there is a direct relationship between the rates of murder and other violent

Table 6.1   Frequency of Female Victimization in Jamaica, 1990–2001

Year	Murders	Attempted Rape	Rape/Carnal Abuse[a]	
1990	n/a	n/a	1,006	
1991	n/a	n/a	1,091	
1992	n/a	n/a	1,108	
1993	n/a	n/a	1,297	
1994	n/a	n/a	1,070	
1995	75	n/a	833	772
1996	90	45	935	872
1997	109	71	875	745
1998	103	70	880	540
1999[b]	81	54	690	690
2000	99		870	434
2001[c]	33		408	152

Source: Compiled from statistics obtained from the Jamaica Constabulary Force, Kingston, Jamaica.

[a] Prior to 1995, the categories of rape and carnal abuse were collapsed.

[b] The 1999 data is based on information available to 12 December 1999.

[c] The 2001 data is for the period ended 3 June 2001.

crimes; consequently, the upward trend in homicides of women increased simultaneously with increases in major crimes. Table 6.1 gives the rate of female victimization between 1990 and 2001, while figure 6.1 gives the breakdown of motives for women killed in 1999. Of the 81 females killed up to November 1999 the mean age was 30, with the median and mode being 26 and 30, respectively. Over a quarter of the women killed (27 per cent or 22 women) were unemployed. As indicated in figure 6.1, 37 per cent of the women were killed in domestic incidents. Harriott (1996) suggests that there is now a qualitative difference in crime and criminals within Jamaica.

While women are victimized in "domestically motivated killings", it should be clarified that "domestic" within the Jamaican context refers to a situation in which the offender and the victim are known to each other. Harriott states that in 1993 the offender was known to the victim in 64 per cent of cases (1996, 70). While members of the same community were involved in 15 per cent of the cases, spouse/paramour and

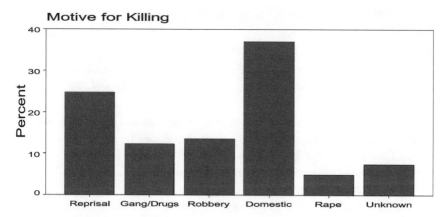

Figure 6.1   Motive for Women Killed in 1999

other family members comprised only 2 per cent. This can be contrasted with the North American definition in which domestic violence generally refers to violence within familial – such as spouse, ex-spouse, boyfriend-girlfriend – relationships. US Bureau of Justice statistics on intimate homicide for the period 1976–2000 indicate that spouses and family members made up about 15 per cent of all victims, but "female murder victims are substantially more likely than male murder victims to have been killed by an intimate". About one-third of female murder victims were killed by an intimate, whereas about 4 per cent of male murder victims were killed by an intimate. The US statistics indicate differences in intimate homicide by race and gender. Within the Jamaican context, class differentiation may be a more distinguishing factor than racial differentiation.

While the majority of cases of female victimization in Jamaica are classified as "domestic" incidents, retaliatory actions also account for a high percentage of women's victimization. The report on urban poverty and violence in Jamaica (Moser and Holland 1997, 33) found that, increasingly, women are targeted as police informers. Reprisal killings comprised the second highest category at 24.7 per cent, with robberies rounding out the top three categories.

According to Jamaican intelligence sources, while females were previously victimized predominantly in domestic incidents, their killings now seem to be centred on specific activities. Increasingly women are being killed because of their active association with drugs or gunmen, as partners or companions, active participants and/or couriers in the drug trade. Of significance too is the increased targeting of women for reprisal killings arising from participation as major players in the drug trade. A newspaper editorial entitled "Teens and Women Most at Risk" discusses women's increased vulnerability to victimization:

> There used to be honour among thieves. Time was when outlaws, even when conducting their most nefarious deeds, abided by a code of ethics that frowned on the killing of women and children. In jail the most reviled inmates were those convicted for molesting and harming children and committing other vicious crimes against women. Although in Jamaica we still hang on to a veneer of civility, the society has sunk to such depths that hardly a week goes by without news report about the slaughter of children, girls and young women. (*Daily Gleaner* 1999)

Political tribalism and drug- and gang-related incidents have repercussions for the high rates of reprisal killings. However, reports indicate that during 2001 reprisal killings and drug- and gang-related activities, rather than political tribalism, were the main causes of the violence, which claimed 278 lives between August and November.[2]

Criminological statistics generally show differences in vulnerability by age, gender, geography and activities. Crime and violence within Jamaica are primarily urban phenomena. Of females killed in 1999, 70.4 per cent were from the metropolitan area, while 29.6 per cent were from rural Jamaica. Even within the urban areas there was a geographical concentration, with female homicides occurring disproportionately in the St Andrew North and South and St Catherine police divisions (see figure 6.2).

When analysed by motive for killing and implement used, differences are revealed. More than half the cases (55.6 per cent, or 45 of 81 cases) involved the use of a gun.

However, only 3 per cent of rural women were killed by a gun; instead, they were more likely to be killed in domestic incidents involving weapons such as a knife or machete. Of the non-gun implements used, machete and knife accounted for 11 and 16 per cent, respectively, while 17.3 per cent were killed by other means.

Media reports indicate that for the ten-year period ending in 2001, 3,500 homicides remain unsolved.[3] The clearance rate, which refers to the proportion of reported crimes that have resulted in an arrest, not a

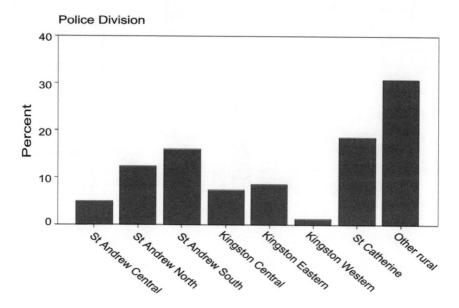

Figure 6.2   Females Killed within Each Police Division, 1999

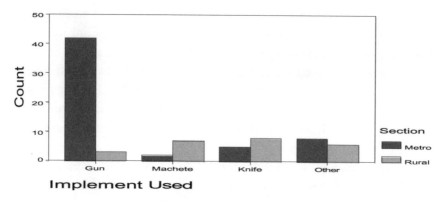

Figure 6.3   Implement Used to Kill Women by Region, 1999

judicial disposition, is in general quite low (see figure 6.4). In 1999 an arrest was made in only 49 per cent of cases of women killed, compared with the United States where the clearance rate for murders is 69 per cent. However, an arrest was even less likely to be made when the implement used was a gun, and was more likely to be made in domestic

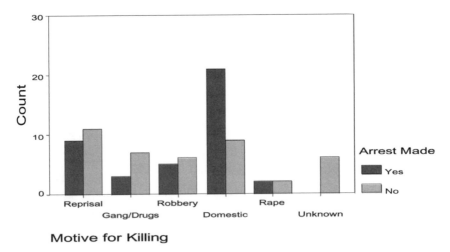

Figure 6.4 Cases in which Arrests Were Made by Motive for Crime, 1999

incidents, which comprised 37 per cent of all cases but 52.5 per cent of arrests.

Sexual Assault/Rape

Another crime category that reflects women's susceptibility to victimization in Jamaica is rape/carnal abuse. Like murder, significant increases have also occurred in the incidences of rape and carnal abuse. Jamaica Constabulary Force statistics indicate that in 1980 the reported incidence of major crimes in this category totalled 767. The numbers steadily increased, and by 1997 the occurrence of rape/carnal abuse had more than doubled, with 1,620 reported incidences. Media reports, citing the Woman Incorporated Crisis Centre for Women sources, noted that approximately six hundred calls or visits were received each month, although they could not state definitively whether this indicated increased offending or increased rates of reporting.[4]

Rape is one of the most under-reported offences. Under-reporting by women is a worldwide phenomenon which transcends social class barriers. Binder (1981), in a study to determine whether more women were reporting sexual assault and whether earlier theories about why women do not report victimizations continued to be valid, found that only 18 per cent of the adult women's rapes and only 11 per cent of assaults endured as children had been reported. Boxley, Lawrence and Gruchow (1995), citing several sources including testimony presented to the US Select Committee on Children, Youth and Families in 1990, note that an estimated 20 to 50 per cent of all rapes occur against adolescents, and six of ten forcible rapes occur before the rape survivor reaches age eighteen. However, less than 5 per cent of these rapes are ever brought to the attention of the police. Current figures on rape reporting indicate that the reporting rate has not improved. The United Nations also estimates that within developing countries the rates of reporting are further affected by several factors, such as economics. It is conceivable, then, that within Jamaica the number of rapes and carnal abuses that are reported is quite conservative.

Rape versus Sexual Assault

Feminist analyses have constantly noted that sexual assault, a major manifestation of women's subordinate position, is all about power (Smart 1989; Brownmiller 1976; Belknap 2000, 212, citing Russell 1984, 153). Similarly, anthropological and social control literature indicates that sexual assault is a primary means of informal social control used against women. This control takes two forms: actual harm and the threat of harm (Grana 2002).

Belknap (2000, 20) notes that prior to the 1980s rape occurrence was measured as the number of rapes reported to the police. However, most jurisdictions have found significant differences among sources such as police reports, hospital records and victimization surveys. Several factors such as definition and age of consent affect both the official statistics and the reporting rate.

Within Jamaica the criminal offence is classified as rape. The common law definition of rape refers to unlawful sexual intercourse between a man and a woman, and the current age of consent is sixteen. Gender is an inherent part of the definition, with carnal abuse defined as sexual intercourse between a male and a female under the age of consent. The mental element in rape is either knowing that the woman did not consent or not caring whether the woman consented (if the consent was procured by force, fear or fraud it is invalidated).[5] However, neither rape nor carnal abuse is defined in the Offences Against the Person Act.

Instead, the act presupposes that these offences already exist at common law, and therefore simply provides for punishment.

The importance of definition is that many women do not define their experiences in the same way that rape is legally defined. Sexual assault, a much broader term, encapsulates any sexual violation of one human being by another; hence, this definition includes more than the use of sexual organs or opposite-sex activities. For example, Belknap notes that when women are asked whether they have been forced to have sex rather than whether they were raped, the rate of occurrence is significantly different. Consequently, in order to introduce some level of clarity, Belknap (2000) suggests that the term forced sexual intercourse should be used. This clarity would improve discrepancies between official statistics and victimization surveys.

Within criminological circles the under-reporting of rape is acknowledged as occurring worldwide. It is interesting, therefore, that the United States Human Rights Country Report issued on 25 February 2000 by the US Department of State criticizes Jamaica and, by extension, Jamaican women when it notes that "violence against women is widespread, but many women are reluctant to acknowledge or report abusive behaviour, leading to wide variations in estimates of its extent".[6]

Without accepting the characterization of low reporting as being culturally influenced, one needs to question whether there are sociocultural factors within the Jamaican environment that increase women's vulnerability to being raped or carnally abused. In other words, is there a rape culture within Jamaica? Like other victims, victims of rape are often blamed for their victimization. However, victim blaming of rape victims is related in part to the rape myth acceptance. Thus, Lonsway and Fitzgerald (1994, 134) note that "rape myths are attitudes and beliefs that are generally false, and that serve to deny and justify male sexual aggression against women".

Although debates abound about the existence of a rape culture, Grana (2002, 143), citing Martha McCaughey, defines a rape culture as one in which

1. rape and other forms of violence against women are common;
2. rape and other forms of violence against women are tolerated (prevalence is high, while prosecution and arrest rates are low);

3. victim blaming and racist myths of rape and other forms of violence against women are common;
4. images of rape and other forms of violence against women abound;
5. images of sex and violence are intertwined;
6. women do not enjoy full legal, economic and social equality with men.

Many, if not all of these elements exist within Jamaican culture and are often romanticized in music and by the media. An example from the media includes depictions of women as "hottie", a word used to describe females in terms of sexual appeal, but more frequently applied to women who are scantily attired.

Under-reporting of abuse is affected by personal factors such as embarrassment; however, as Haniff (1998) notes, the community and the legal system in Jamaica support women's silence. It is important therefore that the extent of victim blaming, an aspect of the second victimization, is examined.

Victim Blaming

Examination of the rape myth hypothesis in the Jamaican context is important because as Belknap (2000) notes, victims of rape and battering are more likely to be blamed than victims of other crimes. Quite frequently they are accused of having provoked the abusive behaviour; this practice is known as victim blaming. Victim blaming emanates from and perpetuates a process called the second victimization which Tarver, Walker and Wallace (2002), citing Walker (2000), define as the reality of the system going about its "business" and the intentional or unintentional mistreatment incidental to the system doing its job precisely. With regard to the (un)intentional mistreatment inherent in the second victimization, a 1993 US Senate Judiciary Committee survey of state criminal justice agencies concluded that: 98 per cent of rape victims will never see their attacker apprehended, convicted and incarcerated; over half (54 per cent) of all rape prosecutions result in either a dismissal or an acquittal; only one in ten rapes reported to the police results in time served in prison; in only one in one hundred rapes (including those that go unreported) is the rapist sentenced to more than one year of incarceration.[7]

The second victimization occurs within personal, institutional and systemic victimization contexts but is most evident in the institutional sphere. Rape shield laws are examples of legislation implemented to address prevalent myths and thereby reduce victim blaming.

In addition to the rape myth, many other myths run rampant. These include the following:

1. Women provoke men to rape by the way in which they dress.
2. Women deserve to be raped.
3. Women say "no" but mean "yes".
4. Women who are raped asked for it.

Myths are held not only by perpetrators but also by other women, who sometimes succumb to socialization and perpetuate victim blaming. Madrid (1997) discusses the personal ideologies that facilitate and encourage the victimization of women who are perceived to have violated society's unwritten rules. In two well-publicized cases involving alleged sexual assault, Mike Tyson and William Kennedy-Smith (Tyson's having resulted in a conviction), many persons, especially women, questioned what the alleged victims were doing with the accused at the hours the incidents allegedly took place.

Derrick Bell, writing about racism, discusses the principle of racial standing. Bell's fourth rule of racial standing states, "When a black person or group makes a statement or takes an action that the white community or vocal components thereof deem 'outrageous,' the latter will actively recruit blacks willing to refute the statement or condemn the action" (1992, 118). One can replace "black" with "female" and extrapolate from Bell's rule to understand female-on-female behaviour and women's co-optation and participation in societal and institutional practices that are often used to subordinate them. The problem is that socialization into these norms is cumulative and unconscious.

There are race, class and gender dimensions to female victimization. For example, Anglos have been the oppressors of Africans while the rich oppress the poor. Women are relegated to the private sphere, where they may assume positions of dominance over other females and children. Thus, women oppress other women, especially those who work in domestic and service sectors. Nonetheless, women's behaviours must be seen as taking place in conditions not of their own choosing.

Conclusion

Both governmental and non-governmental resources exist within the Jamaican context to address women's victimization. The Centre for Investigation of Sexual Offences and Child Abuse, a special investigative unit within the police force, is mandated to foster an environment that encourages victims to report sexual victimization, undertake efficient and effective investigation of allegations of sexual abuse, provide rehabilitation of victims and increase public education on the issue of sexual victimization. The Bureau of Women's Affairs is housed in the Ministry of Labour and Social Services; legislation designed to address violence against women and punishment of offenders includes the Matrimonial Causes Act, act 2 of 1989; the Domestic Violence Act, act 15 of 1995; and the Offences Against the Person (Amendment) Act, act 14 of 1992. Relevant non-governmental agencies include the Association of Women's Organizations of Jamaica, Women's Media Watch and Woman Incorporated Crisis Centres. There is, however, the need for more shelters and the implementation of legislation that will help to ameliorate the disadvantages women face not only in familial settings but also in spheres such as the courts. For example, Sykes (2003) argues that within the courts, the law puts female victims of sexual assault at a disadvantage because of its assumption that women are prone to lie. He argues therefore that the Jamaican legislature needs to implement legislation to "remove the slur against our women".

While there are many similarities in women's life conditions, disparities continue to exist. However, the extent of these disparities is not known, and will not be known until women are allowed to speak of their experiences in their own voice. Whether consequences manifest similarly for women in different jurisdictions, or the degree of difference in such manifestations, needs to be investigated. Consequently, explanations that are posited without speaking with women become, to borrow Karl Popper's term, "bold conjecture". This discussion provides some preliminary information on victimization of females in Jamaica. Because the Jamaican statistics indicate an increase in women's victimization and criminalization, it is recommended that a more systematic criminological study be conducted.

This discussion also raises the importance of exploring women's experiential knowledge. Standpoint feminism, as both epistemology and methodology, advocates speaking with rather than for women. It also advocates research that gives primacy to women's voices. A cursory examination of the Jamaican statistics suggests that while Jamaican women are often killed by someone they know, they are less likely to be killed by an intimate partner. Therefore, research needs to be conducted on women in their respective sites. I recommend that more extensive research be conducted on the particularities of victimization of Jamaican women, with less emphasis on official sources and more on victimization surveys.

Notes

1. See "Ending Violence against Women and Girls". <www.unfpa.org/swp/2000/english/ch03.html>.
2. See "Most Murders Not Politically Motivated". <www.jamaica-gleaner.com/gleaner/20011016/news/news1.html>.
3. See "3,500 Murders Unsolved". <www.jamaica-gleaner.com/gleaner/20010920/ news/news1.html>.
4. Diana McCauley, reporting in the *Jamaica Gleaner Online*, 11 October 1999.
5. Personal communication from the Office of the Director of Public Prosecution, 15 March 2002.
6. <www.usis.usemb.se/human/human1999/jamaica.html>.
7. See <www.nyscasa.org/Resources_Pubs/reports/status/1_status.html>.

References

Belknap, J. 2000. *The Invisible Woman: Gender, Crime and Justice*. Belmont, Calif.: Wadsworth.

Bell, D. 1992. *Faces at the Bottom of the Well: The Permanence of Racism*. New York: Basic Books.

Binder, R. 1981. "Why Women Don't Report Sexual Assault". *Journal of Clinical Psychiatry* 42, no. 11 (November).

Bissessear, A. 2000. "Policy Transfer and Implementation Failure: A Review of the Policy of Domestic Violence in Trinidad and Tobago". *Caribbean Journal of Criminology and Social Psychology* 5, nos. 1–2 (January–July).

Boxley, J., L. Lawrence, and H. Gruchow. 1995. "A Preliminary Study of Eighth Grade Students' Attitudes toward Rape Myths and Women's Roles". *Journal of School Health* 65, no. 3.

Brownmiller, S. 1976. *Against Our Will: Men, Women, and Rape*. New York: Bantam Books.

Daily Gleaner (online). 1999. "Teens and Women Most at Risk". 11 October. <www.jamaica-gleaner.com/gleaner/19991011/cleisure/c1.html>.

Danner, M. 2000. "Three Strikes and It's Women Who Are Out: The Hidden Consequences for Women of Criminal Justice Reform". In *It's a Crime: Women and Justice,* edited by R. Muraskin. Upper Saddle River, N.J.: Prentice Hall.

de Albuquerque, K., and J. McElroy. 1999. "A Longitudinal Study of Serious Crime in the Caribbean". *Caribbean Journal of Criminology and Social Psychology* 4, nos. 1–2 (January–July).

Grana, S.J. 2002. *Women and (In)justice: The Criminal and Civil Effects of the Common Law on Women's Lives.* Boston: Allyn and Bacon.

Greenfeld, L.A., and T.L. Snell. 1999. *Bureau of Justice Statistics Special Report on Women Offenders.* NCJ 175688. December. <www.ojp.usdoj.gov/bjs/pub/pdf/wo.pdf>.

Haniff, N.Z. 1998. "Male Violence against Men and Women in the Caribbean: The Case of Jamaica". *Journal of Comparative Family Studies* 29, no. 2 (Summer).

Harriott, A. 1996. "The Changing Social Organization of Crime and Criminals in Jamaica". *Caribbean Quarterly* 42, nos. 2–3 (June–September).

hooks, b. 1981. *Ain't I a Woman? Black Women and Feminism.* Boston: South End Press.

Human Rights Watch. 2002. "Collateral Casualties: Children of Incarcerated Drug Offenders in New York". Volume 14, no. 3 (June). <www.hrw.org/reports/2002/usany>.

Josephs, J., Z. Weston-Henriques, and K. Ekeh. 1998. "The Legal Response to Domestic Violence in the English-Speaking Caribbean Countries". *Caribbean Journal of Criminology and Social Psychology* 3, nos. 1–2 (January–July).

Lonsway, K.A., and L.F. Fitzgerald. 1994. "Rape Myths: In Review". *Psychology of Women Quarterly* 18.

Madrid, E. 1997. *Nothing Bad Happens to Good Girls: Fear of Crime in Women's Lives.* Berkeley: University of California Press.

Morrow, B.H. 1992. "Afro-Caribbean Women and Domestic Violence". Paper presented at the American Sociological Association Annual Conference, Pittsburgh, Pennsylvania, 20–24 August.

Moser, C., and J. Holland. 1997. *World Bank Report on Urban Poverty and Violence in Jamaica. Latin American and Caribbean Studies Viewpoints.* Washington, D.C.: World Bank.

Pitch, T. 1985. "The Feminization of Social Control". *Research in Law, Deviance and Social Control,* 7.

Population Information Program. 1999. "World Organizations Speak Out". *Population Report: Issues in World Health* 27, no. 11, ser. L (December). <www.jhuccp.org/pr/111/111boxes.shtml#world>.

————. 2003. "Population Report". Centre for Communications Programs, Johns Hopkins School of Public Health. <www.jhuccp.org/pr/l11edsum.shtml>.

Smart, C. 1989. *Feminism and the Power of Law.* New York: Routledge.

Smith, D. 1987. *The Everyday World as Problematic: Feminist Sociology.* Boston: Northeastern University Press.

————. 1990. *Text, Facts and Femininity: Exploring the Relations of Ruling.* New York: Routledge.

Sykes, B. 2003. "Removing the 'Slur' on the Character of Our Women". Unpublished paper, copy on file with the author.

Tarver, M., S. Walker, and H. Wallace. 2002. *Multicultural Issues in the Criminal Justice System.* Boston: Allyn and Bacon.

Tjaden, P., and N. Thoennes. 1998. "Prevalence, Incidence, and Consequences of Violence against Women: Findings from the National Violence against Women Survey". US Department of Justice. <http://www.ojp.usdoj.gov/nij/pubs-sum/172837.htm>.

United Nations Development Fund. *c.*2000. "A Life Free of Violence: United Nations Inter-Agency Campaign on Women's Human Rights in Latin America and the Caribbean". <www.undp.org/rblac/gender/>.

United Nations Population Fund. 2000. "Ending Violence against Women and Girls". <www.unfpa.org/swp/2000/english/ch03.html>.

US Bureau of Justice. Office of Justice Programs. 2003. *Homicide Trends in the US: Intimate Homicide.* <http://www.ojp.usdoj.gov/bjs/homicide/intimates.htm>.

US Census. 2003. "Few Women at High Salary Levels". <news.findlaw.com/ap/a/w/1152/3-24-2003/20030324091502_16.html>.

World Health Organization (WHO). 2002. "Prevalence of Violence against Women by an Intimate Male Partner". Department of Injuries and Violence Prevention Report. October. <www.who.int/violence_injury_prevention/vaw/infopack.htm>.

7

The Impact of Crime on Tourist Arrivals in Jamaica
A Transfer Function Analysis

Dillon Alleyne and Ian Boxill

Tourism analysts in Jamaica have argued that the high crime rate in the country has impacted negatively on tourist arrivals, and in a study of popular perceptions of the tourism industry in Jamaica by Dunn and Dunn (2002), it was found that crime and violence were perceived to be the number one problem affecting the tourism industry.

However, there has been little by way of empirical work to test the nature of the relationship between crime and tourist arrivals.

In fact, the only serious study to have attempted to test the relationship between crime and tourist arrivals in Jamaica is Boxill (1995). In that study the author used a multiple regression model to examine the impact of the rate of violent crime on tourist arrivals. The findings showed that the violent crime rate was not a good predictor of tourism arrivals in Jamaica. In fact, the violent crime rate explained less than 5 per cent of the variation in tourist arrivals in Jamaica. That study had a number of methodological limitations; for example, a linear model was used, which would have been insensitive to possible non-linear relationships between crime and tourist arrivals. This chapter attempts to overcome these limitations by utilizing a transfer function which estimates the immediate and delayed impact of crime on tourist arrivals from 1962 to 1999.

Tourism and Development in Jamaica

Since the 1980s tourism has been one of the leading growth sectors in the global economy. The sector has seen immense growth in revenue and employment as well as the development of new and fledgling markets.

In Jamaica the performance of the sector has been fairly good in absolute terms. For instance, since the slump in visitor arrivals in 1977, when the number was 386,514, the industry rebounded to record 1,903,893 arrivals in 1997, which represented a 4.6 per cent increase over 1996 (Planning Institute of Jamaica 1998). In the 1980s the tourism sector became the country's largest earner of foreign exchange; gross earnings in 1997 were estimated at US$1,140 million (Planning Institute of Jamaica 1998).

Across the Caribbean region there has been considerable expansion in tourism, especially since sugar and bananas have tended to decline. Between 1991 and 1999 the growth of stopover tourist arrivals in the Caribbean as a whole was 4.8 per cent, while for Jamaica the rate of growth was 5.0 per cent over the same period. The implication is that for this period Jamaica performed above the regional average. Jamaica's market share in the Caribbean region has also been steady, with a share of 6.4 per cent of stopovers in 1991 and 6.5 per cent in 1999 (Caribbean Tourism Organization 2001).

Appendix 7.1 shows some major indicators of tourism performance between 1960 and 1999. In table 7.1 the growth rates for total visitors and total stopovers are shown for the period 1960–99, and for sub-periods 1960–80 and 1981–99. The table also reports total visitor expenditure and expenditure per person, and the period of analysis is 1967–99, with sub-periods 1967–80 and 1981–99.

The most dynamic period of growth of visitor expenditure was in the second sub-period, 1960–80, when that figure grew by 7.5 per cent. All the indices except total visitor arrivals generally show higher growth rates in the first sub-period and a lower growth rate in the second, suggesting some stagnation in the industry. (The difference between total visitors and total stopovers is mainly cruise ship passengers.) The average length of stay by visitors has increased gradually – from nearly nine days in the 1960s to between ten and eleven days in the 1990s.

Table 7.1   Growth Rates of Major Indicators of Tourism Performance, 1960–1999

Years	Total Visitors	Total Stopovers	Total Visitor Expenditure	Total Expenditure per Person
1960–1999	5.7	7.2	10.1[a]	4.0[a]
1960–1980	4.5	8.2	11.6[b]	7.5[b]
1981–1999	7.4	6.4	8.4[c]	0.09[c]

Source: Planning Institute of Jamaica, *Economic and Social Survey of Jamaica* (various years).

[a] Period: 1967–1999.
[b] Period: 1967–1980.
[c] Period: 1981–1999.

Naturally the decline in stopovers would be reflected in room occupancy levels. In appendix 7.2 the occupancy levels are reported for Kingston and St Andrew, Montego Bay, Ocho Rios, Port Antonio, Mandeville, the South Coast, and Negril. Jamaica's tourist resorts evolved as enclaves with heavy concentration in a few areas. The most significant areas in terms of visitor concentration are Ocho Rios, Negril and Montego Bay, which together accounted for 83.4 per cent of accommodation in the country in 1997. The occupancy rates for these areas have been on the decline since the late 1980s. In the case of Negril, occupancy levels since 1994 have been in the 62–66 per cent range, which is less than the 70 per cent achieved in the 1980s. While the decline in occupancy rates in Montego Bay and Negril has not been as dramatic, it is still significant. Part of the reason is that the investment in room capacity has not been matched by increasing numbers of visitors. This raises serious issues of the profitability of many hotel properties, and concerns as to why, despite considerable promotion by the government and private sector, there is excess capacity.

The important question is whether this situation reflects a fundamental decline in the industry, or a temporary component of a growth cycle. Butler (1980) identified an S-shaped curve which seems to mirror the experience of many destinations. He identified six phases of the cycle: exploration, involvement, development, consolidation (maturity), stagnation, decline and rejuvenation (appendix 7.3). There has been application of the model to such places as Malta (Oglethorpe 1984) and the Pacific islands (Choy 1992).

The relevant portions of the model are the acceleration or developmental stage, when tourism becomes important as the visitor arrivals increase, and the maturity phase. As the Jamaican data suggest (table 7.1), the trend for visitor arrivals is still upward sloping but growth rates are much lower, especially in the last decade. It may be disputed whether this reflects a maturity or consolidation stage of the product or a process of decline. But even if growth did not falter, the problems of crowding out due to the possibility of reaching capacity, environmental considerations and the problems of waste disposal will undoubtedly place upper limits on tourism growth in Jamaica. It is also clear that the pattern of tourism has been changing. For example, Edwards (1987) has pointed to a shift in the future from sun, sea and beach tourism to an industry in which people will demand to be more active, and one that is culturally satisfying; that is, he foresees an increase in the demand for sustainable tourism with an emphasis on environmental protection. Thus, market segmentation and product differentiation will be important in order to maximize tourism revenue. The growing concern about skin cancer and exposure to the sun also creates the opportunity for developing other forms of tourist attractions.

Still, one possible reason for the inconsistent growth patterns of the Jamaican tourism industry is the rise in the crime rate, particularly the violent crime rate. We now turn to this issue.

Crime and Tourism

The tourism industry in the Caribbean has been beset by the problem of crime over the years (Pattullo 1996). In their seminal work on the link between crime and tourism in the Caribbean, de Albuquerque and McElroy (1999, 968–84) point to a possible link between mass tourism and an increase in certain types of crime. In Jamaica, the Report on the Task Force on Tourism recommended that given the nature of the problem of crime and harassment, "radical steps, far beyond what was has been contemplated up to now, must be taken to strengthen significantly the security presence in the resort areas" (Government of Jamaica 1995, 5).

According to Harriott (2000),

Crime control has become a central developmental issue and an important public policy concern in most Caribbean territories. These tourism-dependent economies have become more vulnerable to violent crime, yet more criminogenic. In the case of Jamaica (which is perhaps the most problematic), the high rates of violent crime and insecurity among all segments of the population are matched by declining public confidence in the criminal justice system and growing cynicism among its functionaries. (p. xv)

One of the main characteristics of studies focusing on crime and tourism in Jamaica is that these studies, to varying degrees, see these problems as a function of the opportunities within the sector as a result of its growth (UWI 1971; Dunn and Dunn 1994; Boxill 1995; Government of Jamaica 1995).

Dunn and Dunn (1994) offer one of the most interesting studies on crime and harassment in Jamaica. The researchers conclude that visitor crime and harassment are problems related to several social, economic, political, cultural and psychological factors. Further,

These problems stem from economic need and the existence of few employment alternatives which offer good potential earnings. The rise in harassment must also be analysed in the context of structural adjustment policies, an undeveloped rural sector, traditional land ownership patterns, the high cost of agricultural inputs and the relatively low returns accruing to small farmers. (p. 76)

Headley (1994) argues,

Most street crimes in Jamaica are generally of a depersonalized nature, since, usually, the assailant consciously suspends whatever personal or firsthand knowledge, if any, he may have of his victim. Actual names and faces of victims are thus objectively less important than the social or material gains (expected and actual) derived from the use of violence. (p. 35)

Drawing from available statistics up to the early 1990s, Headley suggests, more specifically,

Victims, whether they are tourists, shopkeepers, innocent householders, drug-trade competitors, political foes, or vulnerable women, all become expendable targets in a larger, fiercer 'struggle' for goods, status, money and power. All street-level crime and the criminals' tendency towards violence usually indicates problems which, if their root causes are left structurally unattended to, will reproduce themselves. (1994, 36–37)

This view is also consistent with that of Alleyne, Boxill and Francis (1994), who argue that the social problems of the tourism sector are a reflection of larger economic problems at the macro level.

In Jamaica, like many other Caribbean countries, tourism has been a major source of foreign exchange earnings and employment generation. Because of the importance of the tourism sector in Jamaica, there has been a great deal of concern about the impact of crime on tourist arrivals. This, even though official statistics indicate that crimes against tourists have either stabilized or declined over the past two decades. If crime affects the ability of a society to generate income from tourism then what we have is a vicious cycle, one which creates the environment for crime and in turn destroys the very activity that could change that environment. In this regard it is important to determine the nature of the impact of crime on tourism in order to take corrective measures.

However, it must be restated that, so far, there has been little quantitative analysis to support the view that crime has had a significant negative impact on tourism in Jamaica. Consequently this chapter has a clear objective: to clarify the nature of the impact of crime on tourism. Concomitantly, the chapter could permit more constructive intervention in improving the tourism product.

Methodology

The impact of crime on tourist arrivals has generated a great deal of attention at the international level. For example, high-profile terrorist events such as the hijacking of TWA flight 847 in October 1985, that of the Achille Lauro cruise in December 1985 and other incidents caused much concern about whether tourists would change their travel plans (Enders 1995, 286). More recently, the events following the terrorist attack on the Twin Towers in the New York City on 11 September 2001 also sparked much discussion on how this will affect tourism globally and in the Caribbean.

Although it has been made clear through opinion polls that terrorist attacks or crime rates do affect tourism, the extent of this effect has to be discovered through the application of statistical techniques. Enders (1995, 286) points out that polls cannot account for tourists not surveyed, who may be lured back to the troubled spots by lower prices and other incentives.

In estimating the relationship between tourism and crime the modelling strategy employed is that of a transfer function. This is a technique which allows the time path of tourist arrivals to be influenced by the immediate and delayed impact of crime. In a paper on the impact of terrorism on tourism, Enders, Sandler and Parise (1992) examined transnational terrorism and tourism in relation to a number of countries using the transfer function technique. The essential relationship was the logarithmic share of each country's revenue $R_i(t)$ as a function of the number of terrorist incidents occurring in each country $x_i(t)$. As Enders (1995) points out, the important assumption is that there is no feedback from tourism to terrorism; this would occur if the behaviour of tourists forced terrorists to alter their behaviour.

In the case of Jamaica we study the relationship between total tourist arrivals T_t and the number of crimes X_t, where the variables are in logs. The transfer function takes the following form:

$$T_t = \alpha_0 + A(L)T_{t-1} + C(L)X_t + B(L)\varepsilon_t \qquad (1)$$

T_t = Total annual number of tourists in period t
X_t = Total annual number of crimes committed in Jamaica in period t

where $A(L)$, $B(L)$ and $C(L)$ are polynomials in the lag operator L.

There are many steps in this model estimation. The first is to fit an autoregressive moving average (ARMA) model to the X_t sequence. The T_t sequence is then filtered and the best ARMA model is fitted to the $A(L)$ sequence. A model of the form $[1 - A(L)T] = C(L)X_t + e_t$ can then be found and the $\{e_t\}$ sequence can be modelled as an approximation for $B(L)\varepsilon_t$. These various parts of the model $A(L)$, $B(L)$ and $C(L)$ are then estimated simultaneously. Enders (1995, 284–85) carefully sets out the methodology.

We can interpret the model as follows: The coefficients of $[1 - A(L)T]$ yield the (AR) component and $B(L)$ the moving average components of the ARMA model. The polynomial $C(L) = c_0 + c_1L + c_2L^2......$, is called the transfer function and it shows how the movement in X_t affects the time path of tourist arrivals. The first coefficient in $C(L)$

captures the immediate or contemporaneous effect of crimes on arrivals, while subsequent coefficients reflect delayed effects. At the same time, the impulse response function defined as $C(L)/(1 - A(L))$ shows the effect of an X_t shock on arrivals. If after differencing the tourist arrival series T_t it is found to have a unit root, then crime at period t would have a permanent effect on tourist arrivals. The absence of a unit root means that the effect will eventually die out (Enders, Sandler and Parise 1992, 539).

Additional variables were also used to add structure to the model; these are the real advertising budget, $(ADVT_t)$, the United States real gross domestic product $(USGDP_t)$ in 1990 dollars, lags in T_t which are used as proxies for room capacity, and a dummy variable $(Allin_t)$ designed to capture the impact of all-inclusive hotels after 1972.

The US gross domestic product is used as an explanatory variable, since the United States is the largest market and has accounted for significant rates of growth of Jamaica's tourism. We believe that demand for travel by US citizens will increase as the gross domestic product of the United States increases. We expect that the advertising budget of the Jamaica Tourist Board (JTB) may reflect expenditures which, apart from promotion, seek to deflect attention from problems, including crime, in the tourism destination. Thus, increases in advertising expenditure should be positively related to tourist arrivals. We were only able to get data on this variable from 1980 to 1997, and this restricted our sample.

We expect the coefficient on the dummy variable $(Allint_t)$ to be positive, since tourists may feel safer in all-inclusive hotels relative to other types of hotel package. A separate function was also estimated to examine specifically the impact of crime on European arrivals, in order to determine whether this market behaves differently from the overall market.

Data Description

Figure 7.1 graphs the annual growth rates of total crimes (GTTCRIMES) and murders (GMURDER) from 1962 to 1999. In addition, the growth rates of total arrivals (GTARRIVALS) and stopovers (GSTOPOVER) over the period 1960–99 are also reported. The annual

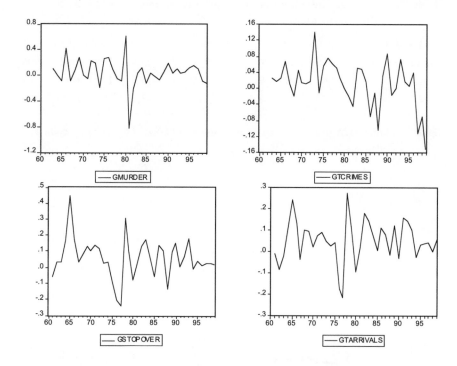

Figure 7.1   Growth Rates of Major Crime Indicators (1962–1999) and Tourism
Indicators (1960–1999)

Source: Planning Institute of Jamaica, *Economic and Social Survey of Jamaica*
(various years).

growth rates of total crimes and total arrivals have been larger in the
first sub-period (1960–80) relative to the period 1981–99. Particularly
interesting are the annual growth rates of murder and total crimes,
which declined in the late 1990s.

Table 7.2 sets out the growth rates of total arrivals between 1960
and 1999 and for sub-periods 1960–80 and 1981–99. The table also
reports the total murder and crime rates for 1962–99. We also examined the trend in tourist arrivals, which was extracted using the
Hodrick-Prescott Filter (Hodrick and Prescott 1997). This trend is used
as a proxy for the tourism industry's potential and is compared with the
actual arrivals (see appendix 7.4).

Table 7.2　Average Growth Rates of Major Tourism Indicators (1960–1999) and Crime Indicators (1962–1999)

Tourist Arrivals	1960–1999	5.7	1960–1980	4.5	1981–1999	7.4
Trend Arrivals	1960–1999	6.2	1960–1980	5.9	1981–1999	6.6
Murder	1962–1999	7.3	1962–1980	15.8	1981–1999	3.1
Total Crimes	1962–1999	1.2	1962–1980	3.5	1981–1999	0.9

Source: Planning Institute of Jamaica, *Economic and Social Survey of Jamaica* (various years).

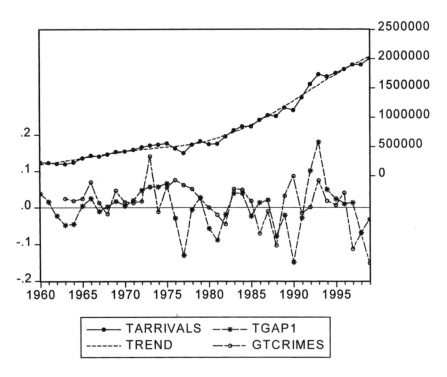

Figure 7.2　Total Arrivals (TARRIVALS), Trend Arrivals (TREND) and Trend Gap (TGAP1), 1960–1999 and Annual Growth in Total Crimes (GTCRIMES), 1962–1999

Source: Planning Institute of Jamaica, *Economic and Social Survey of Jamaica* (various years).

Table 7.3   Major Crimes against Tourists, 1989–1999

Year	Murder	Robbery	Burglary	Rape	Wounding	Total
1989	1	83	17	4	7	306
1990	2	118	23	7	8	438
1991	3	153	33	5	6	553
1992	3	209	51	7	9	612
1993	1	165	21	8	9	433
1994	3	204	29	5	3	469
1995	2	137	31	1	3	370
1996	1	112	28	6	2	286
1997	2	109	16	9	9	247
1998	1	85	17	9	1	185
1999	0	7	13	3	2	124

Source: Tourism Liaison Office, Jamaica Constabulary Force.

When arrivals are above trend we assume that the industry has performed well, and when they are below then there is need for improvement.

The results confirm a decline in growth in overall crime rates and some buoyancy in tourism indicators in the 1990s relative to the 1980s. Figure 7.2 shows the trend in arrivals (TREND) and actual tourist arrivals (TARRIVALS). There were several periods in which arrivals were below trend: 1962–64, 1967, 1976–78, 1980–82, 1985, 1988–91, 1998 and 1999. The interesting thing is that arrivals were below trend in two major periods when the crime rate was crimes were significant, in 1980 and in the period 1998–99. Figure 7.2 also reports the trend gap (TGAP1), which is the difference between actual arrivals and trend arrivals, and the annual crime rate (GTCRIMES).

There seems to be some correlation between the crime rate and the trend gap, especially after 1985. The issue is whether we can attribute these periods of below-trend arrivals to crime and, in addition, are there periods when there were high crimes and arrivals above trend?

Table 7.3 reports crimes against tourists from 1989 to 1999. The table shows a dramatic decline in crimes against tourists. There were 306 incidents in 1989, and this increased to 612 in 1993, then fell in

1999 to a total of 124 incidents. The major type of crime against tourists was robbery, but this category has declined in the last few years.

Given the fact that the actual numbers of crimes against tourists are not significant relative to the national average, it is the news effect of overall crime rates and the perception of the destination at various points in time that create the fear of Jamaica as an unsafe destination. Thus, the US government advisories about an unsafe destination may be more effective than the general news about crimes in a particular destination.

While high crime rates in Jamaica and perceptions about safety may have a negative impact on arrivals, countervailing measures such as increased advertising through the JTB and various discount packages through the hotels may help to lure tourists back to a destination. In addition, the all-inclusive concept may create a greater sense of safety among tourists despite high crime rates in the destination.

Model Estimation

Modern time series analysis suggests that variables used in regression analysis must be stationary in order to avoid a spurious relationship (Dickey and Fuller 1979). The stationarity properties of the data were first checked to determine what level of differencing might be required in order to remove the spurious regression problem. All the variables, total crimes ($Crimes_t$), United States gross domestic product ($USGDP_t$), real advertising expenditures by the JTB ($ADVB_t$) at 1995 prices, total arrivals (T_t) and arrivals from Europe (EU_t), are I(1) or random walks with drift components.

Usually if a group of non-stationary variables has a long run relationship between each other, they are said to cointegrate (Engle and Granger 1987). The Johansen (1988) test found no cointegration among the variables, so changes in the logs were then used for all the series except ($Allin_t$), the dummy variable. A number of models were estimated for the period 1962–99, and the best regression based on minimizing the Akaike information criterion (AIC) was as follows:

$$\Delta T_t = (-0.59L^2 + 0.32L^3) * \Delta T_t - 0.22 * \Delta Crimes_t + 1.08 * \Delta USGDP_{t-2}$$

$$(-2.53) \quad (1.79) \qquad (-0.91) \qquad\qquad (2.47)$$

$$+0.035 * Allin_t + (1 - 0.59L^3)\eta_t$$

$$(2.03) \qquad\qquad (-2.53) \hspace{6cm} (2)$$

$$\overline{R}^2 = 0.25$$

$$AIC = -36.57, \quad SBC = -27.41$$

$$Q(8-1) = 6.56$$

The 't' values are in brackets and the Q statistics for autocorrelation is reported. The model selection criteria, the Akaike Information Criterion (AIC) and the Schwartz Baysean Criterion (SBC) are also reported.

The change in the lag of arrivals, T_t, which is designed to capture capacity effects, has a delay of two and three lags respectively. The first coefficient on capacity (ΔT_{t-2}) is negative and not positive as expected, and highly significant, suggesting that changes in arrivals in the current period are negatively related to changes in arrivals two years before.

The second capacity variable, (ΔT_{t-3}), suggests that changes in arrivals are related to changes in arrivals three years before, but the coefficient is not significant at the conventional 95 per cent level.

The change in real US gross domestic product $(\Delta USGDP_{t-2})$ has the correct sign with a delay of two years and is statistically significant. The results also suggest that changes in arrivals are negatively related to changes in crime rates $(\Delta Crimes_t)$ as expected, but the coefficient is not significant at the conventional level.

The variable $(Allin_t)$ which captures the impact of the all-inclusive hotels is highly significant, with a positive sign as expected. This reflects the fact that the rise of the all-inclusives may have lowered the importance of crime for some tourists.

In addition, the moving average term at lag three, $(1 - 0.59L^3)\eta_t$ from the residual of the transfer function, is highly significant. The explanatory power of the model, as reflected in the $\overline{R}^2$ of 25 per cent, is moderate, suggesting that these variables account for one-quarter of the variation in tourist arrivals.

We believe that the relationship between crime rates and arrivals is mediated by such factors as the level of advertising expenditure and discount packages which are necessary to lure tourists to a destination.

The model was re-estimated to account for the impact on tourist arrivals of the advertising budget of the JTB. This formulation, which was done for the period 1980–97, is as follows:

$$\Delta T_i = 0.57 * \Delta T_{t-1} - 0.15 * \Delta Crimes_{t-1} + (-1.85 + 1.79L) * \Delta USGDP_t$$

$$(2.56) \qquad (-0.48) \qquad\qquad (-2.49) \qquad\qquad\qquad (2.64)$$

$$+0.11 * \Delta ADVB_t + (1 - 0.68L + 0.12L^2)\varepsilon_t \qquad\qquad (3)$$

$$(2.16) \qquad\qquad\qquad (-1.30) \quad (0.23)$$

$$\overline{R}^2 = 0.57$$

$$AIC = -47.5, \quad SBC = -41.7$$

$$Q(3 - 2) = 2.57$$

In this formulation the proxy variable for capacity, (ΔT_{t-1}), has the expected sign and is statistically significant at the 95 per cent level. The results also show that change in the crime rate has the expected sign but is not significant, while change in the US gross domestic product, $(\Delta US\text{-}GDP_t)$, has a negative sign and is significant at the conventional level. The lag of this variable has the expected positive sign and is also statistically significant. It is important to note that change in the advertising budget in the current period is highly significant in explaining overall changes in arrivals and has the expected sign. The explanatory power of this formulation is 57 per cent, which is quite significant. These findings are consistent with Palmer and Ramkisoon (1998), who showed that the advertising budget was an important factor in determining tourist arrivals in Jamaica.

Our results are in line with the expectations for the overall market, dominated by US arrivals, in which the all-inclusive hotels serve to shield visitors from the problems of crime, violence and harassment, either real or perceived. The European market, in which visitors are more interested in being part of the larger environment outside the hotels, may be a different matter, since visitors may have greater exposure to crime. We estimated a separate relationship for the European market to see if crime had a more significant impact on European tourist arrivals. The model results for 1980 to 1997 are as follows:

$$\Delta EU_t = 0.20 * \Delta EU_{t-2} + \{(-2.075L + 2.79L^2) * \Delta Crimes_t / 1 + 0.69\}$$

$$(2.29) \qquad\qquad (-6.75) \qquad (6.75) \qquad\qquad\qquad (5.91)$$

$$+0.09 * \Delta ADVB_{t-2} + (1 + 0.40L - 0.75L^2)\varepsilon_t \qquad\qquad (4)$$

$$(2.93) \qquad\qquad\qquad (3.01) \quad (-5.32)$$

$$\overline{R}^2 = 0.89$$

$$AIC = -34.5, \quad SBC = -30.6$$

$$Q(3 - 2) = 3.38$$

A number of things are outstanding here. First, all the coefficients are statistically significant at the conventional level. Second, the change in the capacity variable ΔEU_{t-2} has a delay of two years. Third, the first coefficient on the autoregressive term for the crime rate variable ($\Delta Crimes_{t-1}$) is negative, as expected, and has a delay of one year, while the sign on the second coefficient is positive. This second term may reflect recovery after two years and the data do give some support for this argument, given the extreme volatility of the European arrival data. Interestingly, the denominator term is 0.69 and significant, suggesting a wavelike effect with no declining memory. The two autoregressive terms $(1 + 0.40L - 0.75L^2)\varepsilon_t$ are from the overall transfer function and these are significant. The overall equation for European tourists is highly significant, suggesting that crime has a severe impact on this market relative to the overall tourism market.

Conclusion

From the foregoing analysis, which is premised on the results of the transfer function, we are able to draw a number of conclusions. First, the Jamaican tourism industry has performed fairly well despite increases in crime. Second, crime impacts negatively on tourism arrivals in both the European and the overall markets, but it has a greater impact on the European market. Third, the impact of crime on the overall arrival market is relatively small, but this is because that impact has been mitigated by increased advertising and promotion and the growth of all-inclusive hotels. What are some of the implications of these results?

In answering this question, it should be noted that the development of Jamaica's tourism industry has been premised on incentives and promotion with a view to encouraging as large a number of tourists as possible. However, factors such as the development of new destinations and the heavy reliance on a single country, in this case the United States, have contributed to a constant share of the regional market. The data suggest that between 1991 and 1993, the US market contributed between 61 and 64 per cent of stopover tourists. Between 1994 and 1999 the United States contribution was between 65 and 69 per cent. No other single market, with the exception of the United Kingdom in 1999, contributed as much as 10 per cent over this period. Between 1983 and 1989 the rate of growth of the US market was 2.1 per cent, while in the period 1990–99 the rate of growth was 4.9 per cent, but the reliance on such a large market share from the United States makes Jamaica heavily dependent on the unfolding of events there. In other words, this approach to tourism is not the best, since a recession in the US economy can have devastating consequences for the Jamaican tourist industry.

Jamaica has simply failed to take advantage of the European market, even though its growth rate of stopovers was 6.2 per cent over the period 1990–99, a faster rate than for the US market. Jamaica has also failed to capitalize on an emerging Caribbean market. The United Kingdom, Canada and the rest of Europe contributed 30.2 per cent of total stopover tourists in Jamaica in 1990, and 24.7 per cent in 1999 (Planning Institute of Jamaica 1998). The inability to achieve higher growth rates in arrivals, therefore, seems to be a structural problem, reflecting the lack of appropriate strategies capable of capitalizing on a growing global industry. Part of the reason for this situation is that the all-inclusive hotels dominate the accommodation sector. For example, the all-inclusives accounted for 24 per cent of rooms in 1997, while the mixed all-inclusive/European plan properties had 8.8 per cent of rooms, European plan rooms were 33.1 per cent and the rest were concentrated in guesthouses, villas and apartments.

The all-inclusive concept is premised on the assumption of high occupancy rates and very little contact outside of the hotels, which limits the encounter between tourists and the community. While in the short run such establishments avoid the problems of harassment and crime, they limit the capacity of the industry to spread benefits outside the controlled environment of the all-inclusive hotel. In addition to the concentration of rooms within a limited number of accommodation types, resort area activities are limited, with very little links to the community.

It should be made clear that despite the emphasis on all-inclusives, as much as 36 per cent of hotel rooms in Jamaica are in small and medium-sized hotels. These types of accommodation have been doing badly when compared to the large all-inclusive hotels. Therefore, the challenge to the Jamaican tourist industry is to find a way to attract more tourists to these small and medium-sized non-all-inclusive hotels, thereby spreading the benefits of tourism to the wider society.

The tourists who are most likely to be attracted to these types of accommodation are European tourists. This category of tourist generally prefers smaller, more intimate settings and greater interaction with the community. This type of tourism tends to bring greater benefits to the larger society, since people outside the hotel often provide additional services to the tourists, unlike the case of the all-inclusives where all of the needs of the tourist are catered to inside the hotel. However, given the results of our study, for this type of tourism to take off the perception of Jamaica as a high-crime destination has to be changed, especially among European tourists.

The all-inclusive sector has been both a blessing (mitigating the impact of destination difficulties, such as high crime) and a curse (reducing the need to deal with improving resort infrastructure and quality). For smaller hoteliers and the wider community to benefit more from tourism this vicious cycle has to be broken; the crime problem must be reduced, or Jamaica will become simply an all-inclusive destination. This type of tourism is likely to further alienate the wider community and perhaps lead to resentment against tourists and, ultimately, to more crime.

In conclusion, we are of the view that for the Jamaican tourism product to maximize its potential, especially in light of the large amounts of tax revenue spent on promoting the destination through advertising, the sector will need to diversify its market, especially in Europe. However, for this effort to succeed the crime rate has to be reduced and the perception of Jamaica as a high-crime destination changed, since these markets are likely to be even more crime sensitive than the non-European markets.

References

Alleyne, D., I. Boxill, and A. Francis. 1994. "Economic Reforms and Sustainable Development in Jamaica". Paper prepared for Institute of Social and Economic Research on behalf of the World Wide Fund for Nature.

Boxill, I. 1995. "Crime and Sustainable Tourism in Jamaica". Unpublished paper, University of the West Indies, Mona, Jamaica.

Butler, R.W. 1980. "The Concept of a Tourism Area Cycle of Evolution: Implications for Management of Resources". *Canadian Geographer* 24, no. 1.

Caribbean Tourism Organization. 2001. *Caribbean Tourism Statistical Report, 1999–2000.* St Michael, Barbados: Caribbean Tourism Organization.

Choy, D.J.L. 1992. "Life Cycle Models for Pacific Island Destinations". *Journal of Travel Research* 30, no. 3.

de Albuquerque, K., and J. McElroy. 1999. "Tourism and Crime in the Caribbean". *Annals of Tourism Research* 26, no. 4.

Dickey, D., and W. Fuller. 1979. "Distribution of the Estimates for Autoregressive Time Series with a Unit Root". *Journal of the American Statistical Association* 74 (June).

Dunn, H.S., and L.L. Dunn. 2002. *People and Tourism: Issues and Attitudes in the Jamaican Hospitality Industry.* Kingston, Jamaica: Arawak Publications

Dunn, L.L., and H.S. Dunn. 1994. "Report on Visitor Harassment and Attitudes to Tourism and Tourists in Negril". Paper prepared for the Tourism Action Plan, the Jamaica Tourist Board and the Negril Resort Board (December).

Edwards, A. 1987. *Choosing Holiday Destinations: The Impact of Exchange Rates and Inflation.* London: Economist Intelligence Unit.

Enders, W. 1995. *Applied Econometric Time Series.* New York: John Wiley and Sons.

Enders, W., T. Sandler, and A. Parise. 1992. "An Econometric Analysis of the Impact of Terrorism on Tourism". *Kyklos* 45.

Engle, R.F., and C.W.J. Granger. 1987. "Cointegration and Error-Correction: Representation, Estimation and Testing". *Econometrica* 55 (March).

Government of Jamaica. 1995. *Report on the Task Force on Tourism.*

Harriott, A. 2000. *Police and Crime Control in Jamaica: Problems of Reforming Ex-Colonial Constabularies.* Kingston, Jamaica: University of the West Indies Press.

Headley, B. 1994. *The Jamaican Crime Scene.* Mandeville, Jamaica: Eureka Press.

Hodrick, R., and E.C. Prescott. 1997. "Postwar US Business Cycles: An Empirical Investigation". *Journal of Money, Credit and Banking* 29, no. 1 (February).

Johansen, S. 1988. "Statistical Analysis of Cointegration Vectors". *Journal of Economic Dynamics and Control* 12.

Oglethorpe, M. 1984. "Tourism in Malta: A Crisis of Dependence". *Leisure Studies* 3.

Palmer, D., and M. Ramkisoon. 1998. "A Path Model to Predict Tourism Arrivals in Jamaica". Unpublished paper, Department of Sociology and Social Work, University of the West Indies.

Pattullo, P. 1996. *Last Resorts: The Cost of Tourism in the Caribbean.* Kingston, Jamaica: Ian Randle Publishers.

Planning Institute of Jamaica. 1998. *Economic and Social Survey of Jamaica.* Kingston, Jamaica: Planning Institute of Jamaica.

University of the West Indies (UWI). 1971. *Report of the Special Committee on Hotel Management.* Mona, Jamaica: University of the West Indies.

Appendix 7.1 Major Tourism Indicators, 1960–1999

Year	Total Visitors	Stopovers	Visitor Exp. M$US	Average Length of Stay	Ratio of Stopovers to Total Visitors	Exp. Per Visitor US$	Annual % Change in Visitor Exp.	Annual % Change in Total Visitors	Annual % Change in Stopovers
1960	226,945	80,420			35.4			-1.1	-5.5
1961	224,492	76,000			33.8			-7.9	3.3
1962	206,838	78,486			37.9			-2.2	3.1
1963	202,329	80,939			40.0			12.4	20.1
1964	227,417	97,230			42.7			32.0	80.8
1965	300,258	175,769			58.5			15.0	21.0
1966	345,288	212,673			61.5			-3.6	10.5
1967	332,838	235,025	57.8	8.6	70.6	173.7	26.6	19.1	10.0
1968	396,347	258,460	73.2	8.6	65.2	184.7	6.4	2.7	7.1
1969	407,105	276,929	77.9	8.5	68.0	191.4	2.2	1.9	11.6
1970	414,720	309,122	79.6	8.1	74.5	191.9	14.1	8.2	16.2
1971	448,564	359,323	90.8	8.1	80.1	202.4	18.8	10.0	13.5
1972	493,488	407,806	107.9	7.9	82.6	218.6	7.3	4.8	2.6
1973	517,410	418,257	115.8	8.3	80.8	223.8	15.3	2.6	3.5
1974	530,726	432,987	133.5	8.4	81.6	251.5	-3.6	4.2	-8.6
1975	553,258	395,809	128.7	8.8	71.5	232.6	-17.8	-14.9	-17.2
1976	470,714	327,706	105.8	8.6	69.6	224.8	-1.2	-17.9	-19.2
1977	386,514	264,921	104.5	8.7	68.5	270.4	41.8	37.9	44.1

1978	532,864	381,818	148.2	8.5	71.7	278.1	31.1	11.4	11.7
1979	593,571	426,540	194.3	8.8	71.9	327.3	24.4	-8.5	-7.3
1980	543,088	395,340	241.7	10.2	72.8	445.0	17.6	1.6	2.8
1981	551,878	406,355	284.3	10.0	73.6	515.2	18.6	21.4	15.1
1982	670,202	467,763	337.2	9.7	69.8	503.1	18.4	16.8	21.0
1983	782,943	566,151	399.2	9.2	72.3	509.9	1.9	7.8	6.6
1984	843,774	603,436	406.6	9.0	71.5	481.9	0.0	0.3	-5.3
1985	846,716	571,713	406.8	9.8	67.5	480.4	26.8	12.7	16.1
1986	954,621	663,593	516.0	10.2	69.5	540.5	15.3	8.7	11.3
1987	1,037,634	738,827	595.0	10.1	71.2	573.4	-11.4	-1.7	-7.3
1988	1,020,293	684,873	527.1	10.3	67.1	516.6	12.5	14.0	4.4
1989	1,163,236	714,771	593.0	11.0	61.4	509.8	24.8	6.3	17.6
1990	1,236,075	840,777	740.0	10.9	68.0	598.7	3.2	8.4	0.5
1991	1,340,516	844,607	764.0	11.0	63.0	569.9	12.3	16.6	7.6
1992	1,563,097	909,010	858.0	11.0	58.2	548.9	9.8	3.4	7.7
1993	1,616,340	978,715	942.0	11.0	60.6	582.8	3.3	4.8	12.2
1994	1,693,323	1,098,287	973.0	10.7	64.9	574.6	9.9	3.5	4.4
1995	1,752,179	1,147,001	1,069.0	10.9	65.5	610.1	5.5	3.9	1.3
1996	1,820,627	1,162,449	1,128.0	11.1	63.8	619.6	1.1	4.6	2.6
1997	1,903,893	1,192,194	1,140.0	10.8	62.6	598.8	4.9	-0.3	2.8
1998	1,898,977	1,225,287	1,196.0	10.9	64.5	629.8		6.0	1.9
1999	2,012,738	1,248,397	1,233.0	10.3	62.0	612.6			

Source: Planning Institute of Jamaica, *Economic and Social Survey of Jamaica* (various years).

Appendix 7.2   Percentage Hotel Room Occupancy, 1980–1994

Year	All Jamaica	Montego Bay	Ocho Rios	Negril	Kingston St Andrew	Port Antonio	Mandeville
1980	44.2	44.8	42.1	65.1	41.2	28.4	42.2
1981	41.5	35.9	45.4	56.3	52.1	22.7	43.0
1982	53.3	51.0	55.9	63.1	60.6	25.7	37.0
1983	58.6	63.1	61.5	74.6	55.9	20.8	37.8
1984	60.4	61.0	65.8	74.8	49.8	23.6	35.2
1985	51.6	52.2	57.7	69.2	36.2	24.9	24.5
1986	57.0	61.2	62.1	74.2	34.6	28.5	35.2
1987	61.7	66.6	66.0	68.5	40.4	38.1	33.4
1988	56.5	58.6	57.8	61.3	48.3	35.7	40.2
1989	59.1	59.0	61.6	70.1	51.3	21.7	41.1
1990	62.0	59.6	70.2	68.6	52.4	23.2	40.4
1991	57.9	56.0	63.1	67.8	45.0	22.2	48.6
1992	60.1	58.9	63.5	70.9	46.5	27.5	46.2
1993	60.3	57.2	66.4	71.1	44.0	32.4	40.5
1994	57.3	49.9	65.0	66.0	52.2	29.0	39.2
1995	60.8	54.9	67.0	67.6	59.0	26.1	37.2
1996	57.7	53.2	64.5	63.5	57.7	22.6	32.6
1997	55.7	54.8	60.7	61.4	45.2	23.4	31.7
1998	58.5	59.6	63.2	62.6	47.2	23.3	37.7

Source: Planning Institute of Jamaica, *Economic and Social Survey of Jamaica* (various years).

Appendix 7.3 Alternative Product Cycle Curves

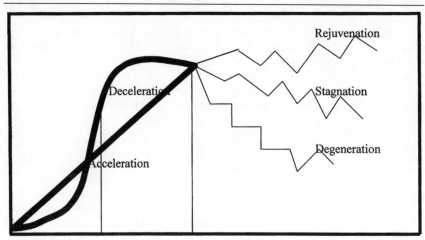

Source: R.W. Butler, "The Concept of a Tourism Area Cycle of Evolution: Implications for Management of Resources", *Canadian Geographer* 24, no. 1 (1980).

Appendix 7.4

The current methodology employs the Hodrick-Prescott filter (1997), which is a smoothing method used to obtain estimates of the long-term trend component of a series. This method begins with the assumption that a time series y_t is the sum of a growth component g_t and a cyclical component c_t, thus $y_t = g_t + c_t$ for t=1,....,T (Hodrick and Prescott 1997). The growth path of g_t is the sum of squares of the second difference, while the c_t's are deviations from g_t, which over long periods is expected to be near zero. The problem is then set out as follows:

$$\min_{\{g_t\}_{t=-1}^{T}} \left\{ \sum_{t=1}^{T} c_t^2 + \lambda \sum_{t=1}^{T} [(g_t - g_{t-1}) - (g_{t-1} - g_{t-2})]^2 \right\}$$

Note that λ is a positive number which penalizes variability in the growth component series so that the larger it is the smoother the series. Hodrick and Prescott show that for a sufficiently large lamda, at the optimum all the $g_{t+1} - g_t$ must be arbitrarily near some constant β and therefore g_t is near $g_o + \beta t$. The implication is that as lambda tends to infinity the limit of the solution is a trend line. Of course the criticisms of such statistical techniques are that they do not consider informed knowledge and other sources of information about trends.

8

Perceptions of Crime and Safety among Tourists Visiting the Caribbean

John W. King

Tourism has been and continues to be a driving force in Caribbean economies. In recent years tourism has become the single most important source of revenue for the region, generating in 1998 US$14.7 billion for some 35 million people. Between 1980 and 1997 tourist arrivals (stayovers) in the Caribbean grew at an average annual rate of 4.8 per cent (*Travel Industry World Yearbook 1998–99*). Throughout the Caribbean the livelihood of residents is heavily dependent on tourism. Some 24.7 per cent of jobs are directly or indirectly tourism related (*Travel Industry World Yearbook 1998–99*).

> Tourism provides not just direct employment in hotels, casinos, restaurants, shops and transport, but also indirect employment in the services and industries spawned by the industry. It also fuels a peripheral 'informal' economic belt where the poor and unskilled strive to earn an income from selling or providing services to tourists on a casual basis. (Pattullo 1996, 52)

As one commentator states, "So phenomenal has been industry growth in recent decades, in fact, that tourism is now 'the tail that wags the dog' in virtually all the Caribbean countries and, increasingly, in Central America, as well" (Goethals 1993, 31).

Tourism itself is a fragile industry, precariously balanced and subject to sudden shifts. Various factors, many of which are unpredictable and not subject to long-term planning, affect the success or failure of the tourism industry throughout the Caribbean region. A particularly devastating hurricane that does significant damage to island infrastructures can set back tourist revenues for several seasons following the disaster. Political instability involving either domestic or international political tensions (sometimes accompanied by violence) can also deter potential visitors to a country or region of the world (Fish and Gunther 1994). The United States Department of State, for instance, issues travel advisories to its citizens identifying places where the level of danger to travellers may reach unacceptable levels. Regardless of the particular problems facing a tourist destination – natural disasters, political instability, or street crime and violence – the effects are the same: a decline in visitors and the accompanying decline in tourist revenues.

Tourism in less developed countries has thrived in places where there is political stability, an adequate infrastructure (roads, water supply, utilities service, airports) and labour force, natural attractions, sufficient accommodation, and the absence of serious social problems which would threaten the safety of visitors. Crime and violence that targets both residents and visitors is one of the more important social factors that impact the tourism industry. It is no surprise, therefore, that government leaders, tourism officials and travel professionals take seriously any potential threat to the life-blood of these delicate economies. Press coverage of incidents that promote a negative image of a tourist destination can quickly spread to the key tourist markets. These images, real or imagined, can paint a picture of a potentially dangerous place where any risk, however remote, is perceived as real and is likely to be a factor in tourist decision making with regard to selecting a vacation destination.

Crime and Tourism: A Brief Review of the Literature

In examining the connection between crime and tourism, a number of questions can be posed. Do crime rates affect rates of tourist arrivals or do rates of tourist arrivals impact levels of crime? Do high levels of crime deter potential tourists from visiting a particular country? Does the deterrent impact vary by type of crime? Does it depend on whether

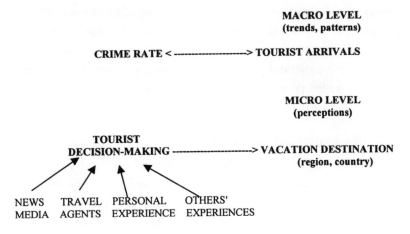

Figure 8.1   Safety Issues and Tourist Travel

tourists themselves are victimized at these vacation spots? Are other factors besides crime more important in choosing a vacation destination? How aware are tourists concerning the actual danger at various tourist destinations? What sources of information do tourists rely on when assessing the potential dangers of travelling to popular vacation destinations?

These questions and others all concern the relationship between crime and tourism, but the path of inquiry takes the researcher in different directions depending on the nature of the question. In order to clarify these divergent paths, one might conceptualize the crime-tourism relationship at two levels (see figure 8.1). At the *macro level,* one might posit that high rates of crime, especially violent crime, result in declines in tourist arrivals. One might further speculate that crimes targeting tourists have an even greater impact on tourist arrivals than crimes against residents of the host country. In addition, it is quite likely that a reciprocal effect may occur – that is, as more tourists flock to a particular destination, there exist more opportunities for criminal victimization of these "suitable targets", resulting in higher rates of crime.

At the *micro level* of analysis, individual *perception* is central in understanding the decision-making process of tourists. This level of inquiry may suggest that despite high levels of crime (or other potential dangers to tourists), tourists may create a perception for themselves that there exists little or no risk in visiting a particular place. How they arrive at this conclusion may vary from person to person. Thus, one might observe significant increases or decreases in vacation destination choices based on the images of a place that are convincing to a large segment of the travelling public. We now turn to a review of the crime-tourism literature that examines this relationship at the two levels of analysis.

Crime Rates and Tourist Arrivals

Only recently has the relationship between crime and tourism been examined in the empirical literature. Interestingly, the majority of these studies have appeared in tourism-related publications rather than the criminological or sociological academic literature. While the relationship between crime and tourism may at times seem obvious, the literature reveals mixed findings. In a frequently cited article that was among the first in this line of inquiry, Jud (1975) examined the impact of foreign tourist business on the crime rate for each of the thirty-two Mexican states. He found that major crimes against property (fraud, larceny and robbery) were strongly related to tourism, but crimes against persons (assault, murder, rape, abduction and kidnapping) were only marginally associated with foreign business travel (Jud 1975, 328). McPheters and Stronge (1974) also found that tourism contributed to levels of property crime during the tourist season in Miami, Florida. A similar seasonality effect was found in the study of resort destinations in Australia done by Walmsley, Boskovic and Pigram (1983).

Some study methodologies have allowed the examination of tourist victimization rates rather than an overall crime rate for a particular geographic area. Chesney-Lind and Lind (1986) in their study of crime against tourists in Hawaii found that tourists in both urban and rural settings were significantly more likely than local residents to be victims of crime. The authors suggest that the patterns are probably due to tourist behaviour, opportunity factors and the structure of the tourism industry. Schiebler, Crotts and Hollinger (1996), in a study involving the ten most visited counties in Florida, also found higher rates of tourist victimization in urban areas (in this case Dade county) and in areas where opportunities for crime are likely to occur. In fact, the majority of empirical studies that examine the impact of tourism on crime use either a "routine activities" (Felson and Cohen 1980) or a "hot spots"

(Sherman, Gartin and Beurger 1989) theoretical framework in interpreting patterns. Both approaches enjoy support in the handful of studies that examine this relationship (Crotts 1996).

In a recent study of crime and tourism in the Caribbean, de Albuquerque and McElroy (1999) were able to examine victimization rates for residents and visitors to Barbados for several property and violent crimes. Consistent with previous studies, they found tourist (or visitor) victimization to be greater for certain property crimes, most notably robbery and personal larceny. Their data suggest that tourists are between four and six times as likely to be robbed than residents. However, unlike some of the previous studies they found no seasonal effect for tourist victimization.

Despite what we might call mixed support for the crime-tourism relationship in the studies cited above, several other studies have found no significant relationship. For instance, in a study that examined the relative impact of tourism (along with a variety of sociodemographic variables) on the crime rate for the fifty states in the United States Pizam found that "tourism has very little or no effect at all on crime" (1982, 10). The author does suggest, however, that these national effects may mask associations between tourism and crime at the community level. Similarly, Pelfrey (1998) found little association between the volume of visitors to Las Vegas, Nevada, and Honolulu, Hawaii (two popular tourism destinations), and the overall crime rate during an eleven-year period. He concludes that "taken as a whole and considering both cities, the data fail to support the justification for fear of or the anecdotal reporting of tourist-related crimes" (301).

The Mass Media and Tourist Decision Making

While much of the often-cited literature on crime and tourism examines the relationships discussed above, the concerns for traveller safety expressed in news stories and anecdotal accounts from tourists rely on individual travel experiences and the perceptions created around these personal accounts. The travel industry takes seriously the impact of these accounts and the potential for negative publicity surrounding incidents of crime and violence at tourist destinations. Central to this line of inquiry are two key questions: Do people consciously consider crime when they evaluate destinations in their travel plans? Do perceived levels of crime in resorts influence travel decisions? (Mathieson and Wall 1982). Studies which examine these issues almost always rely on surveys soliciting the opinions and experiences of travellers, law enforcement officials and individuals employed in the tourist industry. In addition, some studies have analysed the impact of the news media on public perceptions of safety, using content analysis techniques on popular news sources. Referring again to figure 8.1, this *micro level* emphasizes the sources of information that tourists rely on when assessing the relative benefits of one tourist destination over another and making their ultimate selection of a vacation destination.

Demos (1992), in a study that examined the perceptions of safety among tourists visiting Washington, D.C., concluded that the notoriously high violent crime rate in that city was a significant concern for tourists. While most respondents (96.7 per cent) felt that Washington was safe during the day, they tended to travel in groups at night or to remain in their hotel rooms. When asked, "How safe do you feel at night?", 38.8 per cent replied, "Not safe at all", and 20.6 per cent answered, "It all depends. . ." (83). Demos also reports crime and tourism statistics that parallel the concerns expressed by his respondents: during the period 1987–90 crime had increased in Washington and the number of visitors had declined. He attributes these patterns to the perceptions of this city as an unsafe place.

The mass media are without a doubt a powerful force in the shaping of attitudes and opinions. The importance of this force has grown in recent years with the advent of instantaneous communication via satellite relays, the Internet and other digital forms. Given the public's desire for more information more quickly, one can now obtain a wealth of information including news from around the world.

Crime has always been a mainstay news item, regardless of location. One quickly realizes, however, that the actual incidence of crime at a particular time and place is not always in proportion to the public perceptions of risk and safety created by news accounts. Pizam, Tarlow and Bloom (1997, 23) state, "The media traditionally have highly publicized crimes against international tourists in a given destination, even when the number of such crimes are [sic] constantly decreasing. Such media coverage often results in panic among potential visitors." In these cases "perception becomes reality".

An early study by Cuthbert and Sparkes (1978) sought to document the coverage of Jamaica in the US and Canadian press. Using content analysis techniques with a sample of major US and Canadian newspapers, the researchers coded a total of 272 stories for the study period (1976–77). Stories were coded as portraying Jamaica in favourable (positive), unfavourable (negative) or neutral terms. The majority of stories portrayed Jamaica negatively (US = 70.4 per cent, Canada = 73.5 per cent). The most popular news stories were on the topics of "politics" (US = 40.2 per cent, Canada = 39.8 per cent) and "violence/crime" (US = 35.4 per cent, Canada = 51.8 per cent), out of ten topical categories.

Cuthbert and Sparkes supplemented their mass media data with interviews of travel agents in order to better understand the mass media effects on tourist travel. All of the Canadian travel agents and 84 per cent of the American travel agents said that press coverage did affect their clients' interest in travelling to Jamaica in 1976. The newspaper was perceived by the majority of agents to be the medium having the most influence. While half of the Canadian travel agents believed that the press exaggerated the situation, only one-fifth of the American agents expressed this belief (Cuthbert and Sparkes 1978, 216).

A unique study titled "Survey on Crime against Tourists" was commissioned by the Barbados Hotel Association and conducted by Applied Marketing Consultants (1994), an independent research firm in Barbados. The final report contains findings from surveys that solicited the opinions of tourists, law enforcement officials and hotel staff on the issue of crime and safety among tourists visiting Barbados. Among the many areas covered in this multifaceted examination of crime and tourism, two are of particular interest to the present study: the reporting of crime in the media and tourists' experiences and concern about crime: "The majority of law enforcement officials, especially the police (71.4%), felt that reporting of crime by the media in Barbados was too sensational . . . just over one-half (50.5%) of the tourists read about crime in Barbados in a newspaper and a further 48.4% heard about it from a friend/relative" (1–7). Interestingly, although all three groups surveyed expressed concern about crime in Barbados, tourists were less concerned than either law enforcement officials or hotel staff. Of hotel staff, 98.2 per cent said they were "very concerned" about crime against visitors, while 94.4 per cent of law enforcement officers expressed this attitude. The figure for the sample of tourists (47.5 per cent) indicates that there is significantly less concern for safety. It is often said that visitors to a new place, especially a foreign country, are naïve about the potential dangers of their new surroundings, especially while on vacation.

The Current Study

The present study examines the importance of crime and related safety issues in the travel industry. Specifically, we seek to understand the sources of information tourists rely on when planning their vacations, and how these sources shape perceptions of the relative safety of various travel destinations.

Sample and Methods

During fall 2000 a survey was mailed to a random sample of 175 professional travel agencies in New York, New Jersey, Illinois and Florida. These states were selected based on the fact that they are among the most important states in the US travel market for Caribbean vacations. The Airline Reporting Corporation (ARC), based in Arlington, Virginia, provided a random listing for these states from their client database of 39,460 retail travel agencies. ARC is a not-for-profit organization owned by the major US airline carriers, and is the leading financial transaction processing and settlement corporation that facilitates the distribution of travel products and related information.

In addition to the ARC sample, a convenience sample (n = 25) was drawn from metropolitan Cleveland, Ohio, through a selection of travel agencies listed in the telephone directory. Of the two hundred surveys sent to the travel agencies, forty-six were returned (after a follow-up letter). Two surveys were omitted because it was indicated that Caribbean travel was not a part of the agency's business (one travel agency was a "European only" agency). Although the final sample of forty-four is lower than expected or desired, the sample is sufficient to shed light on the key issues of travel safety.

Results

The travel agents who participated in this survey had an average of 13.6 years of experience as professional travel agents. Their years of experience ranged from three to thirty-one. For this sample the average percentage of travel bookings involving trips to Caribbean destinations is 32 per cent. Travel agents also reported that among their clients booking Caribbean vacations, 48 per cent booked at "all-inclusive" resorts and 52 per cent booked "other accommodations". This question was included because of the safety implications of various types of accommodations.

When asked to rank in order of importance (1 = most important) the reasons why clients book at all-inclusive resorts, travel agents listed "attractive pricing" as the most important (mean score = 2.47), followed by "convenience" (2.51). The third most important reason was "reputation of resort" (2.63). Clearly, safety is not a primary factor in selecting this type of accommodation. Most respondents (61 per cent) ranked "safety" fifth most important out of six options (mean score = 4.33). First-time clients may not be aware of the "safety factor" of all-inclusive resorts, that is, the fact that one need not venture beyond the resort for most needs.

In order to determine how perceptions of safety are formed, travel agents were asked to report on the sources of information clients use in planning Caribbean travel. Again, respondents were asked to rank in order of importance six sources of information (resort brochures, newspaper/news magazine articles, Internet sites, travel agents, personal accounts from friends/family and "other"). The various sources may contain a variety of types of information including travel tips, personal travel accounts and travel package options. The respondents indicated that travel agents were the most important source of travel information (mean score = 1.9). Only a few individuals assigned a low level of importance to this source. Personal accounts from family or friends were listed as the second most important source of travel information (2.32), followed by resort brochures (2.79). It should be noted that travel brochures by definition paint a very attractive picture of a travel destination, while the other sources listed on the survey may create either a positive or a negative image. Interestingly, newspaper and news magazine articles were considered a minor source of travel information

Table 8.1   "Based on your experiences as a travel agent (and tourist), how
            important is the issue of crime and safety among tourists visiting
            Caribbean destinations?"

a. Very important = 47.7%
b. Somewhat important = 41%
c. A minor concern = 11.3%
d. Not important at all = 0%

(mean score = 3.3). It is perhaps not surprising that travel agents consider themselves a key source of travel information for their clients.

Several questions in the survey concerned attitudes about and experiences with tourist victimization. We first attempted to gauge the general "fear factor" by asking about their perceptions of the risk to travellers today. When asked how important the issue of crime and safety was among tourists visiting Caribbean destinations, 47.7 per cent of the respondents replied "very important" and 41 per cent said "somewhat important" (see table 8.1). Thus, 88.7 per cent believed that the issue was important to some extent. Another item posed the question, "In your opinion, does the issue of crime and safety among travellers to the Caribbean depend in part on the specific island destination?" Here, 93 per cent replied "yes" and 7 per cent said "no". It is important to note that individual countries were not specifically mentioned in the survey, so as to not prejudice respondents. The responses to this question will become clearer when individual comments by some travel agents are considered.

Two questions attempted to measure changes in tourist safety among international travellers. The results are reported in tables 8.2 and 8.3. The figures in table 8.2 clearly show a consensus on the increased concern for tourist safety: 75 per cent of the respondents believe that the issue of tourist safety *generally* has become more important. The same question was asked concerning travel to the Caribbean region (see table 8.3). Most travel agents stated that the issue really had not changed in recent years (55 per cent), and 43 per cent indicated that the issue had become more important. It appears that travel agents agree that there are many dangers that may befall unwary travellers in various parts of the world but that the situation in Caribbean countries has remained much the same.

Table 8.2   "In your estimation, how has the issue of crime and safety among tourists *generally* (any part of the world) changed in recent years?"

a. The issue has become more important = 75%
b. The issue really hasn't changed = 25%
c. The issue has become less important = 0%

Table 8.3   "In your estimation, how has the issue of crime and safety among tourists to the *Caribbean* changed in recent years?"

a. The issue has become more important = 43%
b. The issue really hasn't changed = 55%
c. The issue has become less important = 2%

The figures mentioned above become clearer when considering some of the individual comments in response to "briefly explain your answer". Respondents who assessed changes in travel safety worldwide seemed to imply that the mass media were a significant factor in shaping public attitudes, as the following comments suggest:

R35: "TV and media coverage of current world events influence travellers today more than they did five years ago."

R34: "I am getting more inquiries from people about safety. People are more aware of safety around the world and question when destinations are in the news."

R11: "Today travellers are more aware of news around the world and they pay attention to government warnings."

R43: "As more information becomes available through the media, more people learn about it. Also, more people are travelling now."

R29: "The media has really hit on stories of crime and victimization among tourists. With more people travelling overseas, it's been in the press a lot."

R14: "News is more sensationalized – one incident gets coverage for days if it is on the news . . . then *20/20,* then *60 Minutes,* then *Dateline.*"

Whether or not these travel agents believe that the news is being accurately and responsibly reported, there appears to be agreement on its impact and the possible effects on tourist decision making. Some of the comments concerned particular countries or regions of the world. These comments reflect both positive and negative attitudes:

R22: "There are some spots, i.e., Holy Land, some Caribbean islands, parts of Mexico, where some people find it [the issue of crime and safety] has become more important."

R36: "Jamaica is the only island people ask about safety as well as Iran and Iraq – but we don't sell that area."

R30: "The Caribbean has always been a safe destination. A lot of their economy depends on tourism so they've made sure it's safe."

R5: "I find the Caribbean very safe – been to 15 islands and never had a problem. Then again, I never travel alone and practice safety."

R17: "Jamaica and Mexico generally get maximum coverage on tourist problems – even though they are considered safe by us."

R18: "There is more crime in some Caribbean islands that you (as a travel agent) have to mention to the clients so they are aware."

R37: "I believe the Caribbean islands have made a strong effort in recent years to lessen the 'harassment' aspect. I personally have been to a number of islands and never had any problems."

R6: "Most of our clients consider the Caribbean 'safe' as opposed to Europe or Asia."

The last group of questions constitutes the core inquiry into criminal victimization among tourists. Here travel agents are asked about their clients' concerns and experiences with victimization. Three questions deal with the frequency and nature of tourists' fear of crime. When asked if their clients have expressed concerns about crime and safety when travelling in the Caribbean, 14 per cent of the travel agents said "frequently" and 63 per cent replied "occasionally" (see table 8.4). Thus, fully 77 per cent of the respondents stated that their clients expressed some level of concern for their safety while planning trips.

A follow-up question was asked that inquired about the nature of these concerns (for those who responded "frequently" or "occasionally" to the previous question). The figures in table 8.5 indicate that the primary concern among travellers visiting the Caribbean is being the target of harassment (79 per cent). Survey respondents were given the following definition of harassment to ensure uniformity in interpretation: "being approached by overly aggressive vendors or others attempting to sell something". The media have covered this issue extensively, so it is not surprising that travel agents are knowledgeable about

Table 8.4   "Have clients planning to visit the Caribbean expressed concerns to you about crime and safety issues during their stay?"

a. Frequently = 14%
b. Occasionally = 63%
c. Rarely = 21%
d. Never = 2%

Table 8.5   "If you answered 'frequently' or 'occasionally' to the previous question, what are the nature of these concerns?" (check all that apply)[a]

a. Theft of money or property = 66.6%
b. Assaults = 36.3%
c. Sexual assaults = 12%
d. Harassment = 79%
e. Drug-related activity = 63.6%
f. Other (please specify) = 9%

[a] Because respondents could select multiple items, percentages do not add to 100.

this threat to tourist satisfaction. While harassment is not a criminal act in the traditional sense, it remains a major issue in the tourist industry. Theft of property or money (66.6 per cent) was listed as the next major concern followed by drug-related activity (63.6 per cent). Travel agents and Caribbean law enforcement officials often warn visitors, especially first-time visitors, that drug possession is illegal in these countries, despite what tourists might believe to the contrary. This is especially the case for marijuana or ganja.

The basis for the concerns expressed above stems from a variety of sources. Eighty-six per cent of respondents said that stories in the mass media were behind the fears of their clients (see table 8.6). This finding is consistent with the individual comments mentioned previously. Information gleaned from the travel experiences of friends and family were also considered an important source in assessing the risk of victimization.

Finally, respondents were asked about their knowledge of *actual accounts* of criminal victimization among travellers visiting Caribbean destinations. The figures are reported in table 8.7 and show that nearly one-third of the sample (30.2 per cent) had no personal knowledge of tourist victimization. Among those travel agents who could recount victimization incidents, 55.8 per cent reported that "harassment" occurred

Table 8.6   "For those travellers expressing concern for their safety, on what do they base these concerns?" (check all that apply)[a]

a. stories in the news media = 86%
b. prior personal experience = 32.5%
c. knowledge of friends/family experiences = 55.8%
d. other (please specify) = 4.6%
e. don't know = 9.3%

[a] Because respondents could select multiple items, percentages do not add to 100.

Table 8.7   "Based on *actual accounts* of travellers known to you, what have been their experiences with tourist victimization at Caribbean destinations?" (Check all that apply)[a]

a. N/A (no personal knowledge of victimization = 30.2%
b. theft of property/money = 44.1%
c. non-sexual assaults = 9.3%
d. sexual assaults = 2.3%
e. harassment = 55.8%
f. approached to buy drugs = 46.5%
g. other (please specify) = 4.6%

[a] Because respondents could select multiple items, percentages do not add to 100.

and 46.5 per cent listed "being approached to buy drugs", closely followed by "theft of property/money" (44.1 per cent). Interestingly, these figures of actual victimization closely resemble the "fear of crime" figures reported in table 8.5.

Discussion

The survey results reported in the previous section allow one to draw some general conclusions about the issues concerning tourist safety. An assumption of this paper, on which conclusions are based, is that it is not crime rates *per se* but rather the perceptions of the risk of criminal victimization that are behind the decisions tourists make in planning their vacations (King 1998). Given the pervasive nature of mass communications and worldwide news coverage, it is not surprising that stories in the news media were identified by a significant majority of travel agents as the primary basis for concerns about travel safety. Headlines in the United States such as "Crime Driving Jamaicans out of Their Homes" (Chacon 1999); "Rising Crime in Bahamas Could Threaten

Tourism" (Emling 1998); "Killings, Cocaine Hurt Bahamas Reputation" (Adams 1998); and "Jamaica Enlisting Soldiers to Curb Recent Crimes" (Bly 1999) all give the impression that these vacation destinations are unsafe places.

Particular incidents that become the subject of intense media scrutiny are likely to be relied on heavily when the public (both residents and visitors) assesses the safety of a place. Two recent events promoted a negative image of Jamaica and served to increase public fears of growing crime and disorder. During the spring of 1999 Jamaica experienced three days of nationwide riots in response to a government tax increase on gasoline. As a result nine people were killed, fourteen policemen injured, sixteen police vehicles damaged and more than 152 people arrested (*Sunday Gleaner*, 25 April 1999). The loss in tourist revenue, estimated at US$7.5 million, may turn out to be much more if Jamaica does not recoup its reputation as an attractive tourist destination. In response to the riots and a US State Department travel advisory, Minister of Tourism Francis Tulloch announced a massive advertising campaign on national cable television in the United States to repair Jamaica's image internationally (*Sunday Gleaner*, 25 April 1999).

More recently, the disappearance of an American travel journalist has resulted in intense media scrutiny. The ABC television news programme *20/20 Downtown* profiled the case on their 4 September 2000 broadcast. Numerous allegations and criticisms were directed at both the Sandals Resort in Negril (the site of the incident) and the producers of the news programme. Regardless of the truth of the allegations, the resulting image of the resort and of Jamaica generally was not favourable. This particular incident appeared in a front-page story in the leading travel industry publication *Travel Weekly* (Myers and Sidron 2000), along with a follow-up article one week later. It is likely that travel agents, who rely on these publications for important developments in the travel industry, are influenced by these sources when advising their clients. Thus, key incidents that are highly publicized are likely to be deciding factors in the formation of favourable or unfavourable perceptions concerning safety.

It should be noted that the world's attention at any given time is usually directed at a particular place, be it a country or a region. If all eyes and ears are riveted to the conflicts in the Middle East, for instance, there is likely to be less attention paid to other places. The perceptions of safety among travellers are thus relative to place and time. One region or country may be perceived as relatively safe, despite its problems with crime and violence, compared with another region or country that for the moment is "ground zero" for intense media scrutiny. These comparisons were confirmed in some of the individual comments offered by travel agents:

> R5: "It [the crime and safety] has only become more important in the areas of Europe/Middle East."

> R2: "Unrest in the Middle East and in some Central and South American countries has increased concern."

Recall also that travel agent respondents believed that the issue of crime and safety in the Caribbean depended in part on the specific island destination. This suggests that the entire Caribbean region is not tainted by negative publicity, but rather that specific nations are associated with incidents of crime and violence.

Some Suggestions for Tourist Safety

Much of the advice offered by experienced travellers and professional travel agents familiar with issues of tourist safety appears to be common sense. These common-sense guidelines, however, are often ignored by tourists caught up in the excitement of their long-awaited vacation escape. In fact, tourists travelling abroad may not follow basic principles of personal safety that they strictly adhere to in urban areas of their own country. The notion of familiarity no doubt explains part of this pattern. Americans, for instance, are quite knowledgeable about the potential dangers when visiting New York, New Orleans, Los Angeles, or Washington, D.C., but when they visit Barbados, Jamaica or the Bahamas they may let down their guard and become attractive targets for crime. Comments from two travel agents in the present study make this point:

> R13: "There is more awareness as to what you can do, what areas and situations you should avoid when you are travelling. The same is true in most places you live today. You have to be aware of your surroundings and to avoid certain situations."

R8: "I believe tourists seem to forget safety precautions when on vacations and are easy prey."

Part of the responsibility for preventing crime against tourists lies with tourists. Securing personal property and valuables, for instance, is essential to preventing theft. Many governments and their tourism agencies distribute booklets that provide safety guidelines for tourists, including police contact information. One such booklet, "Jamaica: Helpful Hints for Your Vacation", is provided by the Tourism Action Plan Limited in collaboration with the Jamaica Tourist Board. The booklet, printed in several languages, outlines "dos" and "don'ts" concerning the use of transportation services, hotel security, shopping and identifying law enforcement personnel. A reminder that the use, sale or possession of certain drugs is illegal in Jamaica and subject to strict enforcement also appears in the booklet. The education of tourists on the issue of tourist safety can also include liaisons with hotels and the use of television and other media outlets (see Applied Marketing Consultants 1994, 1–21).

A police force responsive to the needs of the tourism industry is essential in the prevention and control of crime against tourists. In this regard, the development of liaisons between the police and tourist establishments has been productive in Caribbean venues. The timely reporting of crime and the sharing of information result in greater public confidence and a more effective crime-control effort. The strategic placement of police patrol personnel both serves as a deterrent to crime through a highly visible presence and allows quick law enforcement intervention when incidents of harassment or other offences occur. Tourist areas in Caribbean countries are well defined because they usually include many hotels and other lodging options, shops and craft markets, natural and historic attractions, and restaurants. Given this high concentration of potential victims, Caribbean police forces usually deploy their resources accordingly.

Conclusion

Despite the fact that the actual risk of tourist victimization is remote, especially concerning serious crime, the results of this research suggest that the concern for tourist safety remains high. The examination of travel agents' attitudes towards and experiences with tourist victimization reveals that they perceive the threats to tourist safety as real, largely fuelled by extensive media coverage of particular incidents. Visitor harassment appears to be the primary concern, and has been the subject of extensive discussions within the Caribbean tourism industry. While harassment is comparatively benign as a form of tourist "victimization", the level of concern expressed by tourists suggests that it constitutes a significant threat to the tourism industry and, hence, to the economies of the Caribbean region. In order to better understand the nature and extent of tourist victimization and the fear of crime among visitors, Caribbean governments, tourism boards and the tourism industry itself need to collect the necessary data as a starting point for effective policy prescriptions. In this sense, the study commissioned by the Barbados Hotel Association (cited earlier) can serve as a model for other Caribbean venues. Only with the development of close working relationships guided by a common purpose will we see the improvement in tourist safety that is so vital for this industry to thrive.

References

Adams, D. 1998. "Killings, Cocaine Hurt Bahamas Reputation". *St Petersburg Times,* 29 August.

Applied Marketing Consultants. 1994. *Survey on Crime against Tourists.* Christ Church, Barbados: Applied Marketing Consultants.

Bly, L. 1999. "Jamaica Enlisting Soldiers to Curb Recent Crimes". *USA Today,* 29 January.

Chacon, R. 1999. "Crime Driving Jamaicans out of Their Homes". *Boston Globe,* 26 July.

Chesney-Lind, M., and I. Lind. 1986. "Visitors as Victims: Crimes against Tourists in Hawaii". *Annals of Tourism Research* 13.

Crotts, J.C. 1996. "Theoretical Perspectives on Tourist Criminal Victimization". *Journal of Tourism Studies* 7, no. 1.

Cuthbert, M., and V. Sparkes. 1978. "Coverage of Jamaica in the U.S. and Canadian Press in 1976". *Social and Economic Studies* 27, no. 2.

de Albuquerque, K., and J. McElroy. 1999. "Tourism and Crime in the Caribbean". *Annals of Tourism Research* 26, no. 4.

Demos, E. 1992. "Concern for Safety: A Potential Problem in the Tourist Industry". *Journal of Travel and Tourism Marketing* 1, no. 1.

Emling, S. 1998. "Rising Crime in Bahamas Could Threaten Tourism". *Atlanta Journal and Constitution*, 12 September.

Felson, M., and L. Cohen. 1980. "Human Ecology and Crime: A Routine Activity Approach". *Human Ecology* 8, no. 4.

Fish, M., and W. Gunther. 1994. "Small Island Economies, Tourism and Political Crises". In *External Linkages and Growth in Small Economies,* edited by D.L. McKee. Westport, Conn.: Praeger.

Goethals, H.W. 1993. "Competing for the Tourist $$". *North-South* (August–September).

Jud, G.D. 1975. "Tourism and Crime in Mexico". *Social Science Quarterly* 56, no. 2.

King, J.W. 1998. "The Impact of Crime on Tourism: The Case of Jamaica". Paper presented at the Annual Meeting of the American Society of Criminology, Washington, D.C., 14 November.

Mathieson, A., and G. Wall. 1982. *Tourism: Economics, Physical and Social Aspects*. London: Longman.

McPheters, L.R., and W. Stronge. 1974. "Crime as an Environmental Externality of Tourism: Miami, Florida". *Land Economics* 50 (August).

Myers, G., and J. Sidron. 2000. "Safety: How Cautious Should You Be?". *Travel Weekly,* 7 September.

Pattullo, P. 1996. *Last Resorts: The Cost of Tourism in the Caribbean*. London: Cassell.

Pelfrey, W.V. 1998. "Tourism and Crime: A Preliminary Assessment of the Relationship of Crime to the Number of Visitors at Selected Sites". *International Journal of Comparative and Applied Criminal Justice* 22, no. 2.

Pizam, A. 1982. "Tourism and Crime: Is There a Relationship?". *Journal of Travel Research* 20, no. 3.

———, P. Tarlow, and J. Bloom. 1997. "Making Tourists Feel Safe: Whose Responsibility Is It?". *Journal of Travel Research* (Summer).

Schiebler, S., J. Crotts, and R. Hollinger. 1996. "Florida Tourists' Vulnerability to Crime". In *Tourism, Crime and International Security Issues,* edited by A. Pizam and Y. Mansfeld. New York: John Wiley.

Sherman, L., P. Gartin, and M. Beurger. 1989. "Hot Spots of Predatory Crime: Routine Activities and the Criminology of Place". *Criminology* 27, no. 1.

Sunday Gleaner. 1999. "Protests Cost Tourism US$7.5m". 25 April.

Travel Industry World Yearbook, 1998–99. Spencertown, NY: Travel Industry Publishing.

Walmsley, D., Boscovic, R., and J. Pigram. 1983. "Tourism and Crime: An Australian Perspective". *Journal of Leisure Research* 15, no. 2.

9

Tourist Harassment
Review and Survey Results

Jerome L. McElroy

They are too poor to escape the reality of their lives; and they are too poor to live properly in the place where they live, which is the very place you, the tourist, want to go – so when the natives see you, the tourist, they envy you, they envy your ability to leave your own banality and boredom, they envy your ability to turn their own banality and boredom into a source of pleasure for yourself.

– Jamaica Kincaid, *A Small Place*

Citizens of the planet celebrated the millennium by travelling. According to World Tourism Organization forecasts, total international tourists numbered nearly 700 million and spent $476 billion in 2000 – drawn by the Summer Olympics, the European football championships, the Vatican Jubilee and other special events (Canadian Tourism Commission 2001). This turn-of-the-century travel peak was the culmination of four decades of steady 5 per cent annual postwar growth which has made tourism the largest industry in the world economy. The World Travel and Tourism Council estimates that the visitor industry now accounts for 13 per cent of global exports, 11 per cent of world gross domestic product, 9 per cent of capital investments and 8 per cent of total employment (WTTC 2001).

However, the short-run future outlook for global tourism is clouded by a variety of factors. First and foremost is the sharp slow-down in economic activity emanating from the United States and spreading across major origin markets in Europe and Asia. A second factor is the volatile fuel and energy market, always a danger to transport-intensive tourism. Third, the aftermath of the attack on the World Trade Centre in New York in September 2001, and the expected intensification of political instability in Northern Ireland, the Balkans, Eastern Europe and the Middle East, will likely dampen visitor demand because of the industry's high sensitivity to issues of safety and security. In addition to these external vagaries, contemporary tourism must address an endemic problem that has received scant attention. This is the escalation of tourist harassment in popular destinations across the world, that is, the badgering of visitors by vendors, hagglers, drug and sex peddlers, and would-be tour guides.

Literature

In the theoretical and empirical literature, "tourist harassment" is used in two basically different senses. In the active meaning, harassment commonly refers to visitors aggressively pursuing hosts for drugs and sex. This mainstream view emphasizes the one-way flow of power from the tourist to the host society. In the case of affluent Western visitors to less developed destinations, harassment is one dimension of such power that allegedly "produces negative consequences . . . materialistic consumerism, the commodification of culture, and the one-sided domination and exploitation of members of the visited society by the privileged class" (Cheong and Miller 2000, 372). Examples of this active visitor harassment approach abound in the case of drug demand in Greece (Haralambopoulos and Pizam 1996), the corruption of local women by sex tourism in South Korea (Young-Hee 1998), Thailand (Hall 1996) and India (Saad-Goa 1988), and even guest intrusion in private host space in Malta (Boissevain 1979).

In the passive or so-called Foucauldian view, the approach taken in this chapter, the visitor is portrayed as a target of influences exercised by a variety of tourist brokers. These include travel, transport and customs agents, hotel employees, and formal and informal guides and vendors touting their wares and services. In this sense, visitors are considered vulnerable and insecure, operating on unfamiliar cultural and sometimes linguistic turf and often "stripped of many of their cultural and familial ties and protective institutions" (Cheong and Miller 2000, 380). As a result of this ambiguous status, tourists find their comfort levels transgressed and their freedom circumscribed by local custom and commercial behaviour.

Although there is no consensus yet on the causes of harassment, certainly the service bias of the tourist industry itself, which depends on close personal host-guest interaction, creates a climate conducive to potential misunderstanding and harassment. Clearly a destination's poverty and dependence on tourism is a factor (Pattullo 1996). In addition, sharp visitor-resident socioeconomic and cultural discontinuities provide another major source of friction (Robinson and Boniface 1999). For example, the relatively rich North American tourist may easily take offence at the boisterous and persistent hawking of the relatively poor West Indian vendor, a practice considered socially acceptable by Caribbean norms (Burman 1998). Whatever the source, tourist harassment has cropped up recently as an industry irritant across the globe.

Scope

The present study has five parts. The first briefly reviews the incidence of harassment around the world. The second focuses on the Caribbean, the most tourism-dependent region and site of the most persistent problems. The third examines the case of Jamaica, where harassment has negatively affected the cruise economy. The fourth and most extensive section details results of multi-year harassment surveys in Barbados to improve understanding of this continuing worldwide phenomenon. The conclusion presents lessons and policy implications.

At the outset it should be mentioned that one reason research has lagged is the nature of harassment itself. In most destinations harassment is not considered a crime and therefore is not statistically tracked. Second, it is often subjective and hard to quantify objectively; what is good merchandising to the vendor is badgering behaviour to the visitor. Third, gathering evidence is difficult since perpetrators are often transients, and the burden of proof lies with the short-staying victims who, although bothered, may not feel the discomfort worth reporting. Finally, although tourism officials may know the general contours of the problem, they may be ineffective in controlling harassment because specific data on hot spots and the level, nature and impact of harassment are sorely lacking.

A Global Phenomenon

Visitor harassment is ubiquitous in popular destinations across the international tourist economy, and involves both official and popular types. In Indonesia, for example, British visitors and returning residents often have to bribe local immigration officials to avoid excessive transit detention, intrusive searches and other forms of harassment. In the process they are sometimes subjected to verbal abuse, shouting and character denigration (Jardine 2001). In the recent past tourists of Asian descent have faced similar delays in Vancouver, Canada, because they are often suspected of drug smuggling (Wood 1997). In Acapulco, US tourists, primarily those of Mexican descent, have been subjected to heavy fines and long interrogations by rogue federal police (AP online 2000). Even in the United States, Louisiana sheriff deputies have shaken down out-of-state motorists, who were stopped for routine traffic offences, for cash and property (McGinnis 1997).

However, even more intractable and universal than this type of official harassment is the badgering of tourists by persistent local souvenir hawkers, drug and sex peddlers, would-be tour guides and other hustlers. In Morocco, for example, the relentless harassment of visitors forced the government to clamp down by deploying special plainclothes police to imprison unlicensed (*faux*) tour guides and hustlers (Aizenman 1998). In Bali visitor complaints forced the government to restrict informal beach and street vendors to designated areas, since their presence was perceived as "undermining the quality of the tourist product" (Cukier 1998, 301). The situation has reached crisis proportions on some Kenyan beaches, where hotel guards are sometimes needed to rescue tourists from crowds of traders and beach boys (African News Service 2000). In one instance a hotel had to create its own private beach to curb harassment.

Elsewhere other forms of harassment proliferate. In Turkey the traditional complaint has been badgering by shopkeepers and restaurateurs. Kozak explains this classic clash of cultures this way: "While local shopkeepers see inviting tourists into their shops to buy something as a way to encourage business, Western tourists perceive this as being harassed, because in their culture the customer is expected to make the first move" (2000, 197). In Palestine, Bowman reports on the sexual badgering and exploitation of female visitors by merchants. He notes that in desperation the hassled woman "may, for relief, take up with one of them [the locals] simply to get the others to leave her alone" (1996, 92). Apparently the situation is similar in popular tourist areas in Greece (Zinovieff 1991). In the Northern Marianas sexual harassment of visitors has tarnished Saipan's image as a peaceful and wholesome destination for honeymooners and family travellers, and produced a crackdown on blatant solicitation and peddling escort services (Daleno 2001).

The Caribbean

Nowhere is tourism more important or harassment more visible than in the Caribbean. Conservatively, tourism accounts for 15–20 per cent of regional exports, gross domestic product, capital investment and employment (WTTC 2001). Over half of the world capacity of cruise berths plow these waters (Pattullo 1996, 157). In addition, the importance of tourism has grown markedly on the heels of a decade of unfavourable macroeconomic shocks. These include: the widespread loss of manufacturing investment and labour-intensive employment to Mexico because of NAFTA; the decline in traditional export markets through the consolidation of the European Union; the sharp drop in US aid with the fall of communism; and the recent threat by the Organization for Economic Cooperation and Development to blacklist many island offshore finance centres for allegedly encouraging European firms to escape taxation from their home jurisdictions.

Compounding these external constraints, the Caribbean travel industry itself is plagued by long-standing internal difficulties. The early postwar infrastructure needs refurbishment, but construction costs are 15–30 per cent higher than US levels (*Economist* 2000). The islands have never successfully mounted a sustained, distinctive region-wide marketing campaign to challenge their competitors (Hokstam 2001). The steady deterioration of the euro has blunted the growth of long-staying, high-spending European visitors. Most of all, the Caribbean has never fully embraced tourism because of an age-old ambivalence, perhaps best encapsulated in Trinidadian Eric Williams's preference for "black oil rather than white tourists" (*Economist* 2000, 66). As a result, without a total regional commitment to integrated tourism policy, John Bell, chief executive officer of the Caribbean Hotel Association, warns, "We are always going to be at the bottom of the food chain" (*Barbados Daily Nation* 2001, 2).

As a consequence of these problems, the Caribbean's worldwide comparative advantage deteriorated in the 1990s. The area lost ground to most rival developing regions, including the Middle East, Africa, East and South Asia, and the Pacific (WTO 1999). Rising crime and harassment also played a role in the region's competitive decline. In a survey of major US tour operators, the two most significant factors deflecting visitors away from the Caribbean were fear of crime and harassment (King 2001).

Such perceptions are not unfounded, since harassment by vendors has plagued a number of popular destinations. Police, augmented by armed plainclothes soldiers, have for years been routinely deployed in Jamaica to control harassment of cruise passengers along the north coast (*New York Times* 1999). In Barbados, with its long history of beach boys sexually harassing female tourists, wardens and uniformed police have also been dispatched periodically to beaches and popular nightclubs catering to visitors. In the recent past tourist complaints in Grenada became so serious that a major cruise line threatened to pull out (*Barbados Advocate* 1994). Even in Dominica, where cruise traffic growth has been among the most rapid in the region, harassment has become a major problem. To make visitors feel more comfortable, the legislature voted unanimously to criminalize harassment with fines of nearly US$400 and imprisonment of up to six months (AP Worldstream 2001).

Jamaica

Nowhere has harassment been more persistent and damaging than in Jamaica, where tourism accounts for roughly 15 per cent of gross domestic product and close to one in four jobs. Tourist badgering is an age-old problem. In the early twentieth century, for example, Taylor reports that police were sent to patrol the streets of Kingston to protect visitors from "beggars, unofficial tour guides and vendors . . . and magistrates fined and imprisoned the 'harassing masses'" (1993, 119). Harassment has escalated in recent decades with the expansion of the cruise trade, alongside flat and volatile performance in the non-tourist sectors.

The problem came to a head in 1997 when four cruise lines threatened to leave. A survey at the time indicated that 56 per cent of visitors were harassed by vendors to purchase souvenirs or drugs, badgered for sex, or pushed into taxis. Eight per cent said the experience spoiled their trip (McDowell 1998). The government's response was a fivefold increase in fines for prostitution, abusive or threatening language, indecent exposure, and unlicensed vending; also, police arrested a number of pimps, illegal vendors and taxi drivers (Carroll 1998).

Over the years the main private sector response has been to develop "all-inclusive" hotels where guests are protected on private beaches and facilities only accessible to residents through very high tariffs. Some argue that this "closing of the coastline" has deepened local resentment and intensified harassment, because it severely limits the income-earning opportunities of offsite (non-inclusive) merchants and service providers (Burman 1998). Despite continued official efforts to curb harassment, however, the situation has progressively deteriorated (Davis 2001). As a result, in mid-2001 three cruise lines, citing persistent passenger harassment, decided to drop Jamaica from their itinerary and to include ports in Mexico and Puerto Rico instead (Collins 2001).

Barbados Surveys

Applied Marketing Consultants

Harassment has long been a feature of the Barbados tourism landscape. What distinguishes this destination is official efforts to track its incidence and contours. This section reports the results of three visitor surveys that deal with harassment: a study of visitor perceptions of harassment, an extensive four-year analysis of patterns, and recent summary updates of the latter. In the first case, visitors rated harassment less seriously than local hotel workers and police (Applied Marketing Consultants 1994). However, 58 per cent of females and 39 per cent of males complained, primarily of persistent vendors. Most in the small sample (n = 200) were well-travelled visitors to the Caribbean and relatively young (two-thirds were under fifty years old).

Systems Caribbean Limited

A significantly larger multi-year visitor satisfaction survey was conducted quarterly between 1991 and 1994 and sampled over 9,000 visitors (Systems Caribbean Limited 1995). The detailed results, first recorded in de Albuquerque and McElroy (2001), are worth reporting because they clarify what seem to be the common patterns of harassment around the world. For example, 59 per cent of visitors to Barbados over the four-year survey span indicated experiencing some ("a lot" plus "a little") harassment. According to table 9.1 British tourists reported the highest incidence (69 per cent), largely because of their long average stay (and exposure) of roughly two weeks. Caribbean visitors reported the lowest level (24 per cent), undoubtedly because they were often mistaken by vendors for locals, similar in colour and culture/behaviour, and hence left alone.

Although there were no discernible differences in the level of harassment for male or female visitors (see table 9.1), the former were more likely to be pestered by drug peddlers while the latter were more likely to be harassed sexually. There is also some limited evidence that harassment is age-sensitive, since younger visitors (20–29 years) were three times more likely to report complaints than those aged 60 years and over. This difference largely reflects distinct vacation styles, that is, adventurous youth visiting several beaches and nightclubs versus older tourists either comfortable in their hotels or only venturing beyond their cocoons under the protection of guided tours.

Repeat visitors to Barbados were much less likely to report harassment (50 per cent) than first-time visitors (64 per cent). This difference would suggest that experienced visitors had become somewhat acculturated, knew which hot spots to avoid and perhaps had learned polite ways to deflect vendors. Not surprisingly, the survey also revealed much higher reporting of harassment by guests at south (61 per cent) and west (64 per cent) coast hotels – where most shopping, nightclubs and

Table 9.1   Percentage of Visitors Reporting Harassment by Visitor Characteristics, 1991–1994

Amount of Harassment	By Country of Origin				
	USA	Canada	UK	Other Europe	Caribbean
A Lot	10.6	10.5	20.5	14.0	5.0
A Little	41.9	45.0	48.3	39.3	18.9
A Lot + A Little	52.5	55.5	68.8	53.3	23.9
Not at All	46.4	43.6	30.6	42.5	70.7
No Response	1.1	0.9	0.4	4.2	5.4
Nos. Surveyed	3,516	1,794	3,160	788	516

	By Sex of Respondent	
	Male	Female
A Lot	13.2	13.9
A Little	42.8	41.1
A Lot + A Little	56.0	55.0
Not at All	40.6	41.6
Nos. Surveyed	4,870	4,579

	By Age of Respondent				
	20–29	30–39	40–49	50–59	60+
A Lot	16.8	13.6	10.2	4.3	0.0
A Little	55.8	50.8	45.5	39.1	23.1
A Lot + A Little	72.6	64.4	65.7	43.4	23.1
Not at All	25.4	34.7	44.3	52.2	76.9
No Response	2.0	0.9	0.0	4.4	0.0
Nos. Surveyed[a]	197	118	88	69	26

	By First or Repeat Visit	
	First Visit	Repeat Visit
A Lot	17.1	10.9
A Little	47.1	38.8
A Lot + A Little	64.2	49.7
Not at All	34.9	48.2
No Response	0.9	2.1
Nos. Surveyed	5,389	2,577

Table 9.1   Percentage of Visitors Reporting Harassment by Visitor
Characteristics, 1991–1994 (continued)

Amount of Harassment	By Geographical Location of Hotel		
	East Coast	South Coast	West Coast
A Lot	5.7	16.6	16.0
A Little	41.8	44.4	47.5
A Lot + A Little	47.5	61.0	63.5
Not at All	48.0	37.6	35.6
No Response	4.5	1.4	0.9
Nos. Surveyed	565	3,788	2,805

	By Type of Interview	
	Self-Administered Questionnaire	Interview Administered Questionnaire
A Lot	17.2	11.3
A Little	43.8	33.2
A Lot + A Little	61.0	44.5
Not at All	26.4	47.0
No Response	12.6	8.5
Nos. Surveyed	3,123	3,099

Source: Systems Caribbean Limited, 1991, 1992, 1993 and 1994.

[a] Based on one survey.

attractions are clustered – than by those staying on the east coast (48
per cent), where tourist infrastructure is quite limited. There was also a
significant difference in recorded harassment by type of interview. Self-
administered respondents reported 61 per cent, while interviewed
respondents reported only 45 per cent. This discrepancy may have been
partly due to the natural reluctance of white visitors to complain to
local black interviewers. It also suggests that actual harassment may
have been higher than recorded levels.

According to table 9.2, most harassment (70+ per cent) occurred at
the beach. The low level for Caribbean visitors (28 per cent) may not
only have been due to vendors' mistaking them for locals, but may also
have reflected their preferences for non-beach vacation activities. Other,
less popular locations for harassment were on public streets (49 per

Table 9.2   Percentage of Visitors Reporting Harassment by Country of Origin and Location of Harassment, 1991–1994

Harassment	Location	USA	Canada	UK	Other Europe	Caribbean
					Country of Origin	
	Beach					
Yes		70.3	76.0	76.1	74.4	28.1
No		21.1	22.9	22.7	21.8	63.1
No Response		8.6	1.1	1.2	3.8	8.8
Nos. Surveyed		792	467	1,104	188	57
	Streets					
Yes		47.2	54.2	56.5	50.0	38.6
No		50.5	45.2	42.1	44.7	50.9
No Response		2.3	0.6	1.4	5.3	10.5
Nos. Surveyed		792	467	1,104	188	57
	Town/Shopping					
Yes		39.5	38.3	48.6	31.4	33.3
No		58.2	61.2	50.0	61.7	57.9
No Response		2.3	0.5	1.4	6.9	8.8
Nos. Surveyed		792	467	1,104	188	57
	Hotel					
Yes		8.7	10.5	9.8	10.6	7.0
No		89.0	88.7	88.5	88.3	71.9
No Response		2.3	0.8	1.7	1.1	21.1
Nos. Surveyed		792	467	1,104	188	57

Source: Systems Caribbean Limited, 1991, 1992, 1993 and 1994.

cent) and while shopping in town (38 per cent). The comparatively high levels of harassment experienced by Caribbean visitors in these two venues may partly express the importance of shopping to West Indians on holiday. The uniformly low incidence of harassment at hotels (at 10 per cent) is indicative of the comparative security and protection hotels provide.

Table 9.3 records the main types of harassment by visitor country of origin. Clearly the most common complaint was the persistence of vendors without uniforms, usually on the beach, selling arts, crafts and

Table 9.3   Percentage of Visitors Reporting Harassment by Country of Origin and Type of Harassment, 1991–1994

| Harassment | Type of Harassment | Country of Origin | | | | |
		USA	Canada	UK	Other Europe	Caribbean
	Persistence of Vendors w/o Uniforms					
Yes		80.8	79.1	85.3	66.7	48.7
No		14.8	16.4	12.8	26.7	39.5
No Response		4.4	4.5	1.9	6.6	11.8
Nos. Surveyed		842	402	925	210	76
	Preference for Location of Vendors[a]					
On Beach		14.9	15.2	20.8	28.0	15.5
In Kiosks/Booths		76.6	76.7	70.6	53.5	68.7
No Response		8.5	8.1	8.6	18.5	15.8
Nos. Surveyed		2,804	1,469	2,554	600	355
	Peddling of Drugs					
Yes		27.1	27.1	27.7	31.2	15.0
No		67.4	70.3	70.6	64.7	67.7
No Response		5.5	2.6	1.7	4.1	17.3
Nos. Surveyed		1,609	852	2,005	397	133
	Verbal Abuse					
Yes		13.1	12.4	11.2	20.9	19.2
No		84.0	84.5	86.8	73.2	63.3
No Response		2.9	3.1	2.0	5.9	17.5
Nos. Surveyed		1,447	783	1,775	369	120
	Sexual Abuse					
Yes		6.8	10.5	7.4	11.9	7.7
No		90.0	86.6	90.4	81.8	75.2
No Response		3.2	2.9	2.2	6.3	17.1
Nos. Surveyed		1,447	775	1,775	369	117

Table 9.3   Percentage of Visitors Reporting Harassment by Country of Origin and Type of Harassment, 1991–1994 (continued)

| Harassment | Type of Harassment | Country of Origin | | | | |
		USA	Canada	UK	Other Europe	Caribbean
	Physical Abuse					
Yes		1.8	2.4	1.8	3.3	0.0
No		90.3	93.1	97.9	85.5	77.6
No Response		7.9	4.5	0.3	11.2	21.4
Nos. Surveyed		1,701	869	1,931	421	134

Source: Systems Caribbean Limited, 1991, 1992, 1993 and 1994.

[a] Although not a type of harassment, data were included on preference for location of vendors in this table since it follows from the most common type of harassment mentioned – persistence of vendors without uniforms.

clothing, coconuts and fruit, and other services (massages, hair braiding). Among white visitors "Other Europeans" appeared to be the most tolerant, perhaps because they are more used to goods and services being offered on the beach at Mediterranean and other warm-weather destinations. Survey data provided some support for this contention, since "Other Europeans" expressed the lowest preference (54 per cent as against 70+ per cent) for segregating vendors in booths or kiosks on the beaches. At a distant second, harassment from drug pushers was reported by 28 per cent of the sample. Such hustling is usually focused on young visitors, and peddlers' insistence can sometimes be frightening.

Visitors were also subjected to verbal abuse, especially related to vendor behaviour and circumstances surrounding commercial transactions; an average of 12 per cent of North American and British tourists experienced verbal abuse. The figures were considerably higher for "Other European" (21 per cent) and Caribbean visitors (19 per cent). In the former case some of the abuse may have been due to the frustration vendors, beggars and drug peddlers feel in attempting to communicate with non-English speakers. In the case of the latter, a number of other factors may have come into play. According to de Albuquerque and McElroy:

This is because, as the senior author has observed, they [Caribbean visitors] are more inclined to finger merchandise and bargain, and be less polite than white visitors. When vendors bristle and take offense, Caribbean visitors are less intimidated or reluctant to retort with a few harsh words of their own. (2001, 486)

Almost all incidences of sexual harassment were reported by female respondents. They ranged from 7 per cent of US visitors to 11–12 per cent of Canadian and European visitors. The higher rates reported for the latter two groups might be partly because Barbadian beach boys have traditionally viewed such women as sexually more liberated than their American and British counterparts, and hence more promising (and lucrative) targets (de Albuquerque 1999a). Given the ubiquity of beach boys seeking to proposition tourist women on Barbados beaches (de Albuquerque 1999b), it is possible that sexual harassment was under-reported in the survey. This remains difficult to control since many harassers have legitimate jobs on the beach, and it is difficult to prosecute since tourists often either fail to report or fail to return for trial when perpetrators are apprehended (Price 1993).

Finally, only 2–3 per cent reported experiencing physical abuse (table 9.3). This ranged from simple pushing to more serious assaults involving weapons, as in the commission of a robbery. Unlike other forms of harassment, physical abuse is likely to be a crime and thus much more likely to be reported. Previous research has indicated that visitors to Barbados are much more likely to be victims of property-related crime (theft, larceny, robbery) than of violent crime (murder, rape, serious assault) (de Albuquerque and McElroy 1999).

Caribbean Tourism Organization

Since the early surveys reported relatively high levels of harassment, Barbados tourism authorities recommended a number of control measures; these included the deployment of wardens on popular beaches and regular police patrols at tourist hot spots. They encouraged placing vendor kiosks and booths in designated beach areas, and worked with taxi drivers to organize queues. They also pushed for police training to better deal with visitor complaints. Perhaps as a partial result of these initiatives, reported harassment declined from 65 to 54 per cent over the four-year 1991–94 survey period.

In addition the industry decided to regularly monitor harassment in its routine Barbados Stayover Visitor Survey conducted by the Caribbean Tourism Organization. Early results from mid-1996 indicated patterns quite similar to the previous surveys. For example, close to 60 per cent of visitors reported harassment, mainly by overzealous vendors (CTO 2001). Much lower levels were recorded for drug peddling (27 per cent), verbal abuse (12 per cent) and sexual harassment (9 per cent). Less than 4 per cent of surveyed visitors were victims of crime, primarily the theft of personal property. As previously, most harassment took place on the beach and least occurred at hotel properties. However, somewhat higher levels were recorded for "on the streets" (46 per cent) and "in Bridgetown/shopping" (41 per cent). As earlier, European visitors reported the most harassment while Caribbean visitors reported the least.

Since 1996, however, harassment levels have risen somewhat. For example, average quarterly figures (unweighted) based on data from 1999 and 2000 combined indicate the following. Of those visitors harassed, 80 per cent complained of overzealous vendors, 45 per cent were pestered by drug peddlers, over 20 per cent experienced verbal abuse and roughly 16 per cent complained of sexual harassment (CTO 2001, 66–74). In most cases these numbers exceed earlier survey figures. In addition, the percentage of visitors reporting serious harassment – defined as "harassed a lot" – rose at lease five points between 1996 and 2000. On the other hand, less than 4 per cent of visitors reported being victims of crime, and Barbados continues to be overwhelmingly viewed as a safe or very safe holiday destination. The beach has remained the most common venue for harassment activity, followed by the streets, Bridgetown and other shopping areas, and least of all hotel properties. On the basis of the 1999–2000 data alone, no seasonal pattern of harassment was discernible.

Implications

The new millennium has been marked by the dominance of international tourism in the world economy, in terms of both size and sustained growth. Presently the industry suffers from the threat of US-induced global recession, rising energy and transport costs, increasing political instability, the potential fallout from terrorist activity, and – partly a victim of its own success – continuing visitor harassment. Despite its prevalence at popular destinations around the world, the causes of harassment remain understudied. Casual observation implicates rising visitor densities (and/or overly rapid tourist growth) as well as sharp socioeconomic and cultural cleavages between affluent guests and poor hosts. However, the incidence and patterns of harassment are becoming somewhat clearer.

The three Barbadian survey results presented here suggest that even for popular, successful and safe destinations, harassment poses a continuing problem, one which will likely increase as non-tourist sectors falter and competition intensifies in the globalization of tourism. According to Jean Holder, executive director of the Caribbean Tourism Organization, harassment remains a major long-term threat to regional tourism.

> As Caribbean countries become more dependent on tourism, as other economic sectors fail (putting more and more people out of work), as wealth and poverty are brought into greater proximity, the levels of crime due to need or greed, and harassment of visitors by hard-selling vendors, can be expected to increase. (Pattullo 1996, 100)

The Barbados experience is instructive for other destinations grappling with the problem. Clearly long-run cooperation among all tourism interests appears preferable to criminalization. The strategies followed – tracking visitor complaints, stationing wardens to monitor beaches, deploying police to patrol hot spots, providing vendors with kiosks and taxi drivers with designated queue locations, improving police training so officers can deal effectively with problems of sexual harassment and verbal abuse – all seem to have produced modestly favourable outcomes for all stakeholders (vendors, taxi drivers, hoteliers and visitors). Such collaboration will provide the basis for a more sustainable tourism in the future, that must create a community consensus around the best ways to integrate those at the margin, who are the majority of the harassers, into the economic mainstream.

References

African News Service (online). 2000. "Bookings in Lodges Improve". 27 July. <wysiwyg://bodyframe.167/http:ehostrgw3...>.

Aizenman, N.C. 1998. "Morocco Diarist". *New Republic* 219, no. 10 (7 September).

AP Worldstream (online). 2001. "Harassment Now a Crime in Dominica". 5 April. <wyswyg://bodyframe.200/http://ehostvgw4....anTerm+Caribbean%20and%20Crime&fuzzyTerm=>.

Applied Marketing Consultants. 1994. *Survey on Crime against Tourists: Final Report*. Christ Church, Barbados: Applied Marketing Consultants.

Associated Press (online). 2000. "Mexico Police Harassed U.S. Tourists". 26 April. <wysuwyg://bodyframe.234/http://ehostvgw11...>.

Barbados Advocate. 1994. "Crime Watch Committee Wants Harassment Dealt With". 26 April.

Barbados Daily Nation (online). 2001. "Region Needs New Tourism Policy". 20 June. <www.nationnews.com>.

Boissevain, J. 1979. "The Impact of Tourism on a Dependent Island: Gozo, Malta". *Annals of Tourism Research* 6, no. 1.

Bowman, G. 1996. "Passion, Power and Politics in a Palestinian Tourist Market". In *The Tourist Image: Myths and Myth Making in Tourism*, edited by T. Selwyn. Chichester, UK: John Wiley.

Burman, J. 1998. "Who's Harassing Whom? Tourism and Security in the Jamaican Mass Media". Paper presented to the Twenty-Third Annual Conference of the Caribbean Studies Association, St John's, Antigua, 26–30 May.

Canadian Tourism Commission. 2001. "WTO Announces that 2000 was a Year to Celebrate for the Global Tourism Industry". <www.canadatourism.com>.

Caribbean Tourism Organization (CTO). 2001. *Barbados Stayover Visitor Survey,* 2nd quarter 1996, 4 quarters 1999, 2000. Christ Church, Barbados: CTO.

Carroll, C. 1998. "Jamaica Targets Local Harassers with Big Hikes in Cash Fines". *Travel Weekly,* 25 May.

Cheong, S., and M.L. Miller. 2000. "Power and Tourism: A Foucauldian Observation". *Annals of Tourism Research* 27, no. 2.

Collins, J. 2001. "Cruise Lines Unhappy with Jamaica". *Caribbean Business* 29, no. 17 (26 April).

Cukier, J. 1998. "Tourism Employment and the Urbanization of Coastal Bali". In *Proceedings 1996 World Congress on Coastal and Marine Tourism,* edited by M.L. Miller and J. Auyong. Seattle: Sea Grant Program, University of Washington.

Daleno, G.D. 2001. "Saipan Fights Flesh Trade". *Pacific Islands Report* (online), 12 April. <pidp.ewc.Hawaii.edu/pireport/graphics.htm>.

Davis, G. 2001. "Government Pressed to Stop Tourist Harassment". *Jamaica Gleaner* (online), 28 April. <www.jamaicagleaner.com/gleaner/20010624/news1.htm>.

de Albuquerque, K. 1999a. "Sex, Beach Boys, and Female Tourists in the Caribbean". *Sexuality and Culture* 2.

———. 1999b. "In Search of the Big Bamboo". *Transition* 8, no. 1.

———, and J.L. McElroy. 1999. "Tourism and Crime in the Caribbean". *Annals of Tourism Research* 26, no. 4.

———, and J.L. McElroy. 2001. "Tourist Harassment: Barbados Survey Results". *Annals of Tourism Research* 28, no. 2.

Economist. 2000. "Tropical Blues: Local Ambivalence about Caribbean Tourism Is Damaging the Industry". 29 April.

Hall, C.M. 1996. "Gender and Economic Interests in Tourism Prostitution: The Nature, Development and Implications of Sex Tourism in South East Asia". In *The Sociology of Tourism: Theoretical and Empirical Investigations,* edited by Y. Apostolopoulos, S. Leivadi and A. Yiannakis. London: Routledge.

Haralambopoulos, N., and A. Pizam. 1996. "Perceived Impacts of Tourism: The Case of Samos". *Annals of Tourism Research* 23, no. 3.

Hokstam, M.A. 2001. "CTO Secretary General Jean Holder: Caribbean Can Survive Tourism's Challenges in Partnerships". *St Martin Daily Herald* (online), 1 July. <thedailyherald.com/news>.

Jardine, D. 2001. "Harassment by Immigration Officials". *Jakarta Post,* 10 February.

Kincaid, Jamaica. 1988. *A Small Place.* New York: Farrar, Straus and Giroux.

King, J. 2001. "Perceptions of Crime and Safety among Tourists Visiting Caribbean Destinations". Paper presented at the Second Caribbean Conference on Crime and Criminal Justice, University of the West Indies, Kingston, Jamaica, 14–17 February.

Kozak, M. 2000. "Destination Benchmarking: Facilities, Customer Satisfaction and Levels of Tourist Expenditure". PhD diss., Sheffield Hallam University.

McDowell, E. 1998. "Jamaica Sweeps Off Its Welcome Mat". *New York Times,* 21 June. <www.nytimes.com>.

McGinnis, J. 1997. "Laws Waiting to be Broken". *New Orleans City Business* 17, no. 29 (20 January).

New York Times. 1999. "Jamaica Takes Steps to Protect Tourists". 21 March.

Pattullo, P. 1996. *Last Resorts: The Cost of Tourism in the Caribbean.* London: Cassell.

Price, S. 1993. "Sexual Harassment on the Beaches". *Barbados Sunday Nation,* 17 October.

Robinson, M., and P. Boniface. 1999. *Tourism and Cultural Conflicts*. London: CABI Publishing.

Saad-Goa, B. 1988. *Tourism – Its Effects on Women in Goa: A Report to the People*. Goa, India: Panajii.

Systems Caribbean Limited. 1995. *Barbados Visitor Satisfaction Surveys, 1991–1994*. St Michael, Barbados: Systems Caribbean Limited.

Taylor, F. 1993. *To Hell with Paradise: A History of the Jamaican Tourist Industry*. Pittsburgh: Pittsburgh University Press.

Wood, C. 1997. "A New Chill in Relations". *Maclean's* 110, no. 5 (3 February).

World Tourism Organization (WTO). 1999. *Compendium of Tourism Statistics, 1993–1997*. Madrid: World Tourism Organization.

World Travel and Tourism Council (WTTC). 2001. "Year 2001 TSA Research Summary and Highlights: World". London: World Travel and Tourism Council. <www.wttc.org>.

Young-Hee, S. 1998. "Sexual Violence and Sexual Harassment in a Risk Society". *Korea Journal* 38, no. 1.

Zinovieff, S. 1991. "Hunters and Hunted: Kamaki and the Ambiguities of Sexual Predation in a Greek Town". In *Contested Identities: Gender and Kinship in Modern Greece*, edited by P. Loizos and E. Papataxiarchis. Princeton, N.J.: Princeton University Press.

10

Crime and Public Policy in Jamaica

Don Robotham

This chapter arose from a request from the minister of finance – Dr the Honourable Omar Davies – to consider the causal factors behind crime in Jamaica, in light of a concern expressed by members of the National Planning Council (NPC) that the high crime rates in Jamaica are having a serious deterrent effect on investment and thus on the prospects for economic growth. While this is a legitimate concern, one should be wary of the assumption behind such thinking.

While common sense suggests that there is an inverse relationship between high levels of crime and levels of both local and foreign investment, I am not aware of any study which convincingly establishes such a relationship. There are cases which refute such a relationship – Colombia being one, Mexico a second and Russia a third. In all three very high levels of crime have been sustained along with relatively high levels of both local and foreign investment – and, in the cases of Mexico and Colombia, high rates of economic growth (7 per cent per annum gross domestic product). In other words, the rule generally holds that all things considered, if profit exceeds risk, capital will invest.

Even if there is such a relationship, it is far from certain what the nature and strength of the relationship is. In other words, just what level of crime, what kinds of crime, what kinds of criminals and what kinds of victims are tolerable, and at what point do significant disincentives for the investor set in? Nor is it clear how this mechanism operates with different types of investment, investors or customers, and whether it is with specific parts (or sectors) of a country or the whole. Is the disincentive, if any, due to increased personal risk (as, for example, in tourism), increased insurance costs, increased security costs, increased losses due to pilferage, increased general operating costs (due, for example, to second- and third-country security impositions), a general country stigmatizing effect, or all of the above? Does it apply to reinvestment as much as to first-time investors?

These are far from being academic points, as the outcomes and effectiveness of policy interventions would vary widely according to which relationships proved significant in a given situation. Moreover, there is a tendency in Jamaica to search for special reasons for the relatively low levels of local and foreign investment and of economic growth. Most studies indicate that the key to investment is macroeconomic stability (the holy trinity of low interest rates, a budget surplus and a competitive exchange rate), strong human resources, and an efficient and effective state and legal framework. There is no mystery here, as in a market economy this combination of factors usually means good returns on investment for the investor. It would be a very serious mistake, with incalculable consequences, to fall victim to the frequently expressed view that Jamaica is an exception to the realities which constrain other market economies and to therefore relax our efforts in those critical areas.

Thus, while our violent crime rates are extraordinarily and frighteningly high, it should not be assumed that a reduction in the homicide or shooting rate will by itself lead to a net increase in investment. Economic outcomes are primarily achieved by economic mechanisms. The problem of lack of investment in the Jamaican economy can be quite easily explained by the specific macroeconomic strategy used – the high-interest-rate-uncompetitive-fixed-exchange-rate regime. Crime needs to be reduced urgently not primarily for investment purposes, but because it is destructive to life and property, brings grief and terror to individuals and communities, and is morally abhorrent.

The conclusion arrived at in this chapter is that the causes of crime in Jamaica are such that a combination of socioeconomic, political and law enforcement measures are necessary to address them. Not all crime in Jamaica can be reduced by socioeconomic and community reforms.

In particular, my conclusion is that community policing alone *cannot* solve the violent crime problems of Jamaica. In Jamaica there is and shall remain for some time to come a real "hardcore" crime problem which will not succumb to community policing. There will have to be a role for the use of legitimate force. We will therefore have to address frontally the issue of how to regulate and supervise this legitimate use of force – in other words, how to ensure that it does in fact operate legitimately.

It is well known in Jamaica that this is a conclusion one is not supposed to voice openly. But the remark by the commissioner of police about "iron fist in a velvet glove" gives me licence, if licence were needed.[1] Community policing needs to be combined with strengthening the role of the state – in other words, with the legitimate use of force by the larger society against a hardcore criminal element. The obstacle that we face is that this "iron fist" is not really made of iron, but of something more like copper. In other words, taking a purely pragmatic view, this force is simply too weak to deliver anything except episodic results. Its adventures with the use of force therefore only end up making matters worse.

More to the point, this "iron fist" is arbitrary, indiscriminate and not governed by the rule of law. The problem, in other words, is that we have an instrument which cannot achieve what is needed – neither iron nor velvet – and so the situation goes from bad to worse, with bursts of panic policing following a crime upsurge, followed by hand wringing on all sides, followed by some "report" or the other. What do citizens do when confronted with a state which is unable to enforce laws fairly and impartially, with respect for the civil rights of the people? This latter point is of crucial importance. I myself see no evidence that the police force can be reformed from within. And I say this not out of lack of respect for the force or its core of dedicated officers. This is simply how it is. The force needs transformation more than reform, and that will require strong *external* input if we are to achieve meaningful results.[2]

The Violent Crime Situation in Jamaica in 1999

That having been said, the violent crime situation in Jamaica is clearly acute. The country has the highest homicide rate in the Caribbean and

Table 10.1   Jamaica: Structure of Crime, 1974–1999 (%)

Type of Crime	1974	1993	1999
Violent crimes	10	40	43
Property crimes	78	29	23
Fraud	3	4	4
Drug-defined crimes	9	13	13
Illegal possession of guns	1	3	4
Other	0	11	13

Source: Harriott 1994 (updated).

one of the highest rates in the world. Gun crimes constitute an unusually high proportion of crimes committed, and there are also very high levels of rape. Below are some recent data on rates for the so-called major crimes in Jamaica between 1974 and 1993, drawn from Harriott (1994).

Striking in the Jamaican data, as Harriott has pointed out, is the relative decline in property-related crimes and the general increase in crimes of violence (Harriott 1994). This is very different from the situation in Barbados, Trinidad and Belize, where property crimes continue to significantly outnumber violent crimes. Jamaica used to have this pattern up to the period immediately after independence, but this changed in the late 1970s. Data for 1998 indicate that about 50 per cent of all crimes are now violent crimes, and that property crimes continue to decrease relative to the total.

Another interesting feature of the data is the tendency (from 1998 to the time of writing) for the number of murders (but not of shootings) to experience a small but significant decline. A closer look at the most recent data, however, urges caution: the decline, though significant, is still small. It is also very recent, and therefore it is too early to say if this trend will be sustained. Further, it is localized in the areas of the so-called Peace, especially west Kingston; in other areas, increases are being experienced.[3] Nearly all respondents, including some members of the police force, attributed this decline to the Peace rather than to any newly found effectiveness of police measures.

This points to an issue which we should not lose sight of: everyone is focusing on crimes of violence and homicide. There is a general self-congratulation that both rates seem to be going down recently. But it is possible for these rates to go down *at the same time as a deeper and more insidious corruption of the entire society and its institutions is occurring.*

I would therefore caution against a one-sided and shallow emphasis on temporary movements in the homicide rate, *without carefully analysing the underlying causes and deeper trends.* If the Peace is based on a deeper corruption of our institutions and society via kangaroo courts and a don-administered community stability, we shall truly reap a whirlwind.

Background Causal Factors

The contributory factors to crime can be divided into two groups: background causal factors and specific situational factors. By background causal factors is meant the general demographic, economic, political and social factors which have been found to contribute significantly to the creation of an environment conducive to high rates of violent crime. There is a plethora of such factors: the size and growth of the 15–29 age group; population urbanization and density; housing and social services; levels and duration of unemployment, especially among young males without certification; incidence of female-headed households; parenting; levels of literacy and education; cognitive and moral development; inequality and social distance; growth of the informal-illegal sector; and the particular political economy and value changes in Jamaica in recent years.

By their very nature these are medium and longer-term forces operating differentially in and on the society, with differential impact at various points in time. They are the underlying factors to be addressed in order to achieve a lasting reduction in crime in any society. These are the factors which are addressed by the so-called developmental approach to crime prevention (Tremblay 1995). This I understand to be the approach to be taken in the upcoming Inter-American Development Bank project (IDB 1998). I will select some of the main factors mentioned above as critical for our current crime situation in Jamaica.

But the fact that these are labelled "background" factors could lead to the erroneous conclusion that they need not or cannot be tackled now. I draw the opposite conclusion: if these deeper factors are not

Table 10.2 Jamaica: Population Ages 15–29 by Gender, 1985–2020

Year	1985[a]	1995	1998	2000	2005	2010	2015	2020
Male	348,800	357,700	350,340	364,100	343,800	335,500	328,700	315,200
Female	357,200	359,220	359,600	347,100	327,700	323,000	315,000	301,700
Total	706,000	716,920	709,900	711,200	671,500	658,500	643,000	616,700

Source: Planning Institute of Jamaica 1995, table 7; 1999, table 17.6.

[a] 1985 is the base year and is an actual; 1995 and 1998 are also the actual numbers from the *Economic and Social Survey 1998*. All other figures are Population Policy projections (lowest) using 1985 as the base year.

addressed now, then it will be impossible to make any sustainable headway in addressing our crime problem. We will simply be confined to addressing the symptoms of crime rather than the root causes. I begin the analysis therefore with a discussion of the more obvious demographic, labour force and educational factors which are structurally causative of violent crime in Jamaica. Later I shall discuss three other factors – the economic, political and social values – which are implicated in the cause of crime as well as in the failure to develop viable policies to address crime in Jamaica.

Demographics

I now wish to consider the background factors which I think are of critical importance in understanding violent crime in Jamaica, starting with the most obvious. The first has to do with demographics. The 15–29 age group is responsible for a significant proportion of all violent crimes in Jamaica. In particular, males in this age group are not only the prime offenders, they are also by far the prime victims. It is therefore of critical importance to look at the demographics of this age group in the recent period and the near future.

As table 10.2 indicates, the 15–29 age group has been undergoing significant expansion in Jamaica in recent years. In 1995 the figure hit an all-time high of 716,920, up from 706,000 ten years before. Of this group, 49.8 per cent or 357,700 were males, which was below the proportion projected by the Planning Institute of Jamaica (PIOJ 1995, 1997). In 1998 the total number in this age group fell slightly to 709,900, of which 49.3 per cent were male. While congratulating ourselves on our falling birthrate and our declining percentage in the 0–14 age groups, we have lost sight of the huge throughput into the 15–29 age group – the fruit of past high rates of fertility.

A key causal factor behind our high rates of violent crime is thus the sheer size of this high-risk group. In most countries which have experienced such a bulge, there has been an increase in juvenile and violent crime, especially where guns are easily available. This has a major impact on the social service budget because it means that resources have to be redeployed from other groups (for example, the aged or infants) to the high-risk group.

As the numbers indicate, we are currently experiencing the worst as far as this demographic factor is concerned. However, the good news is that, using the lowest rates of population projection developed, the prospect is for the 15–29 age group to remain large but to steadily decline over the next few decades. In fact, the rate of decline is going to be even more rapid than anticipated by the lowest projections for this group. Already the actual number of males in that age group for 1998 was significantly below that projected to be achieved only by the year 2000. Real relief from this factor, however, does not come until the year 2020, when the 15–29 age group will have declined to 87 per cent of its 1995 size. Over the medium term, therefore, crime rates in Jamaica should follow that of other countries and significantly decline, as the at-risk group declines both absolutely and relatively as a percentage of the total population.

Urbanization

To understand the weight of the demographic factor one must associate it with a second factor: the growing level of urbanization in Jamaica. Clear-cut current data on urbanization are not readily available, but the general trends are clear. Coming from being about 30 per cent urban in 1960, Jamaica was about 60 per cent urban in the year 2000. In addition there was a process of secondary urbanization. St James (3.7 per cent), Mandeville (3.1 per cent), St Ann (2.4 per cent), and Kingston and St Andrew (2.3 per cent) had the largest percentage increases in population between 1996 and 1998 (PIOJ 1999, 17.7).[4] This reflects the continued decline of the rural economy and the growth of secondary urbanization in the tourist and bauxite towns of Montego Bay, Mandeville and Ocho Rios.

All parish capitals are experiencing urbanization, and what this usually means is a replication of inner-city conditions on a smaller scale throughout the island.[5] In other words, we are in a situation where a surge in the size of the 15–29 age group coincides with a period of rapid secondary urbanization, due largely to internal migration. This probably means that the high-risk group is being increasingly compacted in dense, poor, urban neigbourhoods. More analysis of the data on this issue is urgently needed, as it points to a potential for the high crime rates of Kingston and St Andrew and St Catherine to be exported to these other developing urban centres.

Labour Force Participation, Unemployment, Education and Training

The third, fourth and fifth factors to consider are the fall in labour force participation, the high levels of unemployment in the 15–29 age group, and the low levels of education and training. I will leave the discussion of labour force participation for a later point in this chapter, for reasons which will become apparent.

In 1998 the unemployment rate for the 14–29 age group was 26.5 per cent. This is a composite of the rate of 18.9 per cent for young males and 35 per cent for young females (Anderson 1999). The unemployment rate for young males (14–29) in the Kingston Metropolitan Area (KMA) was 17.8 per cent in 1998, compared to 26.5 per cent in "other towns", and 17 per cent in rural areas. While this may suggest that the pressure on young males in Kingston and St Andrew is not so acute, we know from other research that a significant reason for robbery, car theft, pickpocketing and various confidence tricks in the Corporate Area is pressure for economic support from baby mothers, mothers, siblings and other family members (Gayle 1997). Moreover, the very high unemployment rate for young males in "other towns" reinforces the point made above, of a crime disaster waiting to happen in the rapidly urbanizing inner-city areas of Ocho Rios, May Pen, Mandeville, Montego Bay and Savanna-la-Mar.

We focus on the unemployed group, although a study of the Corporate Area provides data which suggest that significant numbers of low-waged employed persons may either indulge in or act as accomplices for crimes such as burglary, pickpocketing, confidence tricks and robbery (Gayle 1997). An important issue in considering the unemployed is the

Table 10.3 Jamaica: Percentage Distribution of
Long-Term Unemployed, by Years
of Secondary Education Completed

Years Secondary	%
No Secondary	16.4
1–3 Years Secondary	15.9
4 or More Years Secondary	67.7
Total	100.0

Source: Anderson 1999.

duration of unemployment. Of the 122,961 unemployed persons in the 15–29 age group in 1998, 31.2 per cent had been unemployed for under six months, 24.3 per cent for between six and eleven months, and as many as 44.5 per cent (54,719 persons) were long-term unemployed. Of the long-term unemployed, 63.2 per cent have never worked. Nevertheless, 67.7 per cent of this same long-term unemployed group have completed four or more years of secondary education (Anderson 1999). Of *all* the youth unemployed (15–29), 73.7 per cent have had no educational certification of any kind, although 26.8 per cent have four years or more of secondary education (Anderson 1999).

What this means is not only that the long-term unemployed is the single largest group among the youth unemployed, but that the dominant group in the long-term unemployed is a group which has received significant secondary education but no certification. Indeed, it is worthwhile noting that the data do lend credence to a view frequently encountered in the inner city, that there are significant groups of unemployed youth with some education and certification. Indeed, 18.5 per cent of the unemployed youth have one or more passes at the GCE/CXC level or higher. This has the effect of undermining the value attached to education by our young people.

It is plausible to assume that these educated, unemployed groups have had their expectations, as well as their levels of knowledge and sophistication, significantly raised by this educational experience. This coincidence of youth, long-term unemployment, dire poverty and significant education (with or without certification) is universally recognized as an explosive one. Again, much more careful study of this group is required if we are to understand the relationship between long-term unemployment, significant secondary education and violent crime.

Anderson has recently analysed the April 1998 labour force survey data to reveal that, of those youth (15–29) with some secondary education, 69.8 per cent left school without obtaining any certification whatsoever. The picture is not different if one considers the data on training. Only 13.4 per cent of the youth unemployed (15–29) reported in 1998 that they had received any vocational training; of this group of 15,331 persons, slightly over one-third (34.3 per cent), reported that they had obtained no certification. The percentage of youth unemployed with technical education is also insignificant – 3.5 per cent, again with about a third (28.6 per cent) of this total having no certification. Of the total of youth unemployed, 77.7 per cent reported in 1998 that they had received no vocational or technical training of any kind (Anderson 1999).[6] These data are a damning indictment of the Jamaican educational system and provide a strong argument for the temporary suspension of the budget of the Ministry of Education until we get to the root of this problem.

Inequality and Social Distance

The most recent published data on inequality in the *Survey of Living Conditions* (SLC) to which I had access at the time of writing was for 1997. What these data show is a substantial increase in the Gini coefficient for 1997. In 1997 the Gini coefficient reached 0.4164 – the highest in the history of the SLC. This exceeds even the previous record of 0.3969 which was recorded during 1991, the year of 80 per cent inflation. The 1997 SLC also indicates that the top 20 per cent of the population accounted for about 49 per cent of all national consumption – an increase in its share. It is clear that the bottom 70 per cent of the population had lost ground and in 1997 accounted for only 38.8 per cent of all national consumption. The SLC explicitly comments on this issue (STATIN 1997, 23). Although one should not attach undue significance to a single year, these are important warning signs that should be taken very seriously.

One of the most interesting questions which has arisen in the discussion of the clear growth of inequalities in Jamaica in recent years is the part played by the government's macroeconomic strategy. The high interest rate regime maintained by the government as a means of maintaining a fixed exchange rate has meant that, as was pointed out earlier, Jamaica (like Brazil) is one of those developing countries in which domestic debt far exceeds foreign debt. This is because over the past eight years the formal economy has essentially been financed by government high-interest-bearing securities, bought by the wealthier strata of Jamaican society. Year after year, enormous amounts in Jamaican dollars have had to be paid out from the government budget to the holders of this government paper and, of course, this money has come from general government revenues – in other words, from taxation. Indeed, data indicate that in the absence of this huge domestic debt, the Jamaican budget might well be in surplus. However, when the large debt-servicing charges (mainly domestic debt service) are factored in, the accounts go into a severe deficit. There can be little doubt that the macroeconomic strategy has been a very efficient income-redistribution machine, distributing income upwards from the poorer and middle-class groups to the wealthier strata.

There are no recent data on the growth of social distance in Jamaica. The only data available are from the 1991 survey by the late Derek Gordon and Dr Patricia Anderson, which showed that there was a marked increase in the *perception* in certain neighbourhoods in western St Andrew and Portmore/Edgewater that spatial polarization between the social classes had grown in recent years (Gordon, Anderson and Robotham 1997). According to this study, 55 per cent of respondents from the middle class questioned in 1991 felt that spatial polarization between the social classes had increased in the previous ten years, relative to the ten years before that. More significant, 70 per cent of the working class and 71 per cent of the poor were of the view that spatial polarization had increased. Given that these responses were obtained at the height of the great 1991 inflation, it is reasonable to expect that with the Gini coefficient for 1997 at a historic height, similar if not larger percentages would be obtained today.

The argument is often made that inequality *per se* does not cause crime. This may well be true when this factor is considered in the abstract, and when it is not accompanied by extreme impoverishment on the one side and substantial wealth on the other. It may also be true for countries such as Chile, Brazil or Mexico which possess an extremely powerful military capacity to enforce inequalities and which do not hesitate to demonstrate the effectiveness of this capacity from time to time. Jamaica is not remotely in such a position and, fortunately, is unlikely ever to be. Jamaica is a country with a 160-year-long history since the end of slavery in 1838. Its modern political history has consisted of twelve general elections and sixty years of national rhetoric promising social and economic advancement to the poorer social classes in return for their vote. This has not happened.

It is common to encounter stories of persons who have achieved great material success by dishonest means but who are nonetheless treated by official society as pillars of the social order. The recent financial crisis and the revelations of the serious financial difficulties of politicians from across the political spectrum have greatly fuelled this already strongly held feeling. In this context the persistence of and increase in inequality, accompanied by severe impoverishment for the majority and a sense that the elite's wealth represents ill-gotten gain, is bound to breed extreme bitterness and deep resentment among the deprived. While research is needed to establish the relationship between a sense of injustice and violent crime in Jamaica, it is reasonable to assume that such a relationship does exist and may be a strong one.

There is much qualitative evidence to suggest that there is a strong feeling that Jamaica is not merely a society in which injustices occur, but is an unjust society in the broadest sense of the term. There is even evidence that this view is held by a majority of the wealthy classes. By "injustice" here one is not referring simply to failures of the judicial system to deliver swift and fair justice. There is a broader sense of endemic unfairness which people seem to have, one which encompasses economic practices, cultural attitudes, and social and personal relationships, privileges and networks. Although one cannot claim that this is a direct causal factor in the high rates of violent crime in Jamaica, it nonetheless creates an environment which at the least is tolerant of crime, since the feeling seems to be that "everybody" does it but only the weak get caught.

Informal or Underground Economy?

I now turn to discussing the issues of political economy and moral economy, as it is fashionable to call it nowadays. What is meant by the somewhat grandiose term "political economy of crime" is two things: first, how economics and macroeconomic policy in Jamaica have affected and will continue to affect violent crime; second, the relationship between the two main political parties in Jamaica and the system of violent crime. The term "moral economy" simply refers to the issue of social values, which has arisen repeatedly in discussion and which clearly is in need of further research. I shall deal with the issue of economics and economic policy first, and the effects which the prevailing policies have had on the growth of violent crime in Jamaica in the last decade.

Harriott has maintained for several years now that the growth of violent crime in Jamaica is clearly related to disputes which arise in the informal sector (see Harriott 1994, 2000). He has himself analysed the violent crime data to show that what the police misclassify as "domestic" crimes are in fact largely disputes between gang members over drugs, payments or turf, or some derivative dispute. In other words his thesis, explicitly maintained, is that the expansion of violent crime is directly related to the expansion of the informal sector of the Jamaican economy.

I have no doubt that this is the case in a general sense, for the data show that "own account" employment in the KMA has increased from 27.6 to 38.9 per cent of the employed labour force between 1991 and 1998 (Anderson 2000, table 2.11). This is a large increase indeed, and focused on the KMA, which is where at least 80 per cent of homicides and violent crimes take place. Nevertheless, I think a more robust distinction needs to be drawn within the informal economy between the legal and underground sectors, and indeed, this distinction is implicit in Dr Harriott's work. Activities such as ganja and hard-drug trafficking, extortion and large-scale illicit imports, manufacturing and tax evasion are to be sharply distinguished from the very visible petty trading of imported "name-brand" clothes and shoes which is commonplace in the markets and sidewalks of the towns of Jamaica.

The need for this distinction becomes apparent when one considers the islandwide labour force data. For while Dr Harriott's thesis certainly holds true for the capital district of the KMA, between 1991 and 1998 the "own-account" non-agricultural self-employed group of the Jamaican labour force – the most reliable statistical measure of the number of persons in the informal sector – grew *islandwide* from 155,248 to 184,000 persons, representing a marginal increase in percentage terms from 24.8 to 25 per cent of the employed labour force (Anderson 2000, table 2.12). Clearly, the distinction between those in underground and those in visible informal activities is a difficult one to make since there are broad overlaps, especially when it comes to wholesaling, retailing, and probably some forms of finance which are really money-laundering operations.

One way of getting some sense of the size of the underground economy group may be to consider the growth in the number and percentage of persons classified as "not in the labour force". As the excellent studies by Dr Patricia Anderson have established, the population, fourteen years and over, who were classified as not in the labour force *increased* from 478,200 to 592,700 between 1991 and 1998. This is an increase from 45.4 to 52.6 per cent of the labour force in the eight-year period (Anderson 2001, table 2). As Anderson has pointed out, "The most pronounced changes in participation rates were found among persons under 25 years." In other words, in the group most involved in violent crime. In the 14–19 age group labour force participation rates for young males declined from 34.3 to 25 per cent between 1991 and 1998. For males of the age group 20–24 participation rates declined also, from 92.1 to 84.6 per cent over the same period. Anderson doubts that such a large decline can be explained by the expansion of enrolment in the education system, especially given the data for the 20–24 age group and that we know from other studies that the male drop-out rate from the formal education system is high (Anderson 2000, 6). It is perhaps here, more than in the relatively marginal growth in the informal economy, that we see reflected the political economy of crime in Jamaica.

From these data I draw the following weighty conclusion, one perhaps too great for the data to bear:

Over the last twenty-five years socioeconomic forces in Jamaica have operated in such a manner that the island has developed a hardcore group enmeshed in a criminal political economy. This group is different from your unemployed youths in your so-called corner gang. It is transnational and not likely to be impressed by community policing methods. It is vital that the two groups not be confused. This group constitutes a grave threat to the state and to the stability of Jamaican society. It also threatens other Caribbean societies, as well as Canada and the United Kingdom.

In my estimation this group will continue to grow over the next five years, simply because the forces which generate it will continue to operate and the capacity to defeat it is not present in Jamaican society. It is also my judgement that Jamaican society and officialdom are naïve about the seriousness of this threat and are largely unprepared to meet it.

Just to give an indication of what is happening with this underground economy in Jamaica, I will point to the fact that according to official data, housing starts and completions were up by 68.7 per cent and 147.9 per cent, respectively, in the first half of 2000, while cement sales rose by 10.2 per cent (Gordon 2001, 11). Clearly there has been a small boom in house construction, visible especially in the rural towns. There has also been a huge expansion in the number of used vehicle imports from Japan to Jamaica in the period, and a proliferation of used car dealers and auto parts shops. Anderson's data show, for example, that self-employment in transportation increased from 23.7 to 29.3 per cent of total self-employed between 1991 and 1998. Yet, due largely to the drought, the Index of Agricultural Production actually *fell* by 19.1 per cent between January and June 2000 (Gordon 2001, 13). This was also the period of the greatest banking crisis in the history of Jamaica. Most telling of all: *we have witnessed prolonged contraction of the formal economy over the very same period that this frenzy of house construction and car buying has occurred.*

In 1991 gross domestic product growth at constant prices was 0.8 per cent. In 1995 it was 0.7 per cent and in 1998, 0.8 per cent. This negative trend has continued into the year 2000 although there is the real prospect of some modest growth (about 1 per cent) for 2001. Where then did this money come from? While some of the expansionary activity is without doubt funded from legitimate sources, especially remittances, one would have to be innocent indeed to believe that this is the only or even the main source for this transportation, retailing and construction boom.

This speaks to the question of the growing overlap between the underground and the formal economy, and a more general spread of corruption across all classes and institutions in the society which may well be underway. This includes corruption of the institutions of law and order to an unprecedented degree.

But Dr Harriott's emphasis on the informal or underground economy – call it what you will – contains a flaw. He points to the growth of this underground sector but does not address the question of *why* it has grown. This is really the crucial question, and to understand this we have to carry our analysis beyond the informal into the formal economy. When we do this it is apparent that the real issue facing Jamaica is the stagnation and contraction of the formal economy. *Why has the formal sector of the Jamaican economy stagnated and contracted for twenty-five years?*

Any analysis of the violent crime situation which does not address this question is scratching the surface. If we stop our analysis only at the expansion of the underground economy, then we will not be able to understand the relationship between our economic problems and our crime problems, with respect to macroeconomic policy in particular. We will not see what the future holds. Most important of all, we shall be unable to use economic policy to combat crime, for we will not truly understand the basis of crime. On the other hand, if we understand that the growth of the underground economy is really a reflection of something else – the stagnation of the formal economy – then this will be the beginning of all wisdom in the policy area.

But what, in turn, is the cause of this formal-sector contraction? Here it is vital to be extremely clear, because Jamaica is in denial on this issue. Some would like to argue that the cause of prolonged formal-sector economic stagnation is the government's macroeconomic policy. But macroeconomic policy, although it aggravated the problem, is not *the cause* of it. The cause is deeper and more intractable. The root problem is that the main sectors of the formal economy in Jamaica are antiquated and uncompetitive, have been so for at least twenty-five years and will become more so in the near future. It is vital for us to understand this latter point, since so many things follow from it.

This is an economy based on the export of raw materials from a beleaguered open-cast mining (bauxite and alumina) industry, a beleaguered sugar industry whose factories and field systems were built between 1934 and 1938, a very vulnerable tourist industry, and a contracting export manufacturing sector. In fact, it would not be too far from the truth to assert that the only sector in which our economy is competitive is that of remittances. Since the late 1960s it has been apparent that this formal economic structure could provide neither the national income nor the individual standards of living to which Jamaicans aspired. But efforts to diversify this formal economy in the 1970s and the 1980s largely failed, for reasons which need not concern us now.

From this fact I draw the following conclusion: Jamaica is unlikely to make significant headway in addressing its problems of formal-sector stagnation in the near term. This means that the chances of reducing the drop-out rate from the labour market are small in the short run.

From this a second conclusion follows: The economic conditions conducive to violent crime in Jamaica will continue in the near and medium term. This is going to be a long haul.

But although it is not the root cause, recent macroeconomic policy in Jamaica (it has now been changed) has clearly aggravated the stagnation and contraction of the formal economy. As is well known, in this programme which, be it noted, was self-imposed and not imposed by the International Monetary Fund (IMF), the reverse repurchase rate rose as high as 33 per cent in November 1996, with inevitably harsh contractions in the formal sector. In particular, this generated a banking crisis, the collapse and near collapse of main-line banks and insurance companies, and a public sector bail-out bill of about US$1 billion.

In fact, it is worth reminding ourselves of the dimensions of this crisis by briefly going over some of the data on debt. Between 1996 and 1999 overall public sector debt, excluding debt from the banking crisis, rose from 97.4 to 119.7 per cent of gross domestic product. If one includes the so-called FINSAC debt, the movement becomes truly horrendous.[7] The total public debt (inclusive of FINSAC) increased from 104 per cent of gross domestic product in 1995–96 to 144 per cent of gross domestic product in 1999–2000. It is also critical for us to note that in 1996 domestic debt was 42.7 per cent of total government debt; by 2000 domestic debt had risen to 57 per cent of total debt (Gordon 2001, 6). One cannot understand the growth in inequality in Jamaica without understanding the dynamics of the growth of this huge domestic debt, owed, of course, to the wealthier strata of Jamaican society.

In addition to this contraction which followed from the high interest rate, over this period Jamaica also maintained an uncompetitive exchange rate. Indeed, it can be shown that between 1996 and 1999 the Jamaican dollar actually appreciated by 35 per cent in real terms against the US dollar (Gordon 2001, 6). The result was not only that Jamaica became an unattractive place to invest in for export; there was actually *dis*investment. A number of investors in the textile industry shut up shop and decamped for Mexico, for example. Indeed, one could say that the recent decision of Alcan (one of the oldest players in the local mining industry) to pull out after sixty years of activity is the culmination of this policy of currency uncompetitiveness, pursued as a part of Jamaica's chosen macroeconomic strategy.

It would take us too far afield to explain here why such a policy was pursued. Elsewhere I have tried to explain how, in a previous incarnation, the government suffered severe inflation and staggering political losses by allowing the exchange rate to float. As a result, they resolved never to repeat the experience and to fix the exchange rate, at whatever costs. Well, the costs have been high indeed. Such a strategy meant no investment in the formal sector; no investment meant no jobs in the formal sector, especially for young males. Hence the reduction in labour force participation rates. Not much of a mystery here.

This strategy has now been abandoned. The track the government has been on since 2000 is one of reducing interest rates, cutting the budget deficit and devaluing the Jamaican dollar. In an open economy like Jamaica's, in present world conditions this is, in fact, *the only way* to get investment and job creation going in the formal Jamaican economy, and it is this new policy which has created the possibility of modest gross domestic product growth for 2001.

But this new macroeconomic strategy, too, will clearly not be painless, as the contretemps around the laying-off of teachers in 2000 indicates. Likewise the rumbling around police salaries in the same year. This is because if we withdraw our debt servicing, nearly all of the rest of our budget is spent on three areas: health, education and national security. Therefore there is no doubt in my mind that we shall be facing cuts in these areas in the near future. The policy of allowing the exchange rate to gradually slip downwards carries obvious social costs in wage controls, price increases and layoffs from the public sector, with the hope of stimulating expansion in the private sector. So it will not give us a reprieve from crime in the short run. Nevertheless it is essential in the long run, for it represents the only hope of getting the formal economy to work and of bringing what I have elsewhere called the "demi-semi-formal economy" back into the formal fold.

From this fact I draw the following conclusion: The situation pertaining to illicit underground economic activity in Jamaica is likely to increase in the near future.

These are all sobering conclusions indeed. Some may say they err on the side of gloom. However, I think that they in fact present a realistic and objective evaluation of the predicaments we find ourselves in. To use the vernacular, "anywhere wi turn, macca jook wi!" In this sense, it does not matter in the least which political party is in power.

Gangs, Drugs, Politics

Probably the most intractable factor contributing to violent crime in Jamaica is the interconnecting network of criminal gangs, drug running, politics and the police. Indeed, this has become so endemic that I have promoted it from being a situational to a broad background factor. Below I recount what research has revealed on this relatively unresearched area.

Although there are about forty-nine active gangs in Jamaica, only a small number (14 per cent) are highly organized (Moncrieffe 1998). Grave consequences follow from neglecting this absolutely vital point made by Moncrieffe. It is of the greatest importance to distinguish the two types of gangs and to adopt different approaches to the two situations. The highly organized gangs are deeply involved in the following activities: trafficking in cocaine, crack and marijuana, both locally and overseas (especially to the United Kingdom and Canada). It is alleged that, apart from such ties, there is significant Colombian drug activity in Jamaica, especially in the numerous rural ports and via cruise shipping. The deep-water ports from the old sugar economy of slavery days are experiencing a revival as a result of these illicit activities.

Extensive involvement in protection and extortion rackets in business districts adjacent to inner-city areas represents another major activity for criminal gangs. Indeed, many informants stated that the basis of the much-lauded Peace was the desire on the part of two gang leaders with opposing political affiliations to have an organized sharing of the protection rackets in downtown Kingston. This latter is with the clear connivance of businessmen in the area, who gain both ways. Their business, themselves and their customers are not robbed, and much of the money paid out for "security" returns to them as custom. This is now an important source of the income of violent criminal gangs. In other words, collusion with extortion by members of the private sector is a significant situational contributor to violent crime in Kingston and lower St Andrew.

It is claimed in their defence that the Peace has brought a dramatic reduction in the number of major crimes, especially murder, in the last two years. This is probably the case. However, no state or society can delegate its fundamental functions of maintaining law and order to a criminal, extra-legal force without facing extremely serious consequences, including social collapse.

It is also claimed, in defence of the highly organized gangs, that they operate a quasi-judicial system, complete with "hearings", witnesses and a rough schedule of punishments, including incarceration and the death penalty. This system, it is said, enjoys popular support and effectively administers justice at the community level in the inner city, where it would not otherwise operate. These claims may well be true, but they are a measure of the decay and collapse of the Jamaican state. This turning of a blind eye to what is being euphemistically called "community justice" is playing directly into the hands of the most violent, wealthy and organized criminal element in the society.

The highly organized criminal gangs are also allegedly engaged in the large-scale illegal importation of goods such as red peas, onions and cooking oil. This, while it may not directly constitute violent crime, nonetheless strengthens these groups economically, weakens legitimate firms, corrupts the state apparatus, and increases the links between criminals and apparently legitimate business people.

Finally, the gangs (or at any rate their leaders) are major beneficiaries of lucrative government contracts, often to provide "security" services; specific examples of such alleged contracts are the Kingston Public Hospital construction and the construction of the wall around the National Stadium. This speaks to the continued close integration of the major gangs and gang leaders with the two leading political parties.

There has been much speculation to the effect that the bond between the gangs and the leading political parties has weakened, as the austerity of macroeconomic policies has drastically reduced (but not eliminated) the "pork" from the budget. While there is apparently some truth in reports that a certain amount of distance has grown on both sides due to the relative financial independence of the gang leaders, arising from the drug trade, extortion rackets and some other complex factors, the relationship still retains great benefits for both sides.

On the side of the gang and gang leader: priority access to government contracts, enhanced authority over the various (very fractious) "corners" in the constituency, and most important of all, police protection and cover. A number of "dons", it was repeatedly alleged, crave the acceptance of official society and see their continued relationship with prominent politicians as an important means to that end, if not for themselves then for their children. The most important benefit which continued political connections have for the gang is protection from the police. How the system works is this: if "your" party is in power, then the gang leader is always forewarned when a major police raid is contemplated. This provides invaluable protection for the gangs. On the other hand, if "your" party is out of power, then you have to attempt to corrupt the police directly, as you can no longer rely on political connections to achieve this on your behalf. On the side of the political parties, they rely on party "soldiers" to deliver the vote during elections or, as recent events vividly demonstrated, to keep the peace during civil disturbances. In other words, both sides – the main criminal gangs and the political parties – have a major stake in maintaining the existing corrupt relationship, even though the main drug gangs are richer and more independent than ever before and do not need the political parties as much as they used to.

Indeed, one issue which must be considered is the extent to which drug funds have been, and will be even more in the near future, the main source of funding for the election campaigns of the main political parties in Jamaica. Certainly, with a financially weakened private sector and a disillusioned middle and upper-middle class (over 60 per cent of the electorate is in abstention mode), it is hard to see from what other sources the large funds will come. In my experience the main political parties are blasé and naïve about this issue, take it lightly and think it of little consequence. This is because they may know some of the people involved to be quite "respectable" citizens in other aspects, and to be viewed as loyal party supporters. But this is dancing with the devil. It will have dire consequences in the further corruption of the state. It will make the reform of the police force impossible. It will make the disengagement of political parties from gangs and garrison communities a lost cause.

It is clearly possible to take measures to reduce the strength of criminal gangs. Legislation in the state of California, for example, now makes membership of a criminal gang to be itself a serious offence. Similar legislation in Jamaica may well be feasible. Likewise, changing the method of awarding government contracts, the terms on which "security" can be provided to business places, and the penalties for colluding with extortion are also quite feasible. What is at issue is whether there is the political will to address such issues frontally. Finally, the fact that the vast majority of gangs are small and disorganized and often operate at the "corner" level should not be lost sight of. It is possible that this relative disorganization leads to more impulsive and excessive violence in acts of crime (Moncrieffe 1998). But the more important point is that these small "corner" gangs are not the source of hardcore criminality in Jamaica. They are very clearly a social rather than a police problem. A different policy approach is therefore needed for them.

However, the most important issue is how to get the political parties to break their ties to hardcore criminal gangs and to garrison communities. One approach may be to legislate public financing and the regulation of the finances of all political parties. Another is for public opinion to make a major issue in future general elections of political parties breaking with criminal gangs and garrison communities. This is one occasion when the Jamaican public has the main political parties at its disposal and, to some extent, at its mercy. Jamaicans should not fail to make the most of this opportunity by demanding that the parties admit to these relationships, publicly discuss them, and publicly set out their plans to break with these gangs and the garrison practices.

"Moral Economy", Social Values and Crime

One of the most interesting experiences for me was the sharp and public disagreement between the minister of finance and myself on the role which changes in social values are playing in the growth of violence and crime in Jamaica. He has always argued that "urban inner-city" values are radically different from those of rural Jamaica, where, of course, he originates and was brought up. He points in particular to differences in the work ethic and in the value placed on human life. What seems to influence him are the apparently trivial incidents which provoke violence and the disproportionality of the violent responses. My attitude, and I dare say the attitude of a majority of social scientists researching the subject, would be to dismiss or to scoff at arguments of this kind.

However, I now believe that this position contains an element of truth, but only an element, and recognizing this is an important part of the struggle to reduce crime in Jamaica. For "rural Jamaica" is also greatly penetrated by these so-called urban, inner-city values. Most important of all, these new trends in values (of course, by no means confined to Jamaica – think of the hostility to American consumerism in Europe, for example) are wrongly identified as "inner-city". As many have pointed out, the so-called inner city is simply following a lead long set by the "outer city". The problem of consumption mania is a serious problem, but it is an islandwide one cutting across all social classes, not a peculiarity of the inner city.

I reproduce below a characterization and critique of these values made by two Rastafarians interviewed as part of the research project conducted in 1999 on crime and the inner city. It is this moral decay – being hooked on Mammon – which, they argue, is at the root of our problems. They exonerate no class from this critique; in fact, their preoccupation is with the impact of this materialism on the poor:

> You see all politician now? I no know if them work. I never too see that dem a work right for the people yet. Them is one of the most persons who attract people with material things. A man still want to drive the car the politician drive, you know? And therefore, fe a man drive that car him have fe go slave real hard. Well me know say that by the time him fe buy the one car, certain system buy all ten off him already. Me no need fe ask. Him have fe go pay the system fe keep that car on the road. You see wha I mean? Him have fe pay the system fe keep the car on the road – insurance and tax. Now, that car itself you know, is not made in Jamaica. So therefore, the money fe the car, or a portion of the money fe the car will have to go where the car industry is. So you know seh is a vast amount of Jamaican money that gone out.

Before you feel seh, if you no have on clothes – because people find themself in insecurity still, you know. If a one naw brandish certain clothes them feel a one naw accept them. So they don't accept themself. So people are waiting on other people to accept them! Fe a man to be accepted by certain society girl, him have fe go drive a car. So therefore, if him no willing to toil and no one naw gi him it – and might be him even going consider to commit a crime to get a car, just to be accepted by some people . . . .

That is insecurity. But material crave, material crave – a it is the problem also. Because, this man set up him system, and him system is not fe benefit I and I. But I and I fine pleasure in him system, which is only temporary pleasure. And yet still, I and I . . . I and I don't remember say a since 1990 certain vehicle start come a Jamaica, you know? And this Earth exists fe billion a years ago without them thing deh. And people live. So?

One of the time the I say to I self, "Many a people don't look further than them eyelash" [*laughing*]. One of the things weh I certain I haffe do is to go into I and I vision and look as far as I can look. And find out which kinda life will endure the longest. Which kinda state of life. Dat mean say if is material things that cannot endure fi the longest, I first haffe start teach I youth dem fi live without material things to a level. The poor man might not know the power him have more time! You know what mi a say? But is because him give himself a headache fi gather material things, it cause impression upon him.

Well one of the main thing weh I and I say is fi people know how fi do things. How to relate to things you know. What is the greatest thing towards a person? What a one feel say can make them become the greatest person? Within themselves. I and I learn that you have inner energies. Once I and I did haffe control the five senses. Don't become a slave to them. And I and I haffe govern the five senses. I five senses nuh fi govern I. So therefore, I can overcome temptation. So that is why a person or a parent have them youth ah dem yard and show them youth how fi go do things and dem youth gaan astray because of lust and greed and jealousy.

The people dem lose track of fi dem vital needs! A want dem start want and desire! Dem nuh know weh really important fi dem, dem no know it. Well, right now the people dem, due to the fact say them get enslaved by them owna senses, where them feel say them can't survive without certain things, them can't survive without the supermarket, them can't survive without electricity inna dem house, them can't survive without telephone bill, telephone . . . and not only the telephone, cause nuff people nah conserve no way right ya now. Dem only want know say dem can go outa proportion wid everything. Use di most water, use the most light, use de most dis and dat and jus as long as dem able fi pay di bill.

But if the people don't know dem real needs and aspirations, seen, dem nah go know who fi really choose fi put in place? Because is "of the people", you know? Dat mean say ah di people ah go put the government in place. But if the people nuh know, if the people nah get nuh vision and know weh dem really want, then how likkle more it ah go go? And a wait pon . . . a wait pon a man fi put him in place and den send him fi find out wah a go gwan, weh him fi do . . . Nah! You fi know wah a go happen and you choose who best fi deal wid dem ting deh and put him inna power. So, I nuh know you hear sah![8]

This – minus the asceticism and the flirtation with a hermit life – is precisely the point which people like Professor Barry Chevannes, Reverend Neville Callam and Ian Boyne have been making for some time. There are without doubt deep-seated cultural and social insecurities abroad in Jamaican society today – in the brown-skinned elite as much as in the upwardly mobile black middle class, in inner and "outer" city. Globalization, deregulation and marketization in Jamaica have led to the revival and strengthening of old insecurities and prejudices to an unprecedented level. Indeed, the problem is by no means confined to these social classes, as the popularity of the idiom of the "browning" attests. Indeed, the opposition party won the 1980 election on the promise that a vote for them would "make money jingle in your pocket". Since then all social classes have become swept up in a mania for "Volvo and video", for "Lexus and Bimmer", skin-lightening creams and name-brand clothes. Although macroeconomic austerity has prevailed, especially after 1993, this has not generated an ethic of saving and productivity but one of crassest consumerism. This, by the way, is not unconnected to recent (in the 1980s and 1990s) Jamaican migration to certain parts of Brooklyn and the South Bronx.

This is, as is usual in Jamaica, captured in some of the lyrics, music, dance styles and overall culture of dancehall music, which interestingly has an appeal across all social classes. Carnival culture, too, is not exempt. This music holds up a mirror to society and official society, not liking what it sees, blames the mirror. The mirror is not altogether innocent, but that is hardly the point. I make the point, however, to indicate that this rabid consumerism is not confined to the higher social classes, although of course its source is to be found there. Nor is it confined to the capital KMA district, although it is naturally strongest there. In other words, the Jamaican status-value and social-mobility systems have been redefined to some extent, in important ways which affect the issue of crime. As many in the old upper and middle class lament, the old colonial values of automatic deference to education and whiteness have undoubtedly diminished.

Also apparently diminished are the deep, black Protestant values of rural Jamaica, based on ambition, thrift, fear of debt, savings, devotion to family, religiosity, individualism and moderation in all things. These values played a critical role in the enormous upward mobility, from the small farming to the middle class, which the late Derek Gordon recorded as occurring between the 1950s and the 1970s. They also have been critical in the success of Jamaican migrants overseas, with their renowned industriousness and high rate of home ownership, in both Britain and the United States. But there has been a change, although we should not exaggerate it: I very much doubt that the old values are gone completely. In fact, I would argue that the old values of black Protestantism are still deeply held and remain the fundamental values of the Jamaican people.

Nevertheless, these older values have been overlaid in Jamaica today by orientations which are much more defined in terms of the vulgar display of certain types of imported material goods. This new self-doubt and crass materialism generates a profound demand for certain types of imported goods, the consumption and bizarre display of which now are held to define "success" and which therefore must be had at all costs. This hunger for "style and fashion" is an important inner and outer social-psychological force which I have no doubt drives people to crime, especially but by no means exclusively white-collar crime.

One of the vital tasks which the cultural and religious movement in Jamaica is therefore in a strong position to undertake is to build on this Rastafarian critique and take up as a priority precisely such an assault on this all-class fixation with vulgar consumption. This is an important issue not only in combating crime but also in restoring a national ethic consistent with the objectives of development, including capitalist development. But a word of caution is necessary here: we must try not to go to absurd extremes.

Anthony Harriott likes to make the point that the turn to violent crime in Jamaica is the result of quite rational processes. There is no need to resort to any hypothesis assuming a special tendency to violence or immorality among Jamaican perpetrators of violence. They are just like the rest of us – with a similar rationality and a similar set of values. I strongly support this view and insist that, while it would be naïve and morally repugnant to romanticize them, we must resist the tendency to be self-righteous and to demonize criminals, including violent ones – which tendency, by the way, is widespread in the society.

Indeed, hard evidence of the adherence to mainstream Jamaican black Protestant moral values among well-known, violent Jamaican criminals can fairly easily be obtained. If we are to deal with our problems a level head and a dispassionate attitude are essential, otherwise we shall not be able to effectively address the obstacles. Moralizing can close off important tools of policy, such as the consideration of pardons and amnesties for selected individuals on a carefully considered basis. This is an area which as far as I know has not been researched, but which seems to me to be a very promising area for future work.

The Police

The state and activity of the police is an important causal factor in violent crime, first of all in the simple sense that the police themselves are often in the news facing allegations of police brutality and corruption. Second, in so far as the security services pursue a so-called hardcore approach to crime reduction which may deeply compromise crime prevention measures in a broader sense.

The chief issues arising in relation to the police are those of corruption and police brutality – in other words, issues of civil and human rights. Recently we have seen allegations from the highest levels of the force, claiming suspicion of corruption at the deputy commissioner level. Evidence is, of course, hard to come by, but there seems to be the general perception that, with the growth of the hard-drug trade and Colombian penetration, corruption has reached very high levels and involves huge amounts of US dollars.

The second related issue is that of police brutality and human rights. This is an issue to which we must change our attitude. The attitude is that it is not possible for policing which uses substantial legitimate force to also be respectful of civil rights. The assumption is widely held, not only by the police but also by the general public, that there is an inescapable trade-off here; this view is not peculiar to Jamaica. I would like to challenge that assumption. I would like to put forward the view that, in fact, strong and effective policing is made *more, not less, effective* when it operates within a regime of strict respect for civil rights. The problem is that such an achievement requires very careful recruiting and screening procedures, intensive training, strong discipline, and institutionalized civilian oversight of the use of legitimate force. Anything else and democracy will go.

Those who cavalierly advocate turning a blind eye to the use of force are ignoring the terrible experience of our sister nations in Latin America – especially the recent experiences of Argentina, Chile and Colombia. Once you set off down the road of repression, there is no telling where it will lead. It may lead to Sierra Leone, for example – with urban dons substituting for the rural warlords and child soldiers who have dismembered that country. There is no easy return from this road, if one can return at all. Those who advocate this "strong state" approach should remember that the Jamaican population has a very deep and prized tradition of individual freedom, and that the Jamaican state and security apparatus is not remotely as strong as its Latin counterparts. We are playing with fire here.

This raises the issue of the reform of the police. There have been at least four comprehensive reports on the police force which have all made convincing proposals for reform. Yet these have remained largely dead letters. The reason for this follows from the situation described above. A politically partisan police force is seen as vital by political parties for electoral purposes. It is one of the links in the chain of voter intimidation, and allows garrison constituencies to be sustained. In this era of budgetary austerity police protection is one of the few scarce benefits which politicians continue to control and have to offer "their" gunmen. Hence there is not the political will to implement the numerous sensible recommendations for police reform.

The problem of police behaviour is also connected to the issue of bitter hostility at the community level towards the police, especially towards the various special units which are established from time to time. "Hardcore policing" is the term which a senior police officer used to describe the following crime-reduction tactics: Build close relationships with the leading dons in the community. Work out a live-and-let-live relationship with them, and delegate routine (and some not-so-routine) "law" enforcement to them at the community level. Also, find ways of contributing to community projects sponsored by the dons, although not directly through protection. Turn a blind eye to extortion as long as it is within customary norms and powerful business people do not lay a specific charge. Tolerate trafficking in ganja as long as this does not get out of hand. In other words, this model of crime reduction is one of partnership between the most aggressive, street-smart police and the leading community gangsters.

The "hardcore" approach is also tolerant of a certain amount of police brutality. The notion here seems to be that in the inner-city context in Jamaica it is necessary to use persistent harassment tactics and excessive force, even where no crimes have been committed. This is justified tactically on the grounds that it has the effect of keeping gunmen off-balance and reminding them who is boss. At the same time it clearly stimulates profound popular hostility and disrespect for the police, and severely hampers their crime-fighting efforts. Any prospect of securing witnesses for serious crimes of violence is severely damaged by these tactics. However, some policemen regard this as a price which has to be paid, given the realities of the Jamaican context.

"Hardcore" seems to be the strategy prevailing at the present time. Off the record, many policemen at all levels will vigorously defend this approach on the grounds that it is the only practicable strategy in the present Jamaican context and that it yields results. However, even where it is not intended, it is deeply corrupting and leads to a merger of gangster and law-enforcement culture at the street level. This includes deep involvement of some policemen in the music and private security industries (favourites of the dons) and, inevitably, in the underground economy. It is not a sustainable strategy.

Finally, a word should be said about the escalation of the use of violent and irregular crime-fighting methods by the security forces – the policy of so-called fighting fire with fire. On a number of occasions allegations have been made that there is an unofficial policy of assassinations of the most "uncooperative" dons, and that the killing of "Hyar Monk" in Grant's Pen is one example of this policy. This is vigorously denied by the security services. Needless to say, I am not in a position to pronounce on such a question. However, it is worth noting some of the reasons why the United States abandoned the use of assassination as accepted state policy after the Kennedy assassination. Two reasons seem to stand out: first, it was discovered that two could play that game and there was no telling where it would end; second, it inevitably led to "blow back" – the euphemistic term used by state security services in the United States to describe the process in which irregulars trained and employed by one's own services later turn their guns on the very state which trained them.

Situational Causal Factors

This now takes us to the issue of situational causal factors. Situational causal factors in crime, to paraphrase a leading criminologist, are those factors which increase opportunities for specific categories of crime by reducing the associated risks and difficulties and increasing the rewards in a given situation (Clarke 1995). These are the factors isolated by situational crime preventers, which tactic has been most effective in reducing crime rates, especially in the United Kingdom. Examples include the widespread use of street surveillance in Britain (closed-circuit television, or CCTV), and so-called target hardening: property marking and tagging and electronic surveillance in stores, steering-column locks, legislation, and even the physical redesign of buildings and areas.

The idea here is to make *ad hoc* but very targeted interventions aimed at specific crimes, which make it very difficult for the offender to execute that particular crime with that particular victim at that particular time and place. It consists of a series of opportunistic but very precisely targeted interventions designed to have a specific effect. It is a short-term approach which seeks to have an impact in the very near term. This approach has had only limited use in Jamaica, although a number of senior police officers and the minister of national security are clearly very interested in utilizing it.[9]

Guns

The most important specific situational causal factor in violent crime in Jamaica is the prevalence of guns in the society. Shootings (and "shottas"

– the telling popular term for the offenders) represent the second largest category of major crimes in Jamaica. In the week of 21–24 June 1999, there were sixteen reported murders and eleven separate cases of reported shootings (Office of the Commissioner of Police 1999). In the first six months of 1996 (1 January–24 June 1996), there were 886 cases of reported shootings, or about 12 per cent of all major crimes in the period. In the similar period for 1998 this figure declined dramatically by 39 per cent, to 538 or 10.5 per cent of all major crimes in the period. However, by 24 June 1999 the number of shootings had again climbed by 3 per cent (to 552) and constituted 13 per cent of all major crimes in the period.

It should also be noted that between 1997 and 1999, consistently between 63 and 68 per cent of all murders were committed using guns. The use of guns in robberies has declined absolutely, but sharply increased in relative terms between 1997 and 1999: in the first six months of 1999 guns were used in 65 per cent of all robberies, compared to 55 per cent of all robberies over the same period in 1997. This even though the number of robberies reported decreased from 931 to 809 (Office of the Commissioner of Police 1999). At the same time the numbers of guns either stolen or recovered did not significantly increase, despite the sharp fall-off in murders and major crimes in general. All this is interesting because the number of murders continues to show a decrease. In other words, the shooting rate and the murder rate seem to be moving in opposite directions.

By definition, the second largest category of major crimes in Jamaica would cease to exist entirely if there were no guns. Also, the above data strongly suggest that, absent guns, the lion's share of murders and violent robberies simply would not occur. This leads to the important conclusion that *guns are a critical independent situational causal factor, not only in murder and shootings but in a wide range of other major crimes as well.* If this is the case, then effective gun control is the key to a sustainable short-term reduction in violent crime in Jamaica.

Situational crime prevention research in the United Kingdom has demonstrated that it is a mistake to think that crimes committed with a gun would be committed anyway, perhaps using another implement – the so-called displacement argument (Clarke 1995). It has been shown, for example, that the simple intervention of replacing the use of toxic

domestic household gas with non-toxic natural gas in the United Kingdom reduced the suicide rate by as much as 40 per cent, and that people
did not seek out other means of committing suicide (Clarke 1995).
Researchers discovered that people were actually facilitated in committing suicide by the convenient availability of a painless, lethal and swift
method of killing oneself in the privacy and comfort of one's home. In
other words, the decision to commit suicide is one thing, the act of committing it another. Key elements of the act of committing suicide in the
United Kingdom turned out to be abetted by situational factors which,
once removed, did not lead to suicide being displaced to other means.
This point is critical, because it undermines the notion that significant
crime prevention can be achieved only by altering the so-called disposition of the personality to commit crimes – by its very nature a long-term
endeavour. It is also important to note that these gains have been sustained.

Following from an analogy with the UK experience with suicide, the
easy availability of guns in Jamaica and their widespread possession by
young males probably build courage and aggressiveness, and increase
the chances in the very rational calculation of the offender that the
intended act of violent crime will achieve success. No doubt some
shootings are impulsive, but we need to know how many and which.
Others may not be and, absent the gun, the chances of failure for the
offender would be dramatically increased, not to mention the chances
of apprehension.

There is a large body of research in the developed countries which
shows that criminals are rationalistic in their approach to crime and
that they carefully weigh the rewards over the risks in any given case –
especially the risk of being caught.[10] We clearly need as a matter of
urgency a similar research programme in Jamaica to enable us, for
example, to understand the detailed chain of the process of criminal
decision making for different kinds of crimes. This will open the possibility of precise and effective situational interventions.

As it is, there is clear but limited qualitative evidence that in Jamaica
the process of criminal decision making for confidence crimes, pickpocketing and petty larceny is highly calculating and rationalistic. For
example, the one known study documents how a confidence trickster
goes through a "week of preparation" before embarking on a particular

trick. In the case of his "water commission man trick" (impersonating a National Water Commission [NWC] employee come to disconnect the water supply for an overdue bill but willing to take a bribe not to disconnect), the con man is careful about the community he chooses in which to commit this particular crime. For example, he reports that one should not go into a community with a don because it is likely to be "too tight" (fear of reprisal). Nor should one go into a high-income community – they are likely to ask too many questions and to call the NWC (fear of being caught).

The most vulnerable communities are those which are "poor but proud", to quote the con man's own words – likely to be overdue but not bold or confident enough to challenge the NWC (Gayle 1999). Likewise there is evidence that Jamaican pickpockets carefully plan their work, considering factors such as the site (especially proximity to a bank or an ATM); the gender and social character of the victim; the days and times; their chances of blending into the crowd (crowded bus stops such as at Half Way Tree); whether it is pay-day or not; the expression on a person's face ("looking too pleased with yourself" near to a bank, as one put it); and opportunities to make a quick getaway (Waltham Park is better than Spanish Town Road because it has more getaway streets).

There is also evidence that certain areas have higher victimization rates than others. For example, the second highest incidence of reported robbery in southern St Andrew is Waltham Park Road (Office of the Commissioner of Police 1999). Exactly where on Waltham Park Road, and why, would be an interesting issue for further research. Data for 1997, 1998 and 1999 also indicate that in the first half of the year, the month of May was consistently the highest month for murders. One senior police officer theorized that the increase may be due to the fact that May represents the end of the financial year and there may therefore be a decline in government contract work, which may in turn stimulate more violent crimes which lead to murder. It would be a useful research project to pursue this issue scientifically.

One shrewd young con man also explained to a researcher that "young brown-skinned girls" are very easy victims, as they are too "proud" to enquire too much into a con or to make a scene if robbed. In the course of the interview he urged the researcher to con a potential victim who "was just begging for it" (Gayle 1999). In other words, if non-violent crime is situationally calculating, violent crime is also likely to be. Only careful research can provide us with some of the answers to these questions.

Solutions

The reality facing policy implementers is that they cannot do everything – the so-called holistic approach is practically useless. Implementation requires priorities and choosing from a theoretically unlimited list of options that limited set of policies which are doable and likely to be effective. Below I try to identify some steps which are feasible. Given the analysis presented above, solutions to crime reduction fall into two broad categories: developmental and situational crime prevention.

It is well to recall the major policy conclusion arrived at here: it is that Jamaica's crime and violence problem requires both socioeconomic measures such as community policing and macroeconomic stability, and the use of legitimate force. How to achieve such a combination effectively and within the framework of the rule of law is the fundamental challenge.

What Doesn't Work

It should first be pointed out that the dominant view in the criminological literature is that worldwide, police services, efficient judiciaries and severe sentencing systems are not significant reducers of crime. Although this assessment may be altered based on recent experiences in the substantial reduction in the rates of violent crime in the United States, even here it is not at all clear that the police services can take credit for the recent crime-rate reductions. The fact that crime reduction is across the continental United States and not a localized phenomenon suggests that local-level police action is not the only or even the primary factor at work.

The reduction has coincided with the longest peace-time boom in the US economy since the immediate postwar period. Unemployment is 3.4 per cent among whites and 7.8 per cent among African Americans. Because of very low inflation and low interest rates, house purchase by all groups, but especially by African Americans, is at an all-time high.

As a result non-employment among young African American males without a college education declined from 48 to 36 per cent between 1992 and 1998 (*New York Times* 1999). At the same time, real wages for this group are estimated to have risen by about 10 per cent. Non-employment rates for single mothers have also fallen from 43 to 31 per cent over the same period, due partly to welfare reform and to the boom. These and other related economic and social factors are probably the critical ones for the recent crime reduction in the United States.

The same negative assessment is made of programmes such as neighbourhood watch and community policing which have been used extensively in the United Kingdom and which we have borrowed from them. The reason presented to explain the failure of neighbourhood watch is that these bodies are usually established in middle-class communities which were low-crime areas in the first place. Nonetheless, it is clear from experience in the United Kingdom that neighbourhood watch enriches citizen-police relations, improves the perceptions that citizens have of the police and enhances their sense of security. Community policing, likewise, is felt to improve citizens' perceptions of the police and their sense of security, but not to contribute significantly to crime reduction and prevention (Tonry and Farrington 1995).

A word needs to be said about community policing here. I am all for this, but one should be clear what one is talking about. In New York City, often held as a model for urban crime reduction, the chief method used was not community policing. The key in New York was the combination of information technology, very focused precinct management and, above all, the stop-and-search regime of the notorious Street Crimes Unit. This unit, in addition to repressing crime mainly in black and Hispanic neighbourhoods, was responsible for the Diallo incident and for an unprecedented deterioration of relations between the black and Hispanic communities, the NYPD and the mayor. If we are proposing community policing in Jamaica, therefore, we must be clear about what we mean.

Developmental Programmes

The impending Inter-American Development Bank project envisages the deployment of an extensive developmental crime-prevention programme in selected inner-city areas in Jamaica. Since these are loan funds, the first thing that the NPC can do is to ensure that the funds are used efficiently and effectively. For developmental crime prevention to be most effective, three factors are usually required: early intervention (that is, at an early age); multiple interventions (for example, cognitive deficit corrections combined with peer group, parenting and school-based interventions); and finally, they need to be prolonged (Tremblay 1995). Some anecdotal Jamaican experience from the Kingston Restoration Company suggests that such intervention without employment generation turns out to be unsustainable.

Not all interventions work equally well, especially in different cultural settings. Many of the programme experts are likely to be foreign consultants, and we have little in the way of an accumulated body of research to help us to select programmes which are more likely to work in Jamaica. In other words, we are flying blind here. Nonetheless, as can be seen from the saliency of background causal factors, developmental crime prevention measures are of the highest importance in Jamaica. This is particularly the case as a frequent charge made by inner-city residents is that official Jamaican society simply does not care about them (Levy 1996).

The NPC should call for a review of the Inter-American Development Bank project to ensure its effectiveness. In particular, the programme should be piloted with the most rigorous evaluation built in, to give us a sense of what is likely to work and what is not.

Macroeconomic Strategy

As indicated above, the only long-term sustainable solution to the violent crime problem in Jamaica is the recovery of the formal economy. It is essential therefore that the government continues, indeed accelerates, its programme of macroeconomic management. This will have short-term negative social consequences, but in the end will lead to more job creation and a reduction in crime.

The government must embark on a programme, however limited, of formal economic activities in the inner city. It is important *not* to adopt a strategy of relying on micro-enterprises as a solution to inner-city economic problems. Micro-enterprises in Jamaica have a failure rate of over 80 per cent. The inner-city economy will achieve sustainable improvements in the same manner as any other part of the Jamaican economy: when it is able to secure steady levels of investment and become integrated with an expanding formal economy. Since the private sector is unlikely to invest heavily in or near the inner city in the near future, the government has to take the lead.[11] Tax concessions and other incentives should be a part of this inner-city economic redevelopment package.

A programme of physical upgrading in the inner city could provide a start, with the clear objective of integrating the inner-city economy with the wider formal economy. This could involve fixing drains; improving sanitation, road surfaces and housing; and beautification. This would add real value to properties in the inner city, as well as generating employment and improving the dreary and demoralizing physical environment. Repeated questioning of inner-city residents indicates that they would gladly accept such programmes – no matter the low wages. They also are adamant that they would ensure that value is given for money, as long as the improvements are being done in their community for their obvious, direct benefit. There are already a number of cases of positive community efforts which support these views (Coe 1999).

Important supporting initiatives, such as the proposed Courts programme of training and employing dressmakers, should be encouraged by the Private Sector Organization of Jamaica (Coe 1999). Although these activities are not likely to have much immediate practical effect, they have the potential to improve the social atmosphere and to create an environment in which other situational measures can be effective.

The Educational System

The failures of the educational system, for both the employed and the unemployed, have to be rectified. In particular, we need urgent research on the causes of the high male drop-out rate, as well as on the misfit between the school curricula and the labour market. A special task force on education and training could be set up by the NPC and given a mandate to begin the necessary and urgent programme of restructuring and reprogramming.

Garrison Communities, Gangs and Political Parties

The nexus between garrison communities and political parties must be broken. The best way to achieve this is for special interest groups and the public at large to make this a major issue for the parties to answer in any general election campaign.

Police Transformation

The reform of the police force is an urgent issue. This is largely a matter of political will. Again, public opinion must hammer the political parties until they commit very clearly to action on this vital issue. It may well be that the force has to be dissolved and rebuilt from scratch, so deep are the problems.

The development of an officer corps with a higher level of education is extremely urgent and, likewise, the modernization of internal administration. Fair and transparent promotion and disciplinary procedures need to be restored. Special attention has to be paid to improving inner-city and police relations and the confidence of the general public of all classes in the police. Civilian review over, and investigation of, allegations of police brutality must be instituted. A serious effort to improve prison conditions must be made.

Strengthening Civil Rights

As argued above, this is an essential ingredient of any approach to reducing crime in Jamaica. A concrete and comprehensive programme of civilian oversight, beginning with civilian oversight of all special squads, is essential. Also critical is the need to look again at the composition, procedures and transparency of the Police Board, its independence from the political process, its methods of appointment, tenure of office and powers of investigation, publicity and sanction.

Consumerism and Values

A critique of consumerism must be mounted. The cultural movement and the churches in Jamaica are well situated to accomplish this.

Gun and Ammunition Interdiction and Control: Sniffer Dogs

The most important immediate measure which can be taken in this area is gun and ammunition control, but views differ on how best to go about this. The first element in this is to cut the supply. Since the view is that guns now enter primarily through informal means in the shipment of household barrels from the United States, it should be a priority to block this source. The importation and installation of x-ray machines is reportedly at an advanced stage. Research in the United Kingdom has shown that the deployment of CCTV on buses considerably reduced vandalism, even on buses which did not install CCTV. There is an important lesson to be learned here. But is this the most effective approach in our circumstances (in interdiction and cost terms)?

Great caution must be exercised in this area. Jamaica, like many developing countries, has an unenviable record of being sold antiquated and ineffective equipment which First World countries have found wanting and have abandoned. We have to ensure that the equipment is of the correct specifications and can do the job in the specific circumstances of Jamaica. There is already some talk (it may only be talk) that the X-ray machines ordered for use in Jamaica cannot effectively accommodate the scanning of barrels. If this is true they would obviously be useless, and we could add this to our already long list of bureaucratic disasters. Persons who make this point argue that well-trained sniffer dogs may be not only cheaper but far more flexible and better adapted to the congested conditions of our customs areas. This issue must be very carefully weighed before a final decision is taken.

Legislation

Also, the NPC should consider proposing legislation similar to the US legislation making airline carriers liable for huge fines, seizure of aircraft and revocation of their licences if drugs are transported on their vessels. The way to do it is to enact legislation holding local importers of barrels to Jamaica similarly liable for guns and ammunition found in barrels shipped through their companies. This will undoubtedly lead to an outcry from these companies, some of which are quite large and presumably make substantial contributions to our political parties. Nonetheless, there is obviously no point in seizing guns or developing gun amnesties if there is a steady, low-risk, low-cost stream of guns and ammunition resupply available. On the basis of these measures, various forms of gun and ammunition amnesties could be developed. These need to be carefully designed and implemented, taking into account present realities and previous experience with such measures.

Information Technology and Research

Finally, the success of crime-prevention strategies in the developed countries is closely tied to the development of capable research units and the widespread deployment of information technology. This is an urgent step, already partially begun, which the NPC should strongly encourage.

Only by research will we know what works, why and how and to what extent it works. This is true for both strategic developmental interventions and situational ones. Jamaica urgently needs an annual crime survey, which is now a standard tool of crime prevention in the developed countries. The NPC should strongly support the initiation of this activity. Information technology – large relational databases of criminals, crime and victims – is a vital tool of research, as well as of strategic planning and day-to-day effective, practical police interventions, especially at the local and community levels in the developed countries.

Acknowledgements

I thank the honourable minister of finance and the National Planning Council of Jamaica (NPC) for permission to publish this article which was written in 2000.

Notes

1. See the presentation made by the commissioner of police, Mr Francis Forbes, at the International Conference on Crime and Criminal Justice in the Caribbean, held at the University of the West Indies, Mona, Jamaica (14–17 February 2001).
2. By "external" I mean external to the existing security institutions. This includes foreign assistance, but this is by no means the primary element.
3. The Peace refers to the recent agreement between dons in Matthews Lane and Tivoli Gardens to end violent actions between these respective communities. This has spread to other areas of Kingston and southern St Andrew, but by no means to everywhere. There is an urgent need for a careful and objective assessment of the merits and demerits of the Peace and the realities of its enforcement and operation.
4. Really St Andrew. Kingston proper continues to experience a steady population decline.
5. For example, the population of Westmoreland (primarily Savanna-la-Mar) grew by 2.3 per cent between 1996 and 1998.
6. It is fairly well known by social policy specialists in Jamaica that the levels of education and training of the unemployed and employed sections of the

Jamaican labour force are very similar. This is one possible explanation for the very low level of productivity that characterizes the economy.

7. FINSAC is the acronym for the Financial Sector Adjustment Company. This was the company set up by the Government of Jamaica to manage the banking crisis of 1996–99.

8. Interview by author, Kingston, Jamaica, 15–16 July 1999.

9. Targeting "deportees" is a clear example of situational prevention. The recent decision to introduce X-ray machines to detect illegal gun imports is another good example of a situational crime prevention initiative.

10. This research also suggests that severe penalties and compulsory sentencing have little apparent deterrent effect, in as much as they do not seem to enter into the criminal decision-making process. These issues are discussed at length in Tonry and Farrington 1995.

11. Near is relative. For example, the Courts initiative is near to one large inner-city area. Richard Coe makes the important point that investment does not actually have to be physically located in the inner city to benefit inner-city residents directly.

References

Anderson, P. 1999. *Analyses of 1998 Labour Force Data*. Kingston, Jamaica: University of the West Indies.

———. 2000. "Work in the Nineties: A Study of the Jamaican Labour Market: Context, Conditions and Trends". Report prepared for the World Bank, Washington, D.C.

———. 2001. "Social Risk Management, Poverty and the Labour Market in Jamaica". Paper presented at the Conference on Reinventing Jamaica, Institute for Research in African American Studies, Columbia University, New York, 2–3 February.

Clarke, R. 1995. "Situational Crime Prevention". In *Building a Safer Society*, edited by M. Tonry, and D.P. Farrington. Chicago: University of Chicago Press.

Coe, R. 1999. Interview by author. Kingston, Jamaica, 25 June.

Gayle, H. 1997. "Hustling and Juggling". Typescript, University of the West Indies, Kingston, Jamaica.

———. 1999. Interview by author. Kingston, Jamaica, 23 June.

Gordon, D., P. Anderson, and D. Robotham. 1997. "Years of Growth, Years of Crisis". In *Urbanization in the Caribbean*, edited by A. Portes, et al. Baltimore: Johns Hopkins University Press.

Gordon, P.J. 2001. "Reinventing the Jamaican Economy". Paper presented at the Conference on Reinventing Jamaica, Institute for Research in African American Studies, Columbia University, New York, 2–3 February.

Harriott, A. 1994. "The Structure of Crime in Jamaica". Typescript, University of the West Indies, Kingston, Jamaica.

———. 2000. *Police and Crime Control in Jamaica: Problems of Reforming Ex-colonial Constabularies*. Kingston, Jamaica: University of the West Indies Press.

Inter-American Development Bank (IDB). 1998. *Workshop of Violence and Crime Mitigation: Summary of Proceedings*. Kingston, Jamaica: Inter-American Development Bank.

Levy, H. 1996. *They Cry "Respect": Urban Violence and Poverty in Jamaica*. Kingston, Jamaica: Centre for Population, Community and Social Change, University of the West Indies.

Office of the Commissioner of Police. 1999. Crime Statistics, 1997, 1998, 1999. Kingston, Jamaica.

Moncrieffe, D. 1998. "Gang Study: The Jamaican Crime Scene". Kingston, Jamaica: Ministry of National Security and Justice.

New York Times. 1999. "How Low the Boom Can Go". 13 October.

Planning Institute of Jamaica (PIOJ). 1995. *A Statement of Population Policy, Jamaica*. Kingston, Jamaica: Planning Institute of Jamaica.

———. 1997. *Economic and Social Survey 1996*. Kingston, Jamaica: Planning Institute of Jamaica.

———. 1999. *Economic and Social Survey 1998*. Kingston, Jamaica: Planning Institute of Jamaica.

Statistical Institute of Jamaica (STATIN). 1997. *Survey of Living Conditions*. Kingston, Jamaica: Statistical Institute of Jamaica.

Tonry, M., and D.P. Farrington, eds. 1995. *Building a Safer Society*. Chicago: University of Chicago Press.

Tremblay, R. 1995. "Developmental Crime Prevention". In *Building a Safer Society*, edited by M. Tonry and D.P. Farrington. Chicago: University of Chicago Press.

Contributors

Anthony Harriott is Senior Lecturer, Department of Government, University of the West Indies, Mona, Jamaica.

Dillon Alleyne is Lecturer, Department of Economics, University of the West Indies, Mona, Jamaica.

Ian Boxill is Lecturer, Department of Sociology and Social Work, University of the West Indies, Mona, Jamaica.

Mark Figueroa is Lecturer, Department of Economics, University of the West Indies, Mona, Jamaica.

Obika Gray is Associate Professor, University of Wisconsin, Eau Claire.

Marlyn J. Jones is Assistant Professor, College of Health and Human Services, Division of Criminal Justice, California State University, Sacramento.

John King is Lecturer, Department of Sociology, Baldwin-Wallace College, Ohio.

Jerome L. McElroy is Professor of Economics, Saint Mary's College, Notre Dame.

Don Robotham is Professor of Sociology, The Graduate Centre, City University of New York.

Amanda Sives is Director, Commonwealth Policy Studies Unit, Institute of Commonwealth Studies, London.